WEBSTER'S NEW WORLD™
ENGLISH GRAMMAR HANDBOOK

Second Edition

WEBSTER'S NEW WORLD™
ENGLISH GRAMMAR HANDBOOK

Second Edition

by Gordon Loberger, Ph.D., and Kate Shoup

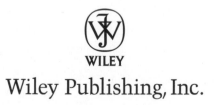

WILEY

Wiley Publishing, Inc.

Webster's New World™ English Grammar Handbook, Second Edition

Copyright © 2009 by Wiley, Hoboken, NJ

Published by Wiley, Hoboken, NJ
Published simultaneously in Canada

For general information on our other products and services or to obtain technical support, please contact our Customer Care Department within the U.S. at 877-762-2974, outside the U.S. at 317-572-3993, or fax 317-572-4002.

Wiley also publishes its books in a variety of electronic formats. Some content that appears in print may not be available in electronic books. For more information about Wiley products, please visit our web site at www.wiley.com.

Library of Congress Cataloging-in-Publication Data
Loberger, Gordon J.
Webster's New World English grammar handbook / by Gordon Loberger and Kate Shoup. -- 2nd ed.
p. cm.
Includes index.
ISBN 978-0-470-41080-6
1. English language--Grammar--Handbooks, manuals, etc. I. Shoup, Kate, 1972- II. Title.
PE1112.L597 2009
428.2--dc22

10 9 8 7 6

ACKNOWLEDGMENTS

I wish to thank two individuals who have been especially helpful to me in preparing the first edition of this text. Kristen Minks White was a very dedicated and efficient project manager for the preparation of the original manuscript, while Jennifer Moore displayed similar efficiency and dedication in making the necessary revisions prior to publication. Both were very able students enrolled in the professional writing program at Murray State University. Also, a number of my students were helpful in pointing out various trouble spots and elusive errors. I hereby thank them all for their assistance.

This edition was subject to many unforeseen obstacles. Trisha Starr and Terri Puckett, both students in Professor Miles Kimball's technical writing class, worked diligently under pressure to prepare the manuscript. Unfortunately, the semester ended before the project was completed. Ms. Puckett graciously consented to continue working through the semester break/Christmas vacation, dividing her time between this project and her duties as wife, mother, grandmother, homemaker, and employee elsewhere. Her concern for the quality of the text and her dedication to the project were truly beyond the call of duty. I know that without her assistance, I would have been nearly helpless at times. I offer her my sincerest thanks for all her help, insights, and for her calm, quiet way of overcoming obstacles. Thank you, Terri.

This latest edition is a result of sharp-eyed students in my classes who detected numerous errors in typing and misplaced answers. The errors and suggestions for necessary corrections were passed on to Terri Puckett, who, once again, worked diligently and efficiently to make corrections. I really cannot thank her enough. As I stated in earlier editions, if any errors occur or remain, I must assume responsibility for them.

Gordon Loberger
Murray State University
Murray, Kentucky

It never ceases to amaze me how many people contribute to the writing, editing, designing, printing, and binding of a single book. Thanks must first go to Dr. Loberger, whose fine text, A Concise Guide to Standard English Usage, serves as the template for this book. Thanks also go to Sherry Gomoll and Roxane Cerda, for providing me the opportunity to make my own contributions to the first and second editions of this title.

Suzanne Snyder's help through this process has been invaluable, as have the sharp eyes of Cathy Debbie Wilson and Lynn Northrup, who helped greatly with the technical accuracy of this book. Thanks very much to all of them for helping us avoid the embarrassment of publishing a grammar book that contains grammatical errors.

Finally, I'd like to thank my daughter, Heidi, who consistently exercises tremendous patience when dealing with her consistently overworked and harried mother. I love you, kid. You're the best.

Kate Shoup
Indianapolis, Indiana

TABLE OF CONTENTS

GET ADDITIONAL FREE CONTENT ONLINE

As an added bonus to this fully revised second edition of the *Webster's New World English Grammar Handbook,* you can visit the companion website at www.wiley.com/go/wnwenglishgrammar.

There, you will find special quick reference sections on the following topics:

- Common punctuation mistakes
- Commonly misused words and expressions
- Commonly misspelled words
- Common variances in spelling among the U.S., the U.K., and Canada

The section on common punctuation mistakes includes a discussion of such issues as using apostrophes to indicate plurals, inserting quotation marks for emphasis, and overusing exclamation points. The commonly misused words and expressions section also includes idioms and slang terms, and shows distinctions between similar words in common use; when it is appropriate to use certain expressions and terms, and when certain expressions and terms are best avoided. Examples of commonly misspelled words include words such as *benefited* or *commission,* in which you might wonder whether the letters *t, m,* or *s* should be single or double. An instance of a common spelling variance among the U.S., the U.K., and Canada is the chemical element spelled *aluminum* in the U.S. and Canada, and *aluminium* in the U.K; this difference and others are presented in the common variances section. These sections provide you with fast, on-the-go answers regarding issues such as those described in this paragraph—as well as other frequently asked grammar questions—and will help you be a better communicator.

Standard English Usage: A Rationale

It should come as little surprise to anyone who has had to struggle through months—even years—of the formal study of grammar in both middle school and high school that certain segments of society place great emphasis on using "correct grammar" and on "speaking correctly." Because the study of grammar was given preeminence in the public-school curriculum (after all, for how many years is one exposed to the basics of English grammar?), nearly every student has been expected to become proficient in such things as diagramming sentences—some of them incorporating uncommon constructions—and in determining the correct use of such forms as who and whom in complex, convoluted sentence patterns.

Needless to say, although such instruction was generally ineffective, it had a certain degree of merit, for knowledge of the subtleties of one's own language can be a very useful tool. But if any students did learn the proper use of who and whom, the learning did not often translate into a functionally meaningful experience. In short, it was usually a failure. Students able to recite rules and employ correct forms failed to incorporate proper usage into their everyday speech. Imagine the chagrin of the hapless teacher of English who for hours inveighed against the use of double negatives, only to hear students employ that usage time and time again, sometimes even when leaving the classroom immediately after instruction. For such a person, the task of teaching grammar probably seems hopeless.

Can, then, proper grammar or standard English usage be taught? Of course it can—and it should be—or this text would not be in existence. But students of grammar must understand the nature of the beast with which they are wrestling, as well as the reasons underlying their efforts.

Students must realize, for instance, that there is a time and place for all things. Attempts by teachers to instill in students a different standard of usage (in effect, a different dialect) to be used at all times and in all places are surely destined for failure. The person who uses who or whom properly at all times and is constantly on guard not to split an infinitive, even in the most informal situations, is using the language in a manner that is just as questionable as the person who misuses who and whom out of ignorance or carelessly splits infinitives in the most formal of situations.

The level of formality one employs in various situations is, then, a matter of dialect. Just as people in one area of a country speak in a way slightly different from people in another area of the country, so too do people in one situation speak differently from the way they would speak in another situation—one that would require greater or less formality. In other words, the formality of one's grammar and usage is a matter of dialect and of adapting one's dialect to a given situation. Just as a doctor or mechanic has more than one instrument or tool with which to perform different tasks, so too ought an effective speaker have different modes of speech for different situations.

Custodians of the Language versus Advocates of Usage

The debate over which grammar to use involves two different philosophies. One school would prescribe certain rules of conduct in matters of grammar and usage. People with this view hold that, in one way or another, speakers ought to maintain the highest standards of formal usage at all times and that to do less reflects discredit upon themselves and their general, overall competence in various matters, whether linguistic or otherwise. This position is the one usually held by teachers of English in many public schools—often encouraged and rewarded by principals and parent groups. The standards to which they would have everyone adhere are, of course, their standards, which reflect their own personal value systems.

Another group is of the opinion that the study of grammar ought to be descriptive in nature, observing and noting the nature of language as it is used by people in general. If, they would maintain, they discover that 75 percent of the speakers of a particular dialect employ split infinitives in their speech—whether formal or informal—that fact should be recorded without any judgment being passed on the appropriateness of the usage. They rightly observe that language is a living phenomenon, growing, spreading, changing, and dying in much the same manner that vegetation grows, spreads, changes, and dies. Attempts to restrain change by establishing artificial constraints or rules, they maintain, are hopeless.

Valid arguments in support of both positions are easy to find. Educated people (and more and more people are obtaining college and university degrees) do indeed have a tendency to hold in mild contempt (at the least) people whose language habits do not meet norms that they or others have established. They see a dichotomy such as that suggested by the title of an article by Thomas A. Knott, General Editor of *Webster's Dictionaries*, in *American Speech* (Vol. IX, April 1934, p. 83). His title is simple and to the point: "Standard English and Incorrect English." The title suggests (though Knott is more tolerant than the title would lead one to believe) that if one does not speak standard English, whatever that happens to be, one is using incorrect English.

In the *Saturday Review of Literature* (14 Nov. 1964, p. 82), Mario Pei, a writer who provided readers a wide range of insights into the phenomena of language through his books and articles, states the following:

> Two voices are raised throughout the land with the same frequency and insistence as that of the Turtle. One is the voice of the Advocates of Usage, the other that of the Custodians of the Language.

The Custodians of the Language, says Pei, "hold that there is a right way and a wrong way of expressing yourself, and that the right way should be prescribed...." The Advocates of Usage, on the other hand, suggest that "language should be subjected to a sort of 'democratic' process similar to the one that prevails in our political life. If enough people say a certain thing in a certain way, that is the way to say it."

This book takes a more moderate approach, neither demanding that all members of society conform to a single set of rules (that is, acknowledging that, in our view, there is a time and a place for formal grammar, and a time and a place for informal grammar, and that different rules sometimes apply to each) nor evangelizing the theory that language must be so elastic that no rules apply. Rather, we seek to gather a useful set of guidelines that writers and speakers can utilize in the boardroom, in the classroom, and in the billiard room.

The Five Clocks

Advocates on both sides of the usage issue have had enough support by writers from various walks of life to fill page after page of numerous magazines for decades. However, in 1961, Martin Joos, a teacher and linguist, published a little book that went far toward creating order out of the chaos of conflicting opinions about language usage. In the book *The Five Clocks* (Harcourt, Brace & World), Joos suggests that speakers of a language (English) modify language usage across five styles, or *clocks*:

- Frozen
- Formal
- Consultative
- Casual
- Intimate

FROZEN STYLE

The first style, *frozen,* is used "for print and for declamation." It is the style of good literature and, consequently, not usually employed in the various speaking situations—except, perhaps, for humorous effect. Obviously, knowledge of this style is a requirement for those whose duties require a degree of facility with language: teachers, editors, writers, formal speakers, attorneys, and others.

FORMAL STYLE

Formal style, according to Joos, is the style of individuals "who are to remain social strangers." It is the style that is employed when a group has grown too large, and participation among members no longer occurs. The formal style demands advance planning and is characterized by the speaker's detachment from the audience. It is, of course, the form of speech that is used in formal lectures or presentations. In this way, it is closely related to the frozen style.

Because of these prestigious uses, the formal style is sometimes viewed as the dialect to be used on all occasions. Unfortunately, many educators tend to stress the importance of this style to the exclusion of the others. The so-called advocates of usage, however, maintain that the formal style is rightly used in formal situations and tend to discount this style for everyday, general usage.

The importance of the formal style should not be underestimated. Often, the confidence one has in oneself as a speaker or writer is directly related to one's ability to use the formal style proficiently. Further, because first impressions often determine the success of a venture, the impression one makes through speech or writing often depends on one's ability to use the formal dialect. Joos, however, makes this observation (and it is well worth remembering): "Formal style is designed to inform... The formal code-labels inform each hearer that he is in a formal frame [and that the hearer] is not to make insertions but must wait until authorized to speak."

In short, the formal style is not the style of general conversation. It is, however, the style of educated speakers and writers; for this reason, those who use the language in any but informal or consultative situations ought to know the proper forms of usage of the formal style.

At the same time, according to Joos, "Good frozen style...lures [one] into educating himself, so that he may the more confidently act what role he chooses" (p. 40); and few would argue the point that knowledge of the formal style (which in many ways is essentially the same) gives the speaker or writer the same self-confidence. In addition, Porter G. Perrin, author of the widely respected Writer's Guide and Index to English (Scott, Foresman, and Company, 1965), states that "People tend to judge us by superficial traits, in language as in other matters" (p. 29).

Beyond those considerations, however, lie other factors. A dialect such as the frozen and formal styles requires insights into the structure of a language, which has practical applications elsewhere—for example, in punctuation. Further, it provides writers and speakers with a wider range of options in expressing themselves than they would have if they were limited to only a single, utilitarian grammatical style. Perhaps with the eye of a prescriptive grammarian, Perrin says that "good Formal English may be the best way (if not the only way) to present certain ideas" (p. 21).

The frozen and formal styles employ restrictions not placed upon speakers of more-informal dialects. As suggested previously, they are most often used in literary and other professional writing and similarly restricted situations, such as addresses (by speakers) on formal occasions. Depending, then, upon what individuals' views of themselves are and what they envision for their futures, they will be more or less concerned with the study of the formal dialect. "Your language," says Perrin, "in the long run represents your personality, and you are responsible for the language you use" (p. 30).

Frozen and formal styles, then, incorporate both similarities and differences. The frozen style, as stated earlier, is the style of formal literary works and declamations. It is not the style of everyday speech, as anyone who has tried to "say" a prepared speech or "orate" informal conversation knows. Frozen, written literary language is a dialect of a special kind, incorporating, of course, the principles of formal English.

Formal style, on the other hand, is the careful speech of persons concerned about their language. The speaker who employs this style makes conscious choices of such things as forms of pronouns, adverbs and adjectives, syntax, verb tenses, and subject-verb relationships. The formal style gains its value from its appropriateness in formal situations other than formal written prose or declamations. It is the style one uses with confidence for self-expression in those situations obviously more structured than the usual informal situations. Probably for this reason, the formal style has received special emphasis at all levels of education.

CONSULTATIVE STYLE

The other styles of usage are not the focus of this book; therefore, they need be mentioned only briefly here. The *consultative style* is that style of language most frequently used for imparting information among individuals. It is generally relaxed and requires a response by the listener(s). According to Joos, in consultative style, "The diction is kept in accurate balance with the requirements: the pronunciation is clear but does not clatter, the grammar is complete but for an occasional anacoluthon, the semantics is adequate without fussiness" (p. 33). In other words, this is the easy-going style of everyday conversation—of business, instruction, on-the-scene reporting, and discussions involving individuals, whether in pairs or larger groups. This is the style the general speaker adopts for his public participation in events; as such, most individuals feel relaxed and comfortable with it.

CASUAL AND INTIMATE STYLES

The other two styles, *casual* and *intimate,* are personal in nature and are of limited general use. In fact, use of these styles by outsiders—by those who are not a part of the "in group," for example—is sometimes looked upon by its "rightful" users as an intrusion or an affront. Identical twins, lovers, close-knit family members, and members of certain fraternal groups may employ various aspects of one or the other of these styles.

That said, the study of these dialects, or "clocks," while interesting in its own right, is not the purpose of this text, even though it has been the focus of hundreds of studies in recent years. As a basis for further study, one would do well to read Joos' little book.

Why the Study of Formal Usage Is Important

One aspect of grammar that we *are* concerned about, however, is the *why* of the study of formal usage. A few reasons have already been suggested, but beyond those reasons lie other considerations. We live in a rapidly changing society, and, cliché though it may be, we must adapt to those changes. No longer can a young person feel secure in the type of world often portrayed by one's parents. This is the age of technology, of mass communications, of computers. It is, in fact, becoming, with increasing emphasis, a "white collar" society. The gulf between those who adapt to those changes and those who do not is widening at an alarming rate, and that gulf will surely grow wider and wider with each succeeding year. What served one's parents and grandparents will no longer serve an individual in the electronic age—and that includes the grammar one uses.

The young person, then, who aspires to a successful life among the educated people of the modern workplace has the responsibility of making sure he or she is prepared to function effectively in an environment that subjects one to close scrutiny via video and the Internet. Obviously, individuals must assume that their grammar—and their general facility with language—will be easily evaluated, and they must take whatever steps are necessary to ensure that their language and grammar reflect positively, rather than negatively, upon themselves.

Fortunately, the formal study of language and specific usages or dialects can be an interesting and intellectually challenging endeavor. Sooner or later, most inquisitive people develop a curiosity about how people say things and what certain things "mean." Further, most educated people recognize a need on their part to use a particular dialect at certain times, just as they recognize lapses in usage among others. We all feel a discomfort—no matter how slight—and even a certain degree of embarrassment when educated people, especially our colleagues, make lapses in usage such as saying "between Billy and I," "they was," "Carl and him were," or "the library is where the book is at." Although we have become more tolerant of various departures from what was once considered standard (the use of *their* rather than *his* with everyone, for example), we still expect a certain degree of language proficiency from educated people. We have, in fact, a reasonable expectation that educated people will speak like educated people. Why should we expect less?

Students must assume the task, then, of acquainting themselves with the varieties of English so that they will be able to choose the dialect that will best serve their purposes, whether it be conversing informally with friends and casual acquaintances or preparing material for formal presentation, either written or oral. One must learn to communicate effectively, and sometimes effectiveness is measured by the respect that is accorded not only the substance of presentation, but also the manner of presentation.

INTRODUCTION

The best way to describe what this book is is to tell first what it is not. It is not, you will discover, a grammar book, although it contains detailed descriptions of grammatical constructions and describes many of the ways in which the English language functions. The purpose of most grammar books is either to analyze the workings of a language in an attempt to offer insight into the language or to prescribe rules about how a language ought to be used by speakers of that language.

The first of these—to describe the language—is the objective of descriptive linguists, language scientists who attempt to remain neutral about what constitutes "correct" grammar and what constitutes "substandard" grammar. Linguists gather detailed information about the workings of a language and piece together an overall picture of that language, much as one would piece together a jigsaw puzzle, until a complete description emerges. Such a task requires the dedicated efforts of hundreds or thousands of scholars devoting their entire lives to their projects. And then, as students of language know, the task is never completed. Language is too complex and is always changing.

The second, as mentioned, is to prescribe rules—lists of *do's* and *don'ts* for writers—as well as to present detailed analyses of writing problems, writing methods, types of discourse, outlining, studies in logic, and so on, all in an effort to make better writers of those students who use the books. Such goals are admirable, and such books have their places. Fortunately, many excellent works of this nature are available to the general public.

This text does not attempt to meet either of these objectives, yet, at the same time, it endeavors, in a limited way, to address both. This book, as you will discover, is intended to be a means of reviewing quickly and effectively basic procedures in sentence analysis, building upon what you already know so that you will be able to write and speak with the effectiveness of an articulate, educated person.

To accomplish this task, we have presented what some may think are too many detailed descriptions of how the English language functions relative to various things—subjects, verbs, and objects, for instance. At other times, you may think we have been too cursory in our presentations or have completely omitted vital material and explanations. But this is a book about standard English usage—practices that often mean the difference between success and failure as a writer or speaker. As a result, this text is meant to be more on the order of a reference book than a standard text.

This book is organized to cover grammar, first at the level of types of words (that is, nouns, verbs, and so on), advancing to cover how those words are used in sentences.

Rules for capitalization and spelling are then presented, followed by one appendix containing tips on improving your writing and a second featuring a handy list of commonly misused words and expressions. Notes, tips, cautions, analysis sections, and sidebars supplement the discussion, alerting you to extra information, providing helpful hints, warning you of pitfalls, and summarizing the key points of each section. To aid you in navigating this information, this book includes a fairly detailed table of contents and an extensive index, enabling you to search for and find quickly specific items about which you need more information. Most of us, when we are writing, do not have the time (nor do we wish to take the time) that is needed to read complete explanations of why something is or ought to be a certain way.

Of course, it should be noted that any author or teacher who attempts to present prescriptive grammar or "standard English" selects those niceties—those rules or ways of saying things—that he or she feels are important. Because of this, a book that presents the study of language from the prescriptive point of view is necessarily selective and presumptuous, presenting those "rules" and usages that the author feels are important enough to be included while omitting others deemed less critical. At the same time, the author imposes his or her own standards upon the material presented, saying, in effect, "If you want to be an effective speaker or writer, do things my way."

A writer of a text such as this cannot avoid these problems, for decisions on what constitutes the most effective way of saying things are not a matter of historical record, revealed truth, or telephone surveys. Rather, "correct usage" is a matter of using a language in precise ways based on what educated speakers and writers have accepted as appropriate over the years. Often, that is a matter of opinion, both on the part of those writers and speakers and on the part of those of us who, at present, examine their uses of the English language. It is a judgment call at best, but a judgment call based on scrutiny of the language used by a variety of educated people. A text such as this one presents guidelines and standards—however arbitrary they may be—in an attempt to help readers develop good language habits, for good language habits are, after all, one means of achieving success and avoiding personal embarrassment.

Language, of course, is in a state of constant change. Words come and go. The word *parenting*, to which many purists object, has already secured a place in our dictionaries and is now accepted as a "real" word. *Cool* once had a meaning similar to "not warm" and "calm," and when used as slang, "great." It has now taken on, in informal usage, a renewed vitality with the meaning of "fine, acceptable," or as a word expressing general approval, as in the expression, "That's cool." *Inflammable* has, by governmental decree, become *flammable*. What is not in one year, decade, or generation is in the next, reflecting the needs of the particular group using the language.

If that be the case, you may ask, why not take an "anything goes" approach? The answer is simple and, we suspect, obvious: Not anything goes. Readers, listeners, employers, and others have certain expectations; those expectations are higher among educated people and professional groups. What is also obvious is that when a person writes or speaks in formal situations, that person is subjecting himself or herself to public scrutiny that could be either beneficial or embarrassing, based on the knowledge of language usage—and that includes vocabulary items. This text has as its main objective the goal of assisting the writer or speaker to use the English language to his or her benefit.

This text does not address all the problems that you may encounter in using the English language effectively. No text can do that. For one thing, this text is highly selective and limited. It presents a brief review of the grammar of the English sentence as a basis for understanding how certain parts of speech (pronouns, adjectives, and adverbs, for example) fit into the overall sentence. This text is also limited in its presentation of words and definitions. Not all troublesome pairs of words are included; for those words and pairs that are, not all definitions are given. Thus, if you believe that a certain word may be used in a way not listed in this text, you should consult a good dictionary to determine the appropriateness of the word or usage in a particular circumstance. A good dictionary is, after all, an important tool for any writer or speaker.

An especially sensitive matter that this text deals with in only a cursory manner is sexism in language. In this matter, an author walks on the prickly cacti of human emotions, for this is an emotional issue. The centuries-old use of *he* as the pronoun of indefinite gender, for instance, is rejected by many writers and groups in today's society. Some of these people advocate eliminating all references to gender, perhaps an admirable goal if the "cleansing" of the language is not carried to extremes (substituting *hystory* for *history,* for example, even though *history* is derived from the Greek word *histor,* meaning "knowing" or "learned," and is gender free). *He* as a pronoun of indefinite gender, however, is often a preferred pronoun in such constructions as "Everyone is expected to hand in his assignment tomorrow." Even so, you can avoid such constructions by recasting the sentence in a manner similar to this: "All students are expected to hand in their assignments tomorrow." At times, though, employing plural nouns can be less effective than using singular nouns. In those cases, you have to decide if you should employ the same nouns, use the awkward *he/she, his/her* combinations, or risk using the *he* pronouns. Because this is a text dealing with standard English usage, and because standard English usage for centuries has employed *he* in such constructions, we have used *he* at times when we thought that other options were less effective. It's a no-win situation at best. Rest assured, however, that we are sensitive to the problem; all the children of both the authors are girls.

Finally, we think we make our position quite clear throughout the text: The level of formality of one's language ought to vary from situation to situation. Not every activity requires correct grammar and formal diction. Standard English—or whatever term is used—is a dialect for formal situations and for less-formal situations in which a speaker may wish to make a positive impression. Grammar—formal or otherwise—is a tool of communication. You should learn to use it wisely and well.

PART I

PARTS OF SPEECH

In a perfect world, people would not forget things, but, as we all know, this is not a perfect world. As but one example, people tend to forget specific details of the formal training in grammar to which they were exposed in their earlier years of schooling. Therefore, a brief refresher course covering some of the basics of grammar may be helpful in dealing with materials presented in later sections of this book. After reviewing the material in this part, you should be able to understand the material in the sections dealing with specific usage problems.

Knowledge of which word or construction to use in a certain place in a sentence often depends upon knowing the function of each word in a sentence or construction. For that reason, a basic understanding of grammar is essential if you wish to speak or write with confidence. Choosing between *who* and *whom*, for instance, or *well* and *good*, depends nearly entirely on the role that these words play in the sentence. Individuals often make errors in usage simply because they are unable to analyze their sentences—or unable to analyze them quickly enough to be effective in making desirable choices of such sentence elements as pronouns, adjectives, and adverbs.

Fortunately, the traditional parts of speech that comprise the English sentence are fairly easily learned. Although it is true that sometimes these parts of speech are used in ways that seem complicated, their basic definitions and usages ought to present very few problems. What follows, then, are definitions and explanations of the parts of speech and discussions of some of the problems associated with them.

Parts of speech, also called *word classes*, include the following:

- Nouns
- Pronouns
- Verbs
- Modifiers
- Function words

Chapter 1

Nouns

A standard definition of a *noun* is a word that names a person, place, or thing.

Persons

Heidi
Jake
man
girl
clerk
Kevin Bacon
typist
brother
Shakespeare
Spaniard
airman
soldier
wife
daughter

Places

Paris
church
cellar
New York
Great Britain
Laos
the South
Texas
the Middle East
home

school
Lake Superior
Earth
the moon
Antarctica

Things

motorcycle
dogs
trip
honesty
love
rhododendron
honor
life
neatness
wisdom
magazine
table
To Kill a Mockingbird
opera
the Pulitzer Prize

Classifying Nouns

Nouns are sometimes classified in the following ways:

- Common
- Proper
- Abstract
- Concrete
- Collective

COMMON NOUNS

Nouns that are the names of things in general are called *common nouns*. A common noun does not begin with an uppercase letter unless it is the first word of a sentence. Some examples of common nouns include the following:

nail
car
teacher
cat
fish
vehicle
racket
bath
match
story

Common nouns are often subdivided into two groups:

- Count nouns
- Mass nouns

Count Nouns

Count nouns are nouns that identify individual items, either singly or as members of groups. In other words, the single entities can be counted. Examples of count nouns include the following:

cat
boxes
tree
fish
herd
class
toe
marble
bean

A *determiner* is a word that introduces a noun phrase. Determiners specify number or quantity (*all, both, two, many, several*) or convey the denotation of a noun phrase (*a/an, the, my, this*). They are discussed in more detail in Chapter 5, "Function Words," under the heading "Determiners."

Determiners patterning with count nouns can be singular or plural, depending on the number of the noun:

That cow is my uncle's favorite.
Those dogs appear friendly.

Mass Nouns

Sometimes called non-count nouns, *mass nouns* identify undifferentiated mass—that is, things not usually considered countable as individual items. Examples of mass nouns include the following:

sugar
grass
water
soda
news
food
dirt
fame
blame
education

Mass nouns are usually singular and modified by words such as *much, more, less,* and *some.*

Although mass nouns are not usually considered countable, countability can be achieved with certain mass nouns through the use of *partitive expressions,* such as *a bit of, some pieces of,* and the like. Following are examples of sentences containing partitive expressions (in italics) with mass nouns (in bold):

Billy offered Jan *a piece of* **advice.**
There wasn't *a shred of* **evidence** to support Joseph's theory about the robbery.

Some partitive expressions work only with certain mass nouns:

a ball of **wax/yarn**
a lump of **coal/sugar**
a cup of **coffee/milk**
a case of **beer/wine**

Measurements can also be used as partitive expressions with mass nouns:

a spoonful of **sugar**
a ton of **manure**

PROPER NOUNS

A noun that refers to a specific thing identified with an individual name is a *proper noun.* The first letter of a proper noun is capitalized. The following are some examples of proper nouns:

Peyton Manning
Rover
Indonesia
Moby Dick
Wisconsin
History 110
Mountain Dew
Skittles
Proverbs
Asia
Grand Prix

ABSTRACT NOUNS

Nouns that name a *quality,* an *attribute,* an *idea,* or anything not having physical properties are *abstract nouns.* Such words as *goodness, love, health,* and *mercy* are included in this category. Many abstract nouns employ the suffixes *-ness* (*goodness*), *-ty* (*loyalty*), and *-th* (*health*) to name ideas and intangible qualities.

CONCRETE NOUNS

Nouns that name things that have physical properties—that is, things that are tangible items—are *concrete nouns.* Some examples of concrete nouns include the following:

wood
rain
Mr. Peterson
ghost
car
wind
pencil
Jennifer
lie
Saturday

Borderline cases exist, such as *ghost* and *lie,* because ghosts, supposedly, can be seen, and lies can be heard.

As you've probably noticed, nouns fit into more than one noun category. For example, *Mr. Peterson* is both a proper noun and a concrete noun.

COLLECTIVE NOUNS

A *collective noun* is a singular noun that refers to more than one thing as members of a single unit. For example, the collective noun *herd* refers to a single unit made up of individual members—cows, for example. Some additional examples include the following:

jury
bunch
throng
committee
company
band
tribe
platoon
family
Congress

Recognizing the Various Types of Nouns

The following sentences contain examples of various types of nouns:

The little puppy that the family obtained from the animal shelter was fun to play with.

puppy: common (count), concrete
family: common (count), concrete, collective
shelter: common (count), concrete

Politicians often make speeches that include such themes as patriotism, love of country, dedication, and self-sacrifice.

politicians: common (count), concrete
speeches: common (count), concrete (you can hear speeches)
themes: common (count), concrete
patriotism: common (mass), abstract
love: common (mass), abstract
country: common (count), concrete
dedication: common (mass), abstract
self-sacrifice: common (mass), abstract

All Americans should help to protect the environment by recycling materials that are reusable.

> **Americans:** proper, concrete
> **environment:** common (mass), concrete
> **materials:** common (count), concrete

Reading these books will fill you with admiration for the talents of the authors.

> **books:** common (count), concrete
> **admiration:** common (mass), abstract
> **talents:** common (count), concrete
> **authors:** common (count), concrete

My parents lived in perfect harmony for years in the same house.

> **parents:** common (count), concrete
> **harmony:** common (mass), abstract
> **years:** common (count), concrete
> **house:** common (count), concrete

The tribe of head-hunters led the explorers through the jungle.

> **tribe:** common (count), concrete, collective
> **head-hunters:** common (count), concrete
> **explorers:** common (count), concrete
> **jungle:** common (count), concrete

The lost hikers felt both joy and relief when they sighted the lodge.

> **hikers:** common (count), concrete
> **joy:** common (mass), abstract
> **relief:** common (mass), abstract
> **lodge:** common (count), concrete

The class sighed with relief when Professor Jones announced that she had postponed the test for a week.

> **class:** common (count), concrete, collective
> **relief:** common (mass), abstract
> **Professor Jones:** proper, concrete
> **test:** common (count), concrete
> **week:** common (count), concrete

Members of our family have always attempted to tell the truth or to remain silent.

> **members:** common (count), concrete
> **family:** common (mass), concrete, collective
> **truth:** common (count) (*truth* is sometimes pluralized, as in "We hold these truths to be self-evident . . ."), abstract

We learned just enough French and German to get by during our stay in Europe last year.

> **French:** proper, concrete
> **German:** proper, concrete
> **stay:** common (count), concrete
> **Europe:** proper, concrete
> **year:** common (count), concrete

Making Nouns Plural

Most nouns are made plural by adding an *s:*

cat	cats
dog	dogs
sneeze	sneezes
tray	trays
file	files

Alas, many nouns do not fit this pattern:

- Nouns that end in *s, z, x, ch,* and *sh* are made plural by adding *es* to the singular form:

bus	buses
mass	masses
buzz	buzzes
fox	foxes
lunch	lunches
wish	wishes
watch	watches

- If a noun's singular form ends in a consonant plus *y,* you must change the *y* to *i* and then add *es:*

baby	babies
fly	flies
sky	skies

Proper nouns that end in *y* are exceptions to the rule to replace *y* with *ies:*

Correct: the Kennedys
Incorrect: the Kennedies

- Some nouns that end in *o* are made plural by the addition of *es:*

hero	heroes
tomato	tomatoes

Because this rule is inconsistent, you should check your dictionary for the correct plural form of nouns ending in *o*.
You should be alert for variant spellings of the plural forms of some nouns. For example, *cargo* can take either the *s* or *es* to form the plural. *Bus* can be spelled with one *s* or two in its plural form (*buses* or *busses*).

- For some nouns that end in *f* or *fe,* the ending is changed to *ves* to form the plural:

wife	wives
shelf	shelves
elf	elves

Because this rule is inconsistent, you should check your dictionary for the correct plural form of words ending in *f* and *fe*.

- Some nouns mutate to form the plural:

man	men
woman	women
tooth	teeth
foot	feet
goose	geese
mouse	mice
louse	lice
brother	brethren
ox	oxen
child	children

A few nouns undergo no visible change, but plurals are implied: *fish, deer, sheep, aircraft,* and so on. With nouns that do not change form when they are made plural, you can determine plurality or singularity by identifying the verb or determiner that patterns with each noun, as in these examples:

One **deer** *is* in the field.
Those **sheep** *are* my uncle's favorite animals.

Some nouns are plural in form but singular in meaning and, therefore, take singular verbs:

Politics *makes* strange bedfellows.
Mathematics *is* an interesting area of study.
The **news** *is* certainly disturbing.

Some plural nouns refer to instruments or items of clothing that consist of two joined parts (*slacks, scissors, pliers, cutters, sunglasses, shorts, briefs, boxers,* and so on). These nouns take a plural verb:

Plaid **trousers** *are* making a comeback.
Helen's **glasses** *were* a little too weak.

Other nouns are plural in form but can be either singular or plural, depending on the meaning intended by the speaker or writer:

Oats *is* a healthful breakfast.
    (The cereal grain, oats, is construed as a single entity.)

The **oats** *are* too wet to harvest today.
    (The grains of oats are construed as individual items.)

Ethics *is* the study of a system of morals.
That man's **ethics** *are* questionable at best.

The word *media* gives many speakers unnecessary problems. *Media* is simply the plural form of *medium*. The following are examples:

The **media** *are* presenting the story inaccurately.
The **medium** favored by many artists *is* painting.

Many words of Latin origin that once formed their English plurals in the traditional Latin manner may now utilize either regular English forms or the Latin forms:

antenna	antennas (or antennae)
curriculum	curriculums (or curricula)
syllabus	syllabuses (or syllabi)
memorandum	memorandums (or memoranda)
narcissus	narcissuses (or narcissi)
cactus	cactuses (or cacti)
radius	radiuses (or radii)

Be careful: *Arbutus* is not usually pluralized with a Latin suffix, while *thesis* still has only the Latin plural form, *theses*.

How can you be certain whether the form of a noun is singular, plural, or both? The answer is simple: Consult a good dictionary.

Making Nouns Possessive

Many nouns are inflected to show possession. When a word shows possession, it indicates a relationship between someone who possesses something and the thing that individual possesses. This inflection typically takes the form *'s*, as in *cat's* tail, *teacher's* book, and *girl's* jacket. The *of* construction can also be used, as in *back of the bus*, *roof of the house*, and *head of the class*.

To make a plural noun possessive, first write the plural form of the noun. Next, add an apostrophe if the plural form ends in *s*; otherwise, add an apostrophe and an *s*:

> the kids' room
> children's toys
> women's shoes

In certain "tongue-twister" words, acceptable shortcuts can be taken. For instance, the possessive form of Venus may be written Venus' and then pronounced "Venus's":

> Venus' diameter and mass are similar to Earth's.

To determine whether this shortcut is appropriate, examine the word in question. If the word is one syllable, add the *'s* inflection; if the word has more than one syllable or ends with a "z" sound, add an apostrophe only:

> Jess's mother answered the phone.
> Mr. Jiminez' car is in the shop.

Inflection refers to an affix (always a suffix in English) that expresses a grammatical relationship, such as the plural *s* in *mothers* and the *ed* ending in *bathed*.

When a noun becomes possessive, it is called a *determiner*. Determiners are discussed in more detail in Chapter 5, in the section titled "Determiners."

Derivational Suffixes

Many nouns are created by adding particular suffixes to other nouns or to other parts of speech. Notice the suffixes (called *derivational suffixes* because they cause a noun to be *derived* from another part of speech) on the following words:

> honesty
> Persian
> truth
> disappointment
> happiness
> departure

Words such as *Asian, Russian,* and *motherhood* are nouns that have been derived from other nouns.

General Observations about Nouns

- A noun is a word that names a person, place, or thing.
- Nouns fit into more than one of the five classifications listed. For example, *tree* is both a common noun and a concrete noun; *justice* is both a common noun and an abstract noun; *English 328* is both a proper noun and a concrete noun.
- A common noun is usually not capitalized unless it is the first word of a sentence.
- Proper nouns are usually capitalized wherever they appear in sentences.
- The name of a school class (*history, geometry,* and so on) is not capitalized unless it is the first word of a sentence, the name of a language (*French, Spanish, English*), or followed by a numeral or letter to form a proper noun (*History 101, Physics B, Astronomy A*).
- Although most nouns are made plural through the addition of an *s* at the end of the word, many nouns do not fit this pattern.
- Some nouns borrowed from other languages can be made plural as they were in the contributing language:

> | crisis | crises |
> |--------|--------|
> | alumna | alumnae |
> | thesis | theses |

- Many nouns are inflected with *'s* to show possession.
- Many nouns are created by adding particular suffixes to other nouns or to other parts of speech.

Chapter 2

Pronouns

A *pronoun* is a word that can be substituted for a noun, noun phrase, or other pronoun without changing the meaning of the sentence or the basic construction pattern of the sentence. Notice the following pairs of sentences. The first sentence of each pair contains a noun or noun phrase that is replaced by a pronoun in the second sentence:

> I saw *John* yesterday. I saw *him* in the library.
> *To Kill a Mockingbird* is an interesting book. *It* was written by Harper Lee.
> *The little boy* went fishing. *He* caught two fish.

Classifying Pronouns

Pronouns are classified in one of seven ways, depending on their uses in sentences. Except for certain uses of the personal pronouns, the pronouns in the various categories cause the average speaker little trouble if the individual speaks English as his or her first language. Here are the categories of pronouns:

- Personal pronouns
- Reflexive pronouns
- Intensive pronouns
- Relative pronouns
- Indefinite pronouns
- Demonstrative pronouns
- Interrogative pronouns

PERSONAL PRONOUNS

Personal pronouns are used when a writer or speaker wishes to use a pronoun to substitute for a word that refers to a person—either himself or someone else (or, in the case of *it*, a thing). Examples of personal pronouns are *I, you, he, she, it, we,* and *they*. Here are some examples using personal pronouns:

You are perfect for the part of Iago!
I painted the living room bright green.
When *he* proposed, Susan nearly passed out.
She doesn't know the answer to the question.
When the moped stalled, *I* gave *it* a swift kick.
We were the last couple standing in the dance contest.
I told Earl and Eunice *they* could go to the movies.

As a general rule, you should avoid using the pronoun *you* in situations clearly calling for a noun or a different pronoun, especially in formal speaking or writing situations.

Incorrect: When *you* are pregnant, *you* shouldn't do any heavy lifting.
Correct: When *a woman* is pregnant, *she* shouldn't do any heavy lifting.

REFLEXIVE PRONOUNS

Reflexive pronouns do what their name implies: They *reflect* the person or thing already identified. They are used when the subject of a sentence performs an action on itself or refers to itself in some other way.

The *subject* of a sentence (or clause) is the noun, pronoun, or noun phrase that normally comes before the verb (for example, *Joann* in "Joann ran the marathon") or, in the case of interrogative sentences, after the verb (for example, *dog* in "Did the dog eat the meatloaf?"). Subjects are covered in greater detail in Chapter 9, "Sentence Parts," under the heading "Subjects and Predicates."

A *reflexive pronoun* is made by combining a form of the personal pronoun and the suffix *self* or *selves* (*myself, himself, yourself, themselves,* and so on). Notice the reflexive pronouns in the following sentences:

You are only fooling *yourself*.
I gave *myself* a manicure.
Roger cut *himself* with the meat cleaver.
My sister saw *herself* in the picture.
The puppy watched *itself* in the mirror.
Janet and Brad are traveling around the world in an attempt to find *themselves*.
I injured *myself* playing miniature golf.

INTENSIVE PRONOUNS

Intensive pronouns are similar in nature to reflexive pronouns; they differ only in their function within the sentence. They are usually found immediately following a noun or pronoun for the purpose of lending emphasis to the noun or pronoun that they follow. Here are some examples of intensive pronouns:

I *myself* witnessed the crime.
The captain *himself* guided the plane.
You *yourself* must do the work.
I shall buy it *myself.*
John *himself* is the culprit.
The players *themselves* voted for the captain.

RELATIVE PRONOUNS

Relative pronouns connect adjective or noun clauses to other elements of the sentence. That is, a relative pronoun substitutes for the noun being modified by an adjective clause and relates that clause to the noun:

The boy **who** *was here* is my nephew.
The person *with* **whom** *I spoke* was the new president.

In the first sentence, *who* substitutes for *the boy*. Without the relative pronoun, the sentence would be constructed as the following:

The boy (the boy was here) is my nephew.

You'll learn more about noun and adjective clauses in Chapter 9, in the section titled "Clauses."

The four most frequently used relative pronouns are *who/whom, which, that,* and *what*. In general, *who/whom* refers to persons, and *which* refers to animals, things, or collective nouns referring to persons. *That* refers to persons, animals, or things. Consider these examples of relative pronouns (in bold) used to introduce adjective clauses (in italics):

The girl **who** *was here* is my sister.
The table **that** *he sold* was a family heirloom.
The dog **that** *bit me* was a family pet.
The cow *for* **which** *you are looking* is in the pasture.
The person *to* **whom** *you were speaking* is the owner.
The worker **who** *injured himself* has gone to the clinic.
The committee **that** *made that decision* has been highly praised.

Sometimes the relative pronoun is omitted from the grammatical construction in which it would normally be found:

Leslie is the person ( ) I wish to see. (*whom*)
Here is the coin ( ) we found. (*that*)

Indefinite Relative Pronouns

Indefinite relative pronouns introduce noun clauses. The indefinite relative pronouns are the following:

who
whom
what
which
whoever
whomever
whatever
whichever

The indefinite relative pronouns have indefinite antecedents, thus their name. Notice the use of the relative pronouns in these two sentences:

The gentleman **who** *gave you that book* is our new librarian.
Whoever *gave you that book* did not give you the right one.

In the second sentence, the relative pronoun *whoever* is an indefinite pronoun because *whoever* has no antecedent. In the first sentence, however, the relative pronoun *who* is not an indefinite pronoun because it has the antecedent *gentleman* and introduces an adjective clause.

An *antecedent* is the expression to which an indefinite pronoun refers. As stated in the preceding paragraph, *gentleman* is the antecedent of *who gave you that book*.

Using Relative Pronouns to Introduce Nominal Relative Clauses

The relative pronouns *who, whoever, whom, whomever, that, which, whichever, what,* and *whatever* can introduce nominal relative clauses—that is, clauses that are used as noun substitutes:

Everyone knew **what** *I wanted for my birthday*
Whoever *wins the race* will receive the scholarship.
Give the keys back to **whoever** *lost them.*
That is exactly **what** *we need for the job.*

Notice that the relative pronouns are inflected for case according to their uses in the various grammatical entities in which they occur. The cases of pronouns are discussed later in this chapter.

INDEFINITE PRONOUNS

Indefinite pronouns are words that are substituted for nouns without referring to a definite person, place, or thing. The most frequently used indefinite pronouns are the following:

anyone
everyone
someone
no one
one
all
some
somebody
anybody
everybody
nobody
every
everything
either
neither
any
many
other
both
none

Indefinite pronouns should not be confused with the indefinite relative pronouns discussed in the section titled "Relative Pronouns."

These pronouns are called *indefinite* because they do not indicate the exact person or thing to which they refer:

Both are acceptable to me.
Everything is fine between Sue and Sam.
Someone has taken my new chemistry book.
Have you told *anyone* about the treasure map?
Somebody ate my sandwich!
Everybody is busy finishing the quiz.
We knew that *no one* had eaten the salami.
I don't have *any,* but John has *some.*
You may have *either*.

Notice that these indefinite pronouns do not introduce clauses, as do the indefinite relative pronouns. Note, too, the difference in usage of the indefinite pronouns in these two sentences:

>   The runner **who** *wins* will earn the prize.
>   (*Who* relates to the noun phrase *the runner* in this sentence, and it introduces the clause *who wins*; it functions as an indefinite relative pronoun.)

>   *Someone* should explain the rules to Bill.
>   (*Someone* has no antecedent and is unrelated to anyone or anything in the sentence. Because it is not related to an antecedent, it is not a relative pronoun.)

Most indefinite pronouns require singular verbs. *Each, either, neither, someone, somebody, anyone, anybody, everyone, everybody, no one, nobody*, and *one* are singular. Prepositional phrases following indefinite pronouns usually do not influence the verb form (prepositional phrases are discussed in more detail in Chapter 9, in the section titled "Prepositional Phrases"):

>   *Each* (of the puppies) **was** healthy.
>   *Every one* (of the workers) **is** ready to eat lunch.
>   *Neither* (of the books) **was** interesting to me.

The exceptions to this rule are in the cases of a fraction or a percentage and such words as *all, most, more, part, some, such, rest, any,* and *none*, which are singular if bulk or a total number or amount is intended and plural if numbers are considered. That is, if the object of the preposition in a phrase modifying the subject of the verb (even if the prepositional phrase is unstated or understood) is a count noun, the verb is plural; if the object of the preposition is a mass noun, the verb is singular:

>   Half *of the water* **is** contaminated.
>   Half *of the professors* **are** members of the organization.

>   Some *of the apples* **are** spoiled.
>   Some *of the soup* **is** cold.

The words *both, few, many, others,* and *several,* on the other hand, are plural and take the plural form of the verb:

>   *Many* **believe** in UFOs.
>   *Both* **have** brown hair.

In formal writing and speaking, indefinite pronouns and noun phrases preceded by indefinite determiners (*each, every, any, either,* and so on) require the singular masculine pronoun form (*he, his, him*):

> *Any* dog worth **his** salt barks when a stranger knocks at the door.
> *Each* student must do **his** own work.

Because of the sensitivity of many people—both writers and nonwriters—and the mistaken notion that gender-based pronouns refer exclusively to males, some writers and speakers make a conscious effort to avoid them. One method of doing this is to make all nouns plural, requiring the use of *they, them, and their:*

> All *students* must do *their* own work.

Because this type of construction is not always the most effective means of expressing oneself, some individuals are attempting to legitimize the use of *they, their,* and *them* as substitutes for the masculine pronoun forms:

> Every student must do *their* own work.

Although this usage may someday be acceptable in formal English, it is not yet recognized as an alternative to the indefinite masculine pronoun. At present, it tends to call attention to itself and may reflect questionably upon the user. It is probably best avoided.

DEMONSTRATIVE PRONOUNS

Demonstrative pronouns serve to point out particular persons, places, or things, even though they may not be named directly. These types of pronouns may sometimes refer to a complete idea expressed elsewhere. The demonstrative pronouns are the following:

> this
> that
> these
> those

Following are some examples of sentences using demonstrative pronouns:

> *This* is the way to kick a football.
> *That* is my new car.
> She told me that *these* are good apples.
> *Those* were the ones she wanted to buy.
> *This* is a good omelet.
> Would you like to try one of *these?*
> I ran the entire way, and *that* is something I seldom do.

INTERROGATIVE PRONOUNS

Interrogative pronouns are pronouns that are used in asking questions. The interrogative pronouns are the following:

who
whom
whose
which
what

Here are a few examples of sentences using interrogative pronouns:

What did you say?
Who did you see in the lobby?
Which bicycle is yours?
Whose shirt is that?
Who was that masked man?
Which topic did you select for your report?

Interrogative pronouns also signal indirect questions in noun clauses:

I asked him *whom* he intended to contact.
We all wondered *what* he intended to do.

Recognizing the Various Types of Pronouns

The following sentences contain examples of various types of pronouns (personal, reflexive, intensive, relative, indefinite, demonstrative, and interrogative):

The little boy injured himself by falling off his wagon.

himself: reflexive
his: personal

Who was that person I saw you talking to yesterday?

who: personal
I: personal
you: personal

That in *that person* functions as a determiner, much as *a* or *the* would. For more information about determiners, see Chapter 5, "Function Words," in the section titled "Determiners."

I call the car that I drive the Kate Mobile.

> **I:** personal
> **that:** relative
> **I:** personal
> **my:** personal

The little girl hurt herself, but she didn't cry at all.

> **herself:** reflexive
> **she:** personal

Everybody was surprised when his vintage motorcycle started without delay.

> **everybody:** indefinite
> **his:** personal

What do you think about the situation in the Middle East?

> **what:** interrogative
> **you:** personal

I suppose I'll have to clean up this mess myself.

> **I:** personal
> **I:** personal
> **myself:** intensive

This in *this mess* functions as a determiner (see the preceding note).

> That poncho belongs to my roommate.
> **my:** personal

That in *that poncho* functions as a determiner (see the preceding note).

The money is gone, but I certainly didn't spend any.

> **I:** personal
> **any:** indefinite

This is a pretty shirt, but no one seems to want it.

> **this:** demonstrative
> **no one:** indefinite
> **it:** personal

Each of you must do your work yourself.

> **each:** indefinite
> **you:** personal
> **your:** personal
> **yourself:** intensive

Somebody is spreading gossip about my friend.

> **somebody:** indefinite
> **my:** personal

The person who stole your bicycle is now in jail.

> **who:** relative
> **your:** personal

We considered ourselves untalented performers.

> **we:** personal
> **ourselves:** reflexive

The Cases of Pronouns

Unlike nouns, which do not change form when they are used in various ways in a sentence (except to indicate possession), certain pronouns—chiefly personal pronouns—do change form depending on their placement in a sentence:

- Pronouns being used as a subject of a sentence or clause are said to be in the *nominative case.*
- Pronouns being used as an object are in the *objective case.*
- Pronouns being used to show ownership or similar relationships are in the *possessive case.*

The following table contains the various cases of personal pronouns. Note that *first person* refers to the speaker talking about himself. *Second person* refers to the person being addressed (the *you* of a sentence). The *third person* is the *he, she,* or *it* about which the speaker is talking.

Personal Pronoun	Nominative Case	Objective Case	Possessive Case
First-person singular	I	me	my, mine
First-person plural	we	us	our, ours
Second-person singular	you	you	your, yours
Second-person plural	you	you	your, yours
Third-person singular	he, she, it	him, her, it	his, her, hers, its
Third-person plural	they	them	their, theirs

Certain relative pronouns can also be inflected for case; the following table shows the various cases of relative pronouns.

Nominative Case	Objective Case	Possessive Case
who	whom	whose
whoever	whomever	whoever's
whoso	whomso	
whosoever	whomsoever	

When a pronoun is made possessive, it is considered a *determiner*. Determiners are covered in more detail in Chapter 5, in the section titled "Determiners."

NOMINATIVE CASE

Examples of nominative-case pronouns include the following:

I
he
she
we
they
who
whoever

A pronoun in the nominative case can function as the following:

- The subject of a sentence:

    They bullied their way into the club.
    I love Parcheesi.

- A subject complement:

    The queen is *I*.
    The winners were *they*.

A *subject complement* is the complement of a linking verb such as *be* or *seem*. You'll learn more about subject complements in Chapter 9 in the section titled "Complements."

- An appositive with another nominative:

    Gymnasts, including *he*, are incredibly nimble.

An *appositive* indicates a relationship between (typically) two noun phrases that refer to the same entity or overlap in their reference. Appositives are discussed in more detail in Chapter 9 under the heading "Appositives."

- A complement of the infinitive *to be* when *to be* has no subject:

    To be *she* would be a hardship.

OBJECTIVE CASE

Examples of objective-case pronouns include the following:

    me
    him
    her
    us
    them
    whom
    whomever

A pronoun in the objective case can function as the following:

- An object:

    Beth's father gave *her* away at her wedding.

- A subject of an infinitive (infinitives are discussed in the section titled "Infinitive Phrases" in Chapter 9):

    I wasn't sure whether *to kiss him* or *to clobber him*.

- An appositive with another object:

    Dora gave James, *her brother*, a tie for Christmas.

- A complement of the infinitive *to be* when *to be* has a subject:

    What I wouldn't give *to be her*.

POSSESSIVE CASE

Examples of possessive-case pronouns include the following:

> my
> your
> his
> her
> its (*never* it's)
> our
> their
> whose

A pronoun in the possessive case can function as the following:

- An adjective:

  My sweater looks better on Julie than it does on me.

- The subject of a gerund:

  Seeing him is painful for Gladys.

A *gerund* is a word that ends in *ing* that shares characteristics of nouns and verbs. For example, in the sentence "Sculpting hedges is Robyn's favorite activity," the gerund *sculpting* requires a direct object (*hedges*) in order to be unambiguous, in the same way many verbs require direct objects. (Direct objects are covered in more detail in Chapter 9, in the section titled "Direct Objects.") At the same time, the phrase *sculpting hedges* acts as the subject of the sentence, much as nouns do. For more information on gerunds, turn to the section titled "Gerund Phrases" in Chapter 9.

Pronouns as Nominals

Pronouns as substitutes for nouns (or *nominals*) may serve the same functions in sentences as nouns. Where nouns serve as subjects, objects, and the like, pronouns may also serve those functions. Unlike nouns, which do not change form when used as subjects or objects, pronouns do; therefore, you should understand the specific uses of pronouns in each sentence or sentence part. Here is a summary of the rules governing pronoun use:

- Pronouns used as subjects, subject complements, and complements of the infinitive *to be* without a subject must be in the nominative case:

  She who sings well will be accepted.
  > (*She* is the subject of *will be accepted*. *Who* is the subject of *sings*.)

The thief was *he who* had the wallet.
> (*He* is the subject complement. *Who* is the subject of *had*.)

The winner was thought *to be I*.
> (*I* is the complement of the infinitive *to be*. A pronoun used in this situation is in the nominative case because *to be* has no subject.)

Give the book to *whoever* asks for it.
> (*Whoever* is the subject of *asks;* the entire clause *whoever asks for it* is used as the object of the preposition *to*.)

You'll learn more about subjects, subject complements, and complements of the infinitive *to be* in Chapter 9.

• Pronouns used as objects of all kinds must be in the objective case:

Give the money to *me*.
> (*Me* is the object of the preposition *to*.)

We found *her* in the subway station.
> (*Her* is the direct object of *found*.)

They gave *us* the map.
> (*Us* is the indirect object of *gave*.)

An *indirect object* is typically placed between the verb and the direct object and typically has the role of recipient or beneficiary of the action. For example, *Maria* in "I told Maria the truth" is the sentence's indirect object. Indirect objects are discussed in more detail in Chapter 9, under the heading "Indirect Objects."

Chasing *us* through the field, the puppy became tired.
> (*Us* is the object of the participle *chasing*.)

A *participle* is a non-finite form of a verb—that is, a verb that does not indicate tense. A participle combines characteristics of a verb with those of an adjective. The present participle of any verb ends in *ing;* the past participle of a regular verb is identified with the past tense, ending in *ed*. Participles are discussed in more detail in Chapter 9, under the heading "Participial Phrases."

Catching *me* can sometimes be difficult.
> (*Me* is the object of the gerund *catching*.)

To find *her*, look near the cafeteria.
> (*Her* is the object of the infinitive *to find*.)

Everyone believed *her* to be *me*.

> (*Her* is the subject of the infinitive *to be*. *Me* is the complement of the infinitive *to be*. Because *to be* has both subject and complement, both pronouns used as subject and complement are in the objective case. See the section titled "Infinitive Phrases" in Chapter 9.)

You'll learn more about objects in Chapter 9.

Bear in mind that sometimes sentences are convoluted and confusing. When you attempt to analyze them, you may stumble through jungles of dense grammatical growth. If, however, a sentence is separated into its constituent parts, the relationship of both the sentence parts and the use of the pronouns can be understood. Consider, for example, this sentence:

> Present the award to (*we, us*) students (*who, whom*) you consider to be the most talented of all (*who, whom*) entered the competition.

To analyze this sentence and to determine the correct pronouns to use in each instance, you need only to consider the sentence constituents. First, examine the first part of the sentence:

> [You] present the award to (*we, us*) students . . .

What sounds right *is* right in this case: Someone will present the award to us. *Us* and *students* both function as the object of the preposition. Objects are in the objective case.

Second, rearrange the second part of the sentence to put the elements into the normal order for an English sentence—that is, subject, verb, object:

> . . . you consider (*who, whom*) to be the most talented of all (*who, whom*) entered the competition.

This part of the sentence can be analyzed in two ways:

- One method is to substitute *he* or *him* for the *who* or *whom* to see if the sentence sounds natural. In this way, you can determine that *You consider he . . .* certainly does not sound right—and it isn't.
- The other—and most reliable—method is to analyze the role of the pronoun in the construction. In this case, the infinitive *to be* has both a subject (*whom*) and a complement (*the most talented*). In such cases, both the subject and complement are in the objective case.

Therefore, the sentence should read as follows:

> Present the award to us students whom you consider to be the most talented of all who entered the competition.

Who versus Whom

Many speakers and writers of English have difficulty determining whether *who* or *whom* is correct in any given situation. One easy litmus test Is to try substituting *he* or *him* for *who* or *whom* to test the pronoun usage. (*He* and *him* are the closest pronouns in spelling to *who* and *whom*. Just omit the *w* and change the vowels.) Consider the following sentence:

Give the bat to him (*who, whom*) cares for the equipment.

In such a case, you first determine whether *who* or *whom* patterns with *him* or functions in some other way. Examine the sentence, determine that *cares* is a verb, and examine *who* or *whom* in terms of that verb—that is, determine which of these sentences makes better sense:

Give the bat to him. *Him* cares for the equipment.
Give the bat to him. *He* cares for the equipment.

Obviously, the second example is correct.

Here's a convoluted sentence along with a detailed analysis to explain the *who-whom*, *he-him* system:

(*He, him*) (*who, whom*) earns the highest score we shall certainly recognize.

First, find the natural beginning of the sentence. In this case, it is *We shall certainly recognize*. . . . Now the next word seems obvious: *him*. A native speaker of English surely would not say "recognize *he*." What's left? (*Who, whom*) *earns the highest score*. Substitute *he* or *him,* and the answer is readily apparent:

He earns the highest score.

Now we can put the sentence back together in its original form with the proper pronoun selections:

Him who makes the highest scores we shall certainly recognize.

Granted, these sentences may be a bit unusual, and few writers—if any—would use such constructions; but this same process may be used in other, less "'rearranged'" sentences. A writer who can analyze these sentences should be able to avoid making mistakes in other situations.

Pronouns after *As, Than,* and *But*

The use of pronouns after *as, than,* and *but* poses some problems. When used in comparisons in formal writing, *as* and *than* function as conjunctions. Therefore, the form of the pronoun after these words depends on the function of the pronoun in the comparative clause.

A *clause* is a sentence or sentence-like construction within another sentence; a comparative clause, then, is a clause containing a comparison. Clauses are covered in more detail in the section titled "Clauses" in Chapter 9.

A *conjunction* is a sentence element that links parts of a sentence together. See the section titled "Conjunctions" in Chapter 5 for more information.

Following are several pairs of sentences. In the first sentence of each pair, the verb in the comparative clause is absent (understood). The second sentence in each pair contains the verb in the comparative clause:

> Her sister talks the same way as she.
> Her sister talks the same way as she talks.
>
> She speaks in public much better than I.
> She speaks in public much better than I speak.
>
> They issued him more credit than me.
> They issued him more credit than they issued me.
>
> We admire Charles more than her.
> We admire Charles more than we admire her.

But is a preposition when it means "except," thus the pronoun following *but* is in the objective case. Notice these two sentences:

> We paid everyone but him. (everyone except him)
> No one but him can bake a cake like that. (no one except him)

As, meaning "in the capacity or position of," functions as a preposition, but its use is distinct from that of *like.* For instance, these two sentences have quite different meanings:

> He spoke *like* a professor who is an authority on bats.
> He spoke *as* a professor who is an authority on bats.

The first sentence states the *manner* of the person speaking, not his actual position or role in life. The second sentence establishes the *authority* of a person who is a professor and an expert on the subject of bats. In both cases, a pronoun in the objective case would be required if a pronoun were substituted for a *professor:*

> He spoke *like* **him** who is an authority on bats.
> He spoke *as* **one** who is an authority on bats.

You would be unlikely to say *as him who. . . ,* but such a construction would be appropriate in some situations because *as* means "in the capacity of."

Selecting the Correct Pronoun

Following are numerous sample sentences that demonstrate the selection of the correct form of pronoun:

Harold, John, and (*I, me*) are going to Graceland next month.
I

I thought that you, (*he, him*), and (*she, her*) would study together.
he
she

The man in the front row was thought to be (*I, me*).
I

(*She, Her*) who wins the spelling bee will receive the trophy.
She

Donna said that it was not (*she, her*) who found the missing money.
she

The guilty parties, (*he, him*) and (*she, her*), confessed readily.
he
she

Did you enjoy (*him, his*) playing the glockenspiel?
his

Give the package to (*whoever, whomever*) comes to the door.
whoever

Ask (*whoever, whomever*) you will, the answer will still be no.
whomever

Why did you believe (*I, me*) to be (*he, him*)?
me
him

I saw the musicians, (*he, him*) and (*she, her*).
him
her

It most surely was not (*he, him*) or (*I, me*) (*who, whom*) you saw.
he
I
whom

Award the prize to (*whoever, whomever*) you believe to be deserving.
whomever

He is 98; can you imagine (*him, his*) jumping rope?
him

Let's you and (*I, me*) look for the lost golf ball.
me

She mistook the woman in the cloak for (*I, me*).
me

Yes, it was (*she, her*) (*who, whom*) you should have seen.
she
whom

Don't you remember (*him, his*) asking us to mow the lawn?
his

No one knows (*who, whom*) he said should get into line first.
who

The teacher always calls upon (*whoever, whomever*) he sees first.
whomever

(*Who, Whom*) did she say called upon her last evening?
Who

We have no objections to (*you, your*) going with us.
your

Was it (*they, them*) (*who, whom*) you asked to finish cleaning?
they
whom

Could it have been (*they, them*) (*who, whom*) you thought would fight?
they
who

No, it was not (*they, them*) about (*who, whom*) I was speaking.
> **they**
> **whom**

Then it must have been (*he, him*) and (*I, me*) (*who, whom*) should have taken the initiative.
> **he**
> **I**
> **who**

It was (*we, us*) graduate students (*who, whom*) you saw.
> **we**
> **whom**

Give it to (*we, us*) contestants (*who, whom*) you deem to be the most diligent among all (*who, whom*) entered the program.
> **us**
> **whom**
> **who**

(*Whoever, Whomever*) is fastest in the race will be the ones (*who, whom*) are rewarded.
> **Whoever**
> **who**

Both Jack and (*she, her*) enjoyed the nurse's anecdote.
> **she**

(*Those, Them*) individuals (*who, whom*) earn the highest scores (*we, us*) shall most certainly recognize.
> **Those**
> **who**
> **we**

Isn't it strange that (*they, them*) were thought to be (*we, us*)?
> **they**
> **we**

Give it to (*whoever, whomever*) asks for it.
> **whoever**

He is generating instructions for (*we, us*) members.
> **us**

Mr. Smith thinks that you, (*he, him*), and (*she, her*) will triumph.
  he
  she

Is it (*we, us*) of (*who, whom*) he thinks this?
  we
  whom

(*We, Us*) early arrivals will have first choice of seats.
  We

Can you envision (*me, my*) doing such a foolish thing?
  my

(*He, Him*), as well as (*she, her*) and (*they, them*), are no better than (*we, us*) are.
  He
  she
  they
  we

Neither (*he, him*) nor his brothers are as tall as (*I, me*).
  he
  I

The men were asked to meet (*he, him*) and (*she, her*) at the theater.
  him
  her

Here come Lewis, Sam, and (*she, her*) with John and (*he, him*).
  she
  him

(*Who, Whom*) could know such a thing about (*we, us*) people?
  Who
  us

(*She, Her*) (*who, whom*) they nominate we shall support.
  Her
  whom

Was it both (*he, him*) and (*she, her*)?
  he
  she

No one enjoyed (*his, him*) lecturing on that particular topic.
    his

The lady in the train was believed to be (*she, her*).
    she

It is up to (*whoever, whomever*) we select to do the work.
    whomever

Neither (*he, him*) nor (*she, her*) studies more than (*they, them*) or (*I, me*).
    he
    she
    they
    I

It was (*she, her*), not (*he, him*), who believed (*we, us*) to be (*they, them*).
    she
    he
    us
    them

Two of the performers, (*he, him*) and (*she, her*), were selected.
    he
    she

Yes, (*he, him*), not (*I, me*), is one of those (*who, whom*) are somewhat older than (*she, her*).
    he
    I
    who
    she

The leaders selected both Beth and (*her, she*).
    her

Why don't you sit between (*she, her*) and (*I, me*)?
    her
    me

It is not (*I, me*) who will go; it is (*he, him*).
    I
    he

Each of you is much wiser than (*he, him*), (*she, her*), or (*I, me*).
> **he**
> **she**
> **I**

Each of (*we, us*) members is asked to invite (*whoever, whomever*) he wishes.
> **us**
> **whomever**

Neither of (*we, us*) officers can go with you, (*she, her*), and (*he, him*).
> **us**
> **her**
> **him**

Many people think that (*I, me*) am (*he, him*).
> **I**
> **he**

Neither of you believes (*I, me*) to be (*he, him*), however.
> **me**
> **him**

None of those people have taken you to be (*I, me*).
> **me**

A girl (*who, whom*) Jack and (*I, me*) thought was (*she, her*) spoke to (*we, us*) today.
> **who**
> **I**
> **she**
> **us**

It could not have been (*he, him*), (*she, her*), and (*I, me*) (*who, whom*) you saw.
> **he**
> **she**
> **I**
> **whom**

It was her best friend (*who, whom*) she was expecting.
> **whom**

She has never found a person (*who, whom*) pleases her entirely.
> **who**

The people with (*who, whom*) he works praise him highly.
whom

Everyone (*who, whom*) the dean called to his office approved the plan.
whom

(*Who, Whom*) was the attorney to (*who, whom*) you spoke?
Who
whom

Give the clothing to (*whoever, whomever*) you believe to need it.
whomever

The small man with the nervous gestures is (*he, him*).
he

Stephen and (*he, him*) were a hilarious comedy team.
he

Everyone except (*she, her*) and (*I, me*) was invited.
her
me

No dictator will govern (*we, us*) Americans.
us

He invited everyone but (*he, him*) and (*I, me*).
him
me

With John and (*he, him*) on the team, we'll advance to the finals.
him

We left without either (*he, him*) or (*she, her*).
him
her

The next victim will probably be Tina or (*I, me*).
I

Everyone in camp but (*she, her*) can swim.
her

Is that piece of cake for Louis or (*I, me*)?
     me

The delegates were Sarah and (*he, him*).
     he

A tap at the door brought Mrs. Jones and (*he, him*) to the window.
     him

Aunt Phyllis invited (*she, her*) and Leslie to New York.
     her

The coach showed George and (*I, me*) a new backhand technique.
     me

(*He, Him*) and (*I, me*) were away for two weeks.
     He
     I

Vote for (*whoever, whomever*) you wish; I shall vote for the one (*who, whom*) I believe can best accomplish our goals.
     whomever
     who

Pronoun Reference

Writers and speakers must be certain that the pronouns they employ refer specifically to the nouns for which the pronouns serve as substitutes. If the noun-pronoun relationship is not clear, the result is a problem in *faulty reference*. To avoid faulty reference, a writer or speaker should either place the pronoun close to the noun for which it substitutes or use a noun rather than a pronoun. Notice the easily detected problem in this sentence:

The professor told Lynne that she had lost her book.

The reference problem in this sentence is obvious: Does *she* refer to Lynne or to the professor? To which one does *her* refer? One way to clarify the sentence is to recast it:

The professor lost Lynne's book and told her so.

Also, avoid using *they* to refer to unknown or unidentified individuals or groups:

I read in the paper that they plan to raise our taxes again. (vague)
I read in the paper that the city council plans to raise our taxes again. (clear)

Finally, readers always appreciate having the antecedent of a pronoun on the same page as the pronoun. A noun on one page and a *he* or *she* on the next page may require a reader to return to the previous page to understand the sentence. Many readers find this annoying and confusing.

General Observations about Pronouns

- A *pronoun* is a word that can be substituted for a noun or noun phrase without changing the meaning of the sentence or the basic construction pattern of the sentence.
- Pronouns are classified in one of seven ways, depending on how they are used in a sentence.
- Unlike nouns, which do not change form when they are used in various places in a sentence, pronouns do change form to show that they are being used as a subject of a sentence or clause, as an object, or to show ownership or similar relationships.
- Sometimes a relative pronoun is omitted from the grammatical construction in which it would normally be found.
- Most indefinite pronouns require singular verbs, even when a phrase following the pronoun contains a plural noun.
- The case of a pronoun (or noun) is determined in each instance by the function of the pronoun or noun in the sentence or phrase of which it is a part.
- A pronoun in the nominative case can function as the subject of a verb, a subject complement, an appositive with another nominative, and a complement of the infinitive *to be* when *to be* has no subject.
- A pronoun in the objective case can function as an object, a subject of an infinitive, an appositive with another object, and a complement of the infinitive *to be* when *to be* has a subject.
- Pronouns in the possessive case can function as an adjective and as the subject of a gerund.
- Pronouns as substitutes for nouns can serve the same functions in sentences as nouns.
- Writers and speakers must be certain that the pronouns they employ refer specifically to the nouns for which the pronouns are substituting. If the noun-pronoun relationship is not clear, the result is a faulty reference.

Chapter 3

Verbs

A *verb* expresses an act, an occurrence, or a state of being.

Because a discussion of verbs must also include a discussion of verb phrases, supplemental discussions of the various forms of verbs are found in other sections of this text—specifically, in Chapter 9, "Sentence Parts," in the section titled "Verbals." The limited presentation that follows should be sufficient to enable you to grasp the essentials necessary to make informed choices concerning standard English usage.

Kinds of Verbs

Verbs may be classified in a number of ways, but for the purposes of this text, they are classified as follows:

- Transitive
- Intransitive
- Copulative
- Auxiliary

TRANSITIVE VERBS

Transitive verbs are verbs that pattern with direct objects—that is, they express an action that directly affects a grammatical unit (usually a noun or pronoun) elsewhere in a clause or sentence. Stated another way, a transitive verb shows an action that is "passed on" to the direct object. In effect, these verbs serve as a *transition* between the subject (the *actor*) and the direct object (the thing acted upon, sometimes called the *patient*). Each of the following sentences contains a transitive verb and a direct object. The transitive verbs are in italics, and the direct objects are in bold:

> The farmer *painted* his old **barn.**
> My cat *caught* a **mouse** yesterday.
> Carl's brother *told* us an interesting **story.**

Active Voice versus Passive Voice

Verbs such as those in the three preceding sentences are transitive verbs in the *active voice*. In sentences with verbs in the active voice, the subject of the verb is the *doer* of the action, or the *actor*. A sentence in the active voice usually patterns in one of the following two orders:

Actor ⇨ Action ⇨ Patient

Subject ⇨ Verb ⇨ Direct Object

Sentences with verbs in the passive voice usually pattern with the actor ⇨ action ⇨ patient elements in a reverse order. In such sentences, the actor remains passive and often patterns as the object of a preposition at the end of the sentence. The element that is the direct object in a sentence in the active voice becomes the subject of the sentence in the passive voice. Each of the following sentences is cast in the passive voice:

The **barn** *was painted* by the farmer.

A **mouse** *was caught* by my cat yesterday.

We *were told* an interesting story by Carl's brother.

Note that in sentences in the passive voice, some form of the verb *to be* (*am, is, are, was, were, been, be*) is used with the main verb, which employs the past-participle form. The following sentences demonstrate the changes that take place when a sentence is converted from the active voice to the passive voice.

Active voice: The sexton rang the bell yesterday.

Passive voice: The bell was* rung** (by the sexton)*** yesterday.

Note the following about the two preceding sample sentences:

*Auxiliary has been added to the verb phrase.

**Main verb assumes past-participle form.

***Actor is the object of a preposition after the verb. The prepositional phrase is in parentheses to indicate that it is often omitted when a sentence is cast in the passive voice. Such sentences as the one following are quite common:

The bell was rung yesterday.

INTRANSITIVE VERBS

If a sentence has a verb that shows action of some sort but does not have a direct object, that verb is known as an *intransitive verb*. Although intransitive verbs do not pattern with direct objects, such verbs may express the same actions or types of actions as transitive verbs. Each of the verbs in the following sentences is intransitive because the sentences do not have direct objects:

The musicians *played* until dark.

The audience *laughed* at the comedian's joke.

The children *gamboled* in the yard.

The ship *disappeared* into the fog.

The mail *arrived* before noon.

The gardener *worked* in the heat of the afternoon.

We *wandered* aimlessly through the forest until dawn.

In the first sentence, for example, the verb *played* is an action verb; but because the sentence does not state what the musicians played, the verb is intransitive rather than transitive.

Most verbs can be used as either transitive or intransitive verbs, as in the following pairs:

> We *worked* the puzzle as a group. (transitive)
> We *worked* inside the hot building. (intransitive)

> The children *played* the piano for their parents. (transitive)
> The children *played* in the muddy water. (intransitive)

A relatively few verbs in English can be either transitive or intransitive but usually not both. The following list includes words that are typically transitive only:

> enjoy
> find
> like (meaning enjoy)
> excuse
> reward
> feed
> sell

Words that are typically intransitive only include the following:

> disappear
> belong
> go
> laugh
> wonder
> giggle
> feast

Of course, these words could be used in some rather unusual sentence constructions, such as, perhaps, in the following question-and-answer sequence:

> **Question:** What do you do for a living?
> **Answer:** I sell.

Such constructions are not common, but the point here is that verbs are usually transitive or intransitive, and few verbs are exclusively one or the other.

COPULATIVE VERBS

A *copulative verb* (also called a *copular verb*) is a verb that usually patterns with a modifier or noun (or noun substitute) that is necessary to complete the meaning of the sentence.

There are two main kinds of copulative verbs:

- The verb *to be*
- Linking verbs

The Verb *To Be*

The forms of the verb *to be*, in addition to *be*, are the following:

am
is
are
was
were
been

Notice how these forms pattern in the following sentences. In the first group, the sentences have adjectives following the form of the verb *to be:*

The water *is* blue.
The suitcase *was* really heavy.
The children *were* dirty and very tired.
The skies have *been* overcast for several days.

In the second group, *be* is followed by a nominal (noun or noun substitute):

Sally *is* the president of the senior class.
I *am* the person responsible for the accident.
You may *be* the driver today if you wish.
Sue and Allison *are* the missing students.

In the final group, *be* is followed by an adverb of time or place or by a phrase that expresses time or place:

The papers *are* not here.
The car *was* in the garage.
The Smiths *were* here yesterday morning.

Adverbs are discussed in Chapter 4, "Modifiers," in the section titled "Adverbs."

Few problems arise in constructing sentences using these different sentence forms—as long as sentences contain nouns and not pronouns after the verb *to be*. When a pronoun is in the third position, the pronoun must be in the *nominative* case, as in the following sentences:

The winner was *he* with the red shirt.
The president is *she* who was elected by the members.
It is *I* whom you wish to see.
The driver must have been *he*.

In informal situations (and even in formal situations upon occasion), you often hear the objective form of the pronoun employed after a form of the verb *to be:*

That's *me*.
It might have been *her*.
It's *him*.

Because the level of usage that is employed in various situations should be governed by the nature of each situation, any pronouncements concerning the acceptability or unacceptability of such expressions as "It's me" would be presumptuous. However, in formal speaking and writing situations, in which you are often judged by the appropriateness of your speech habits, you should strive to take a formal approach to usage. In formal situations, if you err, you should err on the side of formality.

Linking Verbs

Linking verbs are copulative verbs because they require a subject complement to complete the meaning of the sentence. Linking verbs are verbs such as *looked* in the following sentence:

The children *looked* tired after playing in the water.

Any verb that can be substituted in the place of *looked* is probably a linking verb. Some common linking verbs include the following:

appear
become
grow
remain
seem
get
sound
smell
feel
taste
continue

Notice how the verbs function as links between the subjects and the subject complements in the following sentences:

> This meat *smells* rotten.
> The apple at the top of the tree *appeared* ripe.
> The custodian *seems* satisfied with his work.
> That music *sounds* loud and noisy to our parents.
> The soldiers *grew* weary of the training exercise.

Linking Verbs versus the Verb *To Be*

There are some obvious and some subtle differences between linking verbs and the verb *to be:*

- Linking verbs often suggest a possibility rather than offer an absolute observation, as does *be*. Notice:

  > The milk *tasted* sour.
  >> (Although the milk tasted sour, it may not have *been* sour. This is a linking verb.)
  > The milk *was* sour.
  >> (The statement is unqualified. The milk was indeed sour.)

- Linking verbs often imply certain kinds of action or activity, such as smelling, tasting, becoming, and so on. The verb *to be* does not do so directly.
- Linking verbs are not used as auxiliaries in verb phrases, while the various forms of *be* are; and linking verbs do not "stack up" as *be* may (as in the phrase "may have been dancing").

Unusual Linking Verbs

Some words that are not generally thought of as linking verbs perform the same function as linking verbs and therefore should be considered linking verbs:

> go
> stand
> work
> run
> turn
> fall
> lay

(There are a few other linking verbs with limited use.) A few of these words are used in the following sentences:

The prisoner *stands* mute before the court.
The water *lay* calm and peaceful in the moonlight.
The tire *worked* loose from the rim.
Every time the principal enters, the cafeteria *falls* silent.

Linking Verbs and Auxiliaries

Linking verbs may be preceded by auxiliary verbs, as in the following sentence:

The mirror *may have **appeared*** broken to you.

Auxiliaries are discussed later in this chapter, in the section "Auxiliary Verbs."

Modifiers and Linking Verbs

With verbs pertaining to the senses (*feel, taste, become, smell, sound, grow, look, appear,* and the like), an adjective form is required if the modifier relates to the subject; an adverb form is required if the modifier relates to the verb.

Linking verbs are followed by a subject complement. When the same words are followed by *adverbials,* the words are not linking verbs; rather, they are action verbs. For example, the verb in the second sentence of each pair below is not a linking verb:

The detectives *looked sleepy* from working all night long.
> (*Looked* is a linking verb, not an action verb; thus, the modifier is an adjective, not an adverb.)

The detectives *looked sleepily* at one another.
> (In this sentence, *looked* is an action verb and *sleepily* indicates the manner in which they looked, not how they looked as in the first sentence; thus, the modifier is an adverb.)

The climbers *grew* weak from lack of water.
The trees *grew* quickly from all the sun and rain.

Leslie *appears* wise and competent.
Peter *appears* nightly, guitar in hand, to serenade Naomi.

See Chapter 4 for more information about these types of modifiers.

Following are several sample sentences, with the correct modifier indicated

Neither John nor Nathan seems (*angry, angrily*). Each has shaken the other's hand.
>**angry**

Sarah looked (*angry, angrily*) at Ruth and me when Joe entered the room.
>**angrily**

Ben looks (*bad, badly*) because of his illness.
>**bad**

Raj wanted (*bad, badly*) to go to the concert.
>**badly**

Each of the girls looks (*beautiful, beautifully*) wearing her new clothes.
>**beautiful**

That milk tastes (*sour, sourly*) to both him and me.
>**sour**

From where we were sitting, the thunder sounded (*loud, loudly*).
>**loud**

The roses in the vase smell (*sweet, sweetly*) to her and me.
>**sweet**

You must grill the meat (*tender, tenderly*) so that it will taste good.
>**tender**

The masonry instructor taught us students to build a wall (*strong, strongly*).
>**strong**

His moving to another state makes us friends feel (*sad, sadly*).
>**sad**

Boil the eggs (*soft, softly*) while he and she set the table.
>**soft**

She looked (*angry, angrily*) because I believed her to be him.
>**angry**

The engine runs (*smooth, smoothly*) because Dad and I overhauled it.
>**smoothly**

While Eric and I were on the mountain, the whistle of the train sounded (*faint, faintly*) in the distance.
>**faint**

The mother looked (*proud, proudly*) as the committee honored her daughter.
>**proud**

Each of the students feels (*unhappy, unhappily*) about failing his examinations.
> **unhappy**

Harry, as well as they, seems (*happy, happily*) to be home again.
> **happy**

He looked (*sad, sadly*) at his co-workers as he announced his resignation.
> **sadly**

The father looked on (*proud, proudly*) as his son received the award.
> **proudly**

A rose by any other name would smell as (*sweet, sweetly*).
> **sweet**

This meal tastes (*delicious, deliciously*).
> **delicious**

Puppies appear so (*playfully, playful*) in pet stores.
> **playful**

Both men felt (*strange, strangely*) after the accident.
> **strange**

The incense smelled (*fragrant, fragrantly*).
> **fragrant**

The patient looked (*hopefully, hopeful*) at the doctor.
> **hopefully**

AUXILIARY VERBS

An *auxiliary verb* is one of a small set of verbs that combine with a main verb to express various shades of meaning, usually of time or voice. (Refer to the discussion of active and passive voice earlier in this section.) The three primary auxiliaries are *be, have,* and *do*. Others include the following:

- **Modal auxiliaries:**

    may
    might
    can
    could
    shall
    should
    will
    would
    must

- **Marginal auxiliaries:**

    dare
    need
    ought to
    used to

- **Semi-auxiliaries (auxiliary-like verbs):**

    be going to
    have to
    had better

You must be careful when examining sentence patterns not to confuse sentence patterns with *be* as the main verb with sentence patterns with *be* as an *auxiliary* or *helping* verb because forms of the verb *to be* are often used as auxiliaries. The first of each pair of the following sentences employs *be* as the main verb, while the second employs *be* as an auxiliary. The main verbs in the sentences are italicized.

Carl *is* a basketball player.
Carl is *playing* basketball.

The men *were* here by noon.
The men were *planning* to be here by noon.

These *are* the plans I have submitted.
We are *submitting* these plans.

Recognizing the Various Types of Verbs

The following sentences contain examples of various types of verbs:

All the children were standing in line and waiting for ice cream.

were: auxiliary
standing: intransitive
waiting: intransitive

If you see my roommate, ask her to bring my notes to class.

see: transitive (active)
ask: transitive (active)

The children were excited about their grandmother's impending arrival.
    were: to be

We were washing the car when the storm arrived.

    were: auxiliary
    washing: transitive (active)
    arrived: intransitive

The floor had been scrubbed to a high gloss by the new recruits.

    had been: auxiliary
    scrubbed: intransitive

Try catching a fly with your hands; it is really difficult.

    try: transitive (active)
    is: to be

We waited until four o'clock, then we left without James.

    waited: intransitive
    left: intransitive

The group left Stan sleeping in a car in the parking lot.

    left: transitive (active)

We considered the alternatives and then made our decision.

    considered: transitive (active)
    made: transitive (active)

Before we leave, we want to congratulate you on a job well done.

    leave: intransitive
    want: transitive (active)

The children watched the toy sailboats on the pond.

    watched: transitive

We all thought about the lost hunting party.

    thought: intransitive (*about the lost hunting party* is a prepositional phrase)

My brother gave Mother a pretty weak excuse.

> **gave:** transitive

Some people dream about frightening things.

> **dream:** intransitive

Some people have no dreams at all.

> **have:** transitive

Verb Tenses and Aspects

Tense refers to the time of a situation. English makes use of two tense categories, which are indicated by the form of the verb:

> **Present:** walks, is walking, has been walking
> **Past:** walked, was walking, had been walking

Tense is indicated by the inflection of the first or only verb in the verb phrase:

- Present tense for all verbs (except modal auxiliaries—that is, *may, might, can, could, shall, should, will, would, must*) is indicated by the *s* form for third-person singular and by the base (uninflected) form for others:

  > Edward *saves* cereal box tops to collect prizes. (third-person singular)
  > I *save* fabric scraps in order to make quilts. (all other forms)

- Regular verbs (and many irregular verbs) employ the *ed* inflection to indicate past tense:

  > We *saved* the man's life by administering CPR.
  > Auxiliaries are also used to make clear distinctions in time. For example, auxiliaries such as *will* and *be going* indicate that the action expressed by the main verb will occur sometime in the future.

Unlike tense, which indicates a verb's location in time in absolute terms (past or present), a verb's *aspect* refers to the way the time of the situation is regarded. Aspects are expressed by a combination of an auxiliary and a main verb. In English, two types of aspects apply:

- **Perfect aspect:** This aspect is used to indicate the time of one situation in relative terms to the time of another situation.

  > I *have climbed* this mountain many times before now.

- **Progressive aspect:** This aspect indicates the duration of a situation.

  > I *am strolling* the boardwalk.

Aspects always appear in sentences in conjunction with tenses to form the following:

- **Present perfect:** has walked, have walked
- **Past perfect:** had walked
- **Present progressive:** am walking, is walking, are walking
- **Past progressive:** was walking, were walking

The perfect and progressive aspects can be combined, as in the case of *has been walking*.

Irregular English Verbs

Although the vast majority of verbs in the English language have a predictable pattern when it comes to indicating tense, there are, alas, numerous verbs that differ in this regard. Except in the case of the highly irregular verb *be*, which has eight forms, irregular verbs may have as many as five different forms:

- Base
- *s* form
- *ing* form
- Past
- *ed* participle

The *ed* participle is used in conjunction with *had, has,* or *have* to indicate past-perfect or present-perfect tense.

Except in the case of *be*, the *s* and *ing* forms are predictable for all irregular verbs. For your reference, the following table indicates the base, past forms, and *ed* participles of several irregular verbs:

Base	Past	*ed* Participle
begin	began	begun
bend	bent	bent
bite	bit	bitten
bleed	bled	bled
blow	blew	blown
break	broke	broken
build	built	built
burn	burned or burnt	burned or burnt

(continued)

(continued)

Base	Past	*ed* Participle
burst	burst	burst
buy	bought	bought
cast	cast	cast
come	came	come
cost	cost or costed	cost or costed
cut	cut	cut
deal	dealt	dealt
dig	dug	dug
dive	dived or dove	dived or dove
dream	dreamed or dreamt	dreamed or dreamt
drink	drank	drunk
drive	drove	driven
feed	fed	fed
feel	felt	felt
fight	fought	fought
find	found	found
fit	fitted or fit	fitted or fit
get	got	got or gotten
hang	hung or hanged	hung or hanged
have	had	had
hear	heard	heard
hide	hid	hidden
hit	hit	hit
hold	held	held
hurt	hurt	hurt
keep	kept	kept
kneel	kneeled or knelt	kneeled or knelt
lay	laid	laid
lean	leaned or leant	leaned or leant
leap	leaped or leapt	leaped or leapt
learn	learned or learnt	learned or learnt
let	let	let
lie	lay	lain
light	lighted or lit	lighted or lit
lose	lost	lost
make	made	made

Base	Past	*ed* Participle
mow	mowed	mowed or mown
put	put	put
quit	quitted or quit	quitted or quit
read	read	read
rid	ridded or rid	ridded or rid
ring	rang	rung
run	ran	run
saw	sawed	sawed or sawn
say	said	said
see	saw	seen
set	set	set
sew	sewed	sewed or sewn
shear	sheared	sheared or shorn
show	showed	showed or shown
shrink	shrank	shrunk
sing	sang	sung
smell	smelled or smelt	smelled or smelt
speak	spoke	spoken
speed	speeded or sped	speeded or sped
spell	spell or spelt	spell or spelt
spoil	spoiled or spoilt	spoiled or spoilt
stand	stood	stood
sting	stung	stung
strike	struck	struck
sweat	sweated or sweat	sweated or sweat
swell	swelled	swelled or swollen
swim	swam	swum
take	took	taken
tear	tore	torn
wed	wedded or wed	wedded or wed
wet	wetted or wet	wetted or wet
win	won	won
wind	wound	wound
write	wrote	written

> ## Irregularities within Irregularities: Cost/Costed and Hang/Hanged
>
> *Cost* in the sense of "estimate the value or cost of" is a regular verb; *cost* in the sense of "to require expenditure or payment" or "to require effort, suffering or loss" is an irregular verb. When the word *cost* is used to mean "estimate the value or cost of," its past tense and past-participle forms are *costed*.
>
> **Incorrect:** Rescuing the drowning child nearly *costed* Edgar his life.
> **Correct:** That house *cost* me an arm and leg.
>
> **Incorrect:** Evelyn *cost* the antiques on our behalf.
> **Correct:** Joseph *costed* the car at $4,100.
>
> The verb *to hang* has multiple meanings; the regularity or irregularity of the various verb forms depends on the intended meaning. *Hang* denoting suspension by the neck (as in an execution or a suicide) is a regular verb (*hang, hanged, hanged*); all other forms are irregular and use the forms listed above.

Moods of Verbs

In English, writers employ three *moods* or *modes* to indicate various relationships or conditions:

- Indicative
- Imperative
- Subjunctive

THE INDICATIVE MOOD

The *indicative mood* is employed to state a fact or to ask a question and is the form common to most sentences, whether declarative or question:

We *visited* some friends last night.
Did Roger *ask* his father for advice?
Everyone *was waiting* for the rain to stop.

THE IMPERATIVE MOOD

The *imperative mood* is employed when a sentence states a request, command, or suggestion:

Call me in the morning.
Stop playing with your food!
Please *remain* in your seats until the bell rings.

THE SUBJUNCTIVE MOOD

The *subjunctive mood* is employed to express a condition contrary to fact, a wish, a supposition, a prayer, or a doubt, as well as in *that* clauses. The subjunctive mood is most commonly employed, however, in contrary-to-fact statements such as the following:

> I wish I *were* young again.
> If we *were* rich, we could buy a vacation home.

Notice that in the subjunctive mood, *were* is used for both singular and plural subjects. The same holds true for sentences containing *if* clauses reflecting past events:

> If Miss America *were* there, she would be recognized.

When expressing a doubt, the verb *to be* is employed:

> If that *be* the situation, I'm leaving.
> If there *be* any doubt, check the map.

The *present subjunctive* occurs with verbs such as *insist*:

> I insist that you *take* these leftovers.
> The TSA representative insisted that she *remove* her shoes before passing through the metal detector.

Certain idiomatic expressions also require the subjunctive mood:

> *Come* spring, I'll be in the mountains.
> He appeared, as it *were,* ready to fight for nothing.
> Torpedoes *be damned!* Full speed ahead!

An *idiomatic expression,* or *idiom,* is an expression that is peculiar to itself grammatically or that has a meaning that cannot be derived from the conjoined meaning of its elements.

As if clauses are contrary to fact and take the subjunctive:

> He acts *as if he were* God's gift to women.

Making Verbs Negative

Sentences are typically negated through the verb via the insertion of *not,* or, in informal speech or writing, by attaching not's contraction, *n't,* to the end of the first or only verb. In sentences containing auxiliary verbs, *not* follows the auxiliary, or *n't* is attached to the auxiliary:

Shelley *should not* think twice about asking for a raise.
The queen *must not* concern herself with such trivial details as cleaning.

If a sentence contains no auxiliary verb, then the appropriate form (based on tense and person) of the auxiliary *do* is inserted to indicate a negative expression:

Do not dream of leaving us here!
Katherine *did not panic*, despite Stephen's obvious injuries.

EXCEPTIONS TO THE RULES

A few verbs do not adhere to these rules:

* The verb *to be* requires no auxiliary when being converted to express a negative thought:

    Cats *are not* as loyal as dogs.
    Greg *was not* the best candidate for mayor.

* The verb *to have* allows for both alternatives. All the following sentences are considered acceptable negations of the sentence "Heidi has her own room":

    Heidi *has not* her own room. (formal)
    Heidi *hasn't* her own room. (informal)

    Heidi *does not have* her own room. (formal)
    Heidi *doesn't have* her own room. (informal)

EXPRESSING NEGATION OTHER THAN THROUGH THE VERB

Words such as *no, not,* and the like can be used to negate a sentence without making the verb negative. Compare the following pairs of sentences. The first sentence in each pair employs the traditional negation (through the verb); the second sentence in each pair uses an alternative means to convey the same negative idea:

Britney *hasn't* a clue about the Civil War.
Britney *has no* clue about the Civil War.

Mother *did not speak* a word of my being grounded.
Mother *spoke not* a word of my being grounded.

DEALING WITH DOUBLE NEGATIVES

A double negative occurs when a sentence contains two negative ideas, thus effectively canceling out both ideas:

> I *don't listen* to *nobody*.
> I *don't have nothing* to do today.

Although sentences such as these are quite common in informal speech, the meaning they express is in fact a positive idea—the opposite of what most speakers intend:

> I *listen* to *somebody*.
> I *do have something* to do today.

Although you should, in general, avoid such constructions, certain double-negative constructions have gained acceptance in contemporary speech:

> Josie's new glasses *did not go unnoticed*.
> Ian *wasn't unhappy* with his choice of suits.
> Jane is *not unlike* her sisters in that respect.

To the trained ear, however, such constructions sound somewhat stilted or affected. Perhaps a more effective way of stating the same ideas in formal situations would be the following:

> Josie's new glasses *were noticed*.
> Ian was *relatively happy* with his choice of suits.
> Jane is *somewhat like* her sisters in that respect.

Subject-Verb Agreement

One fundamental requirement for every sentence you write or speak is that the subject and verb of the sentence agree. That is, if the subject of your sentence is plural, that should be reflected in the verb form—regardless of tense, aspect, or mood. Because of the inherent complexity of the English language, however, it is sometimes not clear how such agreement is achieved. For this reason, several rules concerning subject-verb agreement follow:

- A verb must at all times agree with its subject in both person and number.
- Most indefinite pronouns require singular verbs. *Each, either, neither, someone, somebody, anyone, anybody, everyone, everybody, no one, nobody,* and *one* (and *a person*) are singular. *Both, few, many, others, several, we, you,* and *they* are plural and take the plural form of the verb.

- Prepositional phrases following indefinite pronouns usually do not influence verb number:

  > *Each* of the puppies **was** healthy.
  > *Neither* of the books **was** interesting to me.

The exceptions to this rule are in the cases of a fraction or a percentage and such words as *all, most, more, part, some, such, rest, any,* and *none.* These are singular if bulk or a total number or amount is intended and plural if numbers are considered. That is, if the object of the preposition in a phrase modifying the subject of the verb (even if the prepositional phrase is unstated or understood) is a count noun, the verb is plural; if the object of the preposition is a mass noun, the verb is singular:

  > Twenty percent *of a person's body heat* **is** lost through the top of his head.
  > Twenty percent *of the diplomats* **are** members of the delegation.
  > The rest *of the laundry* **is** in the dryer.
  > The rest *of the guests* **are** on their way.

- The word *number,* if preceded by *a* and followed by *of,* takes a plural verb. When *number* is preceded by *the,* it takes a singular verb:

  > *A number* of students **are** in the lobby.
  > *The number* of defects in the product **is** disappointing.

When preceded by the word *any, number* is singular when it refers to a single item and plural when it refers to more than one item:

  > *Any number of guests* **is** too many if the host has already gone to sleep.
  > *Any number of guests* **are** expected at the party.

- Two or more subjects connected by *and* require a plural verb, except in the case of singular subjects connected by *and,* which require a *singular* verb if the subjects denote the same person or thing:

  > The *winner and loser* **are** both tired.
  > The *winner and* defending *champion* **is** James P. Sullivan.

In addition, singular subjects joined by *and* require a singular verb if the subjects denote foods commonly served together as one dish:

  > *Biscuits and gravy* **is** my favorite breakfast dish.

This is an especially perplexing concept because much of what is visualized as consisting of a single entity is in the language user's mind. Items being served (as on a food line, for instance) are not a meal, thus:

  > *Ham and eggs* **are** being served this morning.
  > *Ham and eggs* **is** Carl's favorite morning treat.

In situations where such usage may sound awkward or stilted, you have the option of simply reversing the sentence order:

> Carl's favorite morning treat is ham and eggs.

- Expressions indicating quantity or amount to be considered as a unit require a singular verb. These expressions often refer to amounts of money, units of time, or measurements:

> *Five dollars* **is** the price of that shirt.
> *Two hundred yards* **is** a long way to crawl.

- Nouns plural in form but singular in meaning require a singular verb:

> *Mumps* **is** very uncommon in the United States today.

- *There, here,* and *where* are not usually subjects. If these words begin a sentence, the number of the verb is determined by the number of the nominal (noun) following them:

> *There* **are** four cats in my bedroom.
> *There* **is** one cat too many for me to tolerate.

- When the correlative conjunctions *both-and* join the parts of a compound subject, the verb is plural:

> *Both* the lion *and* the tiger **are** friendly animals.

- Two or more singular subjects joined by *or* or *nor* require a singular verb:

> Either John *or* his sister **is** the hall monitor.
> Neither the storm *nor* the hail **frightens** us.

- When the words *or, either-or, nor, neither-nor,* or *not only-but also* join the parts of a compound subject, the verb must agree with the nearer subject:

> *Either* the cat *or* its *kittens* **are** eating the food.
> *Not only* his neighbors *but also John* **has** a new pool.

- Intervening phrases and clauses not introduced by coordinating conjunctions do not affect the number of the verb. These phrases and clauses often begin with words such as *including, as well as, no less than, together with, with,* and *accompanied by:*

> My *mother, together with* my sisters, **is** at the store.
> The *chief, accompanied by* six officers, **has** talked to the protesters.

- If two or more subjects are joined by *and* and are preceded by *each* or *every,* the verb is singular:

> *Each* person *and* his guest **is** expected to arrive promptly.
> *Every* worker *and* her tools **is** needed for this new task.

- If one subject is used affirmatively and the other negatively, the verb agrees with the one that is used affirmatively:

  John, not the workers, **is** responsible for the error.
  Not the team but the *coaches* **are** late for the game.

- A verb is *never* affected by a subject complement:

  The *gift* he gave his friend **was** books.
  (*Books* is the subject complement.)

- If a verb has a relative pronoun (*who, that, which*) as its subject, the verb must agree with the antecedent of the relative pronoun:

  The group of children *who were* here is going to the new school.
  (The antecedent of *who* is *children,* not *group;* thus, children *were,* and group *is* going. If *group* is intended as the antecedent, then *was* is the correct form of the verb.)

  The man parked his old cars in the barn *that was* abandoned.
  (The antecedent of *that* is *barn,* not *cars.*)

You must be very certain that you understand the relationship of the sentence parts and the role the relative pronoun plays in some sentences—especially in sentences that contain the word *only*. Notice the difference in meaning of the following two sentences:

  She is one of the **seniors** *who were* absent from class.
  (In this sentence, the relative *who* refers to *seniors;* thus you would rightly employ a plural verb form, *were.*)

  She is the only one of the seniors *who was* late.
  (Only one senior was late. Who? *She was.* The *who* refers to *she,* not to *seniors.*)

Although these sentences can be confusing, one way to determine the antecedent of the relative pronoun is to try to locate the word *only* or similar words. Such words are often a giveaway for the use of the relative. Also, try restructuring the sentence by placing the prepositional phrase first:

  Logical: Of the seniors who were absent from class, she is one.
  Illogical: Of the seniors who were absent from class, she is the only one.
  (How could seniors [plural] be absent from class if she was the only one?)

You'll learn more about how sentence parts relate to one another in Chapter 9.

- When the subject is a title of a book, newspaper, or work of art; a clause; a direct quotation; or a name of a firm or an organization, a singular verb is required:

> "The Chrysanthemums" **is** a story by Steinbeck.
> *Weekly Ramblings* **is** a high school newspaper.
> Gittlejax and Wallentine **is** representing our interests.
> "Who Would Count Eternity in Days" **is** from a poem by Theodore Roethke.

- The expression *many a* requires a singular verb:

  > *Many a* day is required to complete some tasks.

- A relative pronoun used as a substitute for the first-person pronoun (*I*) requires a verb form that is consistent with the form of the verb that would be used with the personal pronoun:

  > Give the prize to *me* who **am** the winner.
  >   (*Who* equals *me* equals *I*, which takes *am*. ["I am the winner."])

  > It is *I* who **feel** guilty about the confusion.
  >   (*Who* equals *I*, which takes *feel*. ["I feel guilty."])

- Elements of modifying clauses that come between a verb and its subject do not influence subject-verb agreement:

  > The *air controller* whom you saw guiding the planes **was** rewarded for her excellent work.

- Appositives, including parenthetical expressions, do not affect subject-verb agreement:

  > The work *crew*—John, Rolinda, and their brothers—**was** already at work when we arrived.
  > My *daughter*, the person who wrote the stories, **is** an English major.

- The pronoun *none* is often used in place of *no one* or *not one*. *None* may be either singular or plural but is now more commonly plural:

  > *None* of the students **have** finished their work.
  > *None* of the oranges **are** ripe yet.

Logic would seem to dictate the use of a singular verb because *none* means less (or fewer) than one, but idioms often defy logic. In this case, however, a simple substitution test can be helpful: *None* can be construed as singular if *not one* or *no one* can be substituted for it. *None* can be considered plural when *no persons* or any of a group of things or people can replace it—that is, oddly, when *none* applies to more than one:

> He received no reward, and *none* **was** expected.
> *None* (*no persons*) **are** more insecure than victims in hostage situations.
> (*None* refers to *victims*, which is plural; thus the plural verb is used.)

When *none* precedes a singular noun, use a singular verb:

None of the *cake* **is** left on the table.

From A.D. 1450 to 1650, *none is* was the preferred usage by a margin of three to one; from 1650 to 1917, *none are* was preferred seven to four; from 1917 to the present, *none are* is preferred, but usage is varied, as noted.

When in doubt about the use of verbs with idioms (words and expressions peculiar to a language), consult a good dictionary.

Selecting the Correct Verb Form

Following are numerous sample sentences that demonstrate the selection of the correct verb forms:

Robert, as well as John and his sister, (*was, were*) late today.
   was

Neither David nor she (*was, were*) able to go to Alaska.
   was

(*Has, Have*) either Frank or she studied Greek?
   Has

Here (*come, comes*) Tina and her friends.
   come

James and I thought it to be LuAnn and her; however, neither (*was, were*) there.
   was

(*Was, Were*) you and she at home when Tom and he called?
   Were

Every one of the girls (*was, were*) at the station to meet Joe and me.
   was

There (*is, are*) Leslie and Anita, as well as she, walking with Frank and him.
   are

(*Has, Have*) her brother and she decided to go with you, him, and them?
   Have

The dean, as well as the professors, (*is, are*) kind to John and me.
   is

John, Tom, and I (*is, are*) the committee.
> **are**

A number of the members (*has, have*) visited Lynne and me.
> **have**

Neither the dean nor the professors (*advise, advises*) you and me to study French this semester.
> **advise**

You, not he, (*is, are*) the one whom we chose.
> **are**

Neither Mr. Black nor his son (*was, were*) able to assist us students.
> **was**

John, together with the rest of us seniors, (*was, were*) in Dayton last week.
> **was**

Every man and woman (*is, are*) responsible for what has happened.
> **is**

The team (*has, have*) agreed upon a practice time.
> **has**

Measles (*is, are*) very contagious.
> **is**

Spaghetti and meatballs (*was, were*) on the menu.
> **was**

Ten percent of the students (*is, are*) absent.
> **are**

The number of people absent (*is, are*) smaller than expected.
> **is**

Ten miles (*is, are*) a rather long distance to walk with someone who is unable to walk far.
> **is**

She is one of those people who (*is, are*) always late.
> **are**

Many a person (*has, have*) been disappointed by someone in whom he placed his confidence.
> **has**

Eleanor is the only one of those workers who (*is, are*) resting.
> **is**

The Merry Wives of Windsor (*is, are*) usually enjoyed by all who have the opportunity to see the play.
>**is**

Books (*is, are*) always an appropriate gift for us readers.
>**are**

Two thirds of the material (*has, have*) been wasted.
>**has**

Both you and he (*is, are*) accountable to someone whom you consider to be most capable of handling authority.
>**are**

Betty is one of those readers who (*skips, skip*) to the last page.
>**skip**

Do you believe that $100 (*is, are*) too much to pay for this item?
>**is**

Here (*come, comes*) those you believe are troublemakers.
>**come**

The team (*is, are*) on its way to Louisville.
>**is**

Corned beef and cabbage (*is, are*) one of his favorite dishes.
>**is**

This is one of those books that (*is, are*) usually popular with people who you think are avid readers.
>**are**

That he drives no better than we (*is, are*) an accepted fact.
>**is**

Each junior and senior (*is, are*) insistent upon seeing someone they believe can answer their questions.
>**is**

The fact that you were believed to be she and that I was believed to be he (*is, are*) difficult to comprehend.
>**is**

Where (*is, are*) those candidates whom you have declared to be eligible?
>**are**

Do you think the preserves (*is, are*) good on toast?
>**are**

Not only he but also she (*think, thinks*) that you are the guilty one.
thinks

Bread and butter (*is, are*) his favorite snack.
is

Neither Sue nor her many friends (*has, have*) studied Latin.
have

She, not her sisters, (*is, are*) attending the conference.
is

Each of the 20 cousins (*was, were*) at the reunion.
was

He is the only one of the swimmers who (*needs, need*) water wings.
needs

Each of you (*is, are*) to be congratulated.
is

The girl whom you saw talking to my brothers (*was, were*) she whom you have long admired.
was

Three freshmen—you, he, and she—(*was, were*) selected.
were

The committee (*is, are*) John, Joe, Sue, and they.
is

You, as well as I, (*is, are*) older than she.
are

Mine is one of the papers that (*is, are*) late.
are

No, it is not I who (*is, am, are*) the guilty one.
am

Each of you (*knows, know*) that it was I who called.
knows

Neither of them (*believes, believe*) it was he who wrote the book.
believes

Neither she nor they (*is, are*) so young as I.
are

We teachers, as well as they, (*has, have*) promised to help.
have

Ice cream and cake (*is, are*) his favorite dessert.
is

A man's best friend and companion (*is, are*) his dog.
is

The father and husband (*was, were*) considerate of his family.
was

Five kilometers (*is, are*) the length of the race.
is

Some of the food (*has, have*) already been thrown away.
has

Most of the students (*has, have*) already left campus.
have

Activities such as this (*is, are*) not permitted.
are

Here (*go, goes*) he, she, and I to take the test.
go

The family (*is, are*) planning to meet in Toledo.
is

Isaac is the only one of those students who (*was, were*) willing to help.
was

Dennis is one of those players who (*takes, take*) the game seriously.
take

Troublesome Verbs

Three sets of verbs are somewhat troublesome, even to native speakers of English:

- Lay/lie
- Sit/set
- Raise/rise

The easiest and most practical way to learn the correct usage of these troublesome verbs is to learn the exact definition of each, and, when you are in doubt about which word to use, substitute the definition for the word. If this method is used, making errors is nearly impossible.

Lay/Lie, Sit/Set, Raise/Rise

To *lay* means to "put" or "to place." To *lie* means "to rest" or "to recline."

Lie in this context should not be confused with *lie*, meaning "to fib." That form of *lie* is not an irregular verb.

To *sit* means "to rest." To *set* means "to put" or "to place."

To *raise* means "to lift." To *rise* means "to come up" or "to ascend."

Also, in their usual meanings, *lie, sit,* and *rise* are always intransitive (have no direct objects), and *lay, set,* and *raise* are usually transitive and therefore have direct objects to complete the meaning. Note these examples:

> I *laid* the book on the shelf.
> Let us *lie* here and rest.

> She *sits* by the window to read.
> I *set* the vase on the table.

> Did you *raise* the flag?
> The flames did not *rise* very high.

In addition, the verbs *lay* and *set* may be used as intransitives in certain of their secondary meanings:

> The hen *lays* well.
> The sun *set* at six o'clock.
> The cement did not *set* well.
> The boys eagerly *set* out on their camping trip.

You should be certain that the principal parts of these verbs are firmly fixed in your mind as a means of avoiding usage problems:

Present Tense	Past Tense	Past Participle
I lay	I laid	I have laid
I lie	I lay	I have lain
I set	I set	I have set
I sit	I sat	I have sat
I raise	I raised	I have raised
I rise	I rose	I have risen

MAY/CAN, SHALL/WILL

The verbs *may/can* and *shall/will* often give people trouble. *Can* implies ability, while *may* denotes permission or possibility:

> I *can* lift that bundle.
> Mother says I *may* go to the game tonight.
> I *may* go swimming; I'm not certain.

Shall is used with the first-person pronoun:

> I *shall* sing to you.

Will is used with second- and third-person pronouns:

> You *will* be the first speaker tomorrow evening.
> He *will* lend you the money.
> The robin *will* build a nest in the tree.

Although usage is changing, traditional use of *shall* and *will* incorporates a few more subtleties, some of which can be confusing at times:

- If you wish to express determination, desire, or promise, reverse the normal order given previously and use *will* in the first person and *shall* in the second and third persons:

> I *will* go to Atlanta. No one can stop me!
> You *shall* do as you are told.
> They *shall* be punished as I promised.

- In asking questions, *shall* is used in first-person constructions. In second- and third-person constructions, the choice depends on the correct form that would be used in the *response* or answer to the question:

> *Shall* (not *can*) I do this task for you?
> *Shall* you finish this test on time?
>   (The response or answer is "I shall.")
> *Will* that dog bite?
>   (The response or answer is "He will.")

- *Shall* is used in all persons in noun clauses that serve as objects after verbs such as *deciding, demanding, insisting, willing,* and *wishing* if the subjunctive mood is not employed:

> He demands that the insurgents *shall* surrender immediately.
> He demands that the insurgents *surrender* immediately.
>   (The subjunctive mood of the verb is employed in this sentence.)

- In indirect quotations (where the speaker's thoughts are presented but not his exact words), the tense form that is employed is the one that would be correct for the speaker.

> The president said that he *shall* retire soon.
> (His actual words were, "*I shall* retire soon.")

As stated previously, usage of *shall* and *will* is changing, and many writers and speakers use the various forms of *shall* and *will* interchangeably. In fact, the preceding statements are probably only vaguely known—if known at all—to many writers. Nevertheless, students, writers, and speakers who are concerned about the quality of their speech, especially in formal situations, should be familiar with these forms of standard English.

SHOULD/WOULD, MAY/MIGHT

The uses of *should* and *would* correspond to those of *shall* and *will*. For example, for expressing simple future, you use *should* with the first person and *would* with second and third persons:

> I *should* like to tell you the story of my life.
> The workers *would* need more water in the noonday sun.

The past tense form of *may* is *might*. The past tense form of *shall* is *should*:

> I *may* go to the game; I'm not certain.
> (*May* expresses present or future intentions or possibility.)

> I *might* have done it; I don't remember clearly.
> (*Might* expresses past situations.)

> I *shall* finish my work tomorrow.
> (*Shall* expresses a present or future situation.)

> I *should* have retired while I still had the chance.
> (*Should* expresses a past situation.)

Might is used in other special situations. For instance, *might* is used to state hypothetical situations:

> If the moon were nearer, we *might* be able to drive without lights.

Might is also used to express weaker possibility or probability than *may*:

> Martha *may* become an attorney some day.
> (A reasonable possibility exists.)

Of course I can jump 30 feet. I *might* be able to pole-vault to the moon, too. (The possibility is weak or nonexistent.)

BRING/TAKE

The verbs *bring* and *take* are sometimes misused, although the formal rule governing the use of these two verbs is quite simple: Use *take* to indicate direction *away* from the speaker; use *bring* to indicate direction *toward* the speaker:

I shall *take* these books to the library when I go.
Bring your work to class when you come next Friday.
When you go to Washington, *take* light clothing.
I shall *bring* my dog when we come hunting here tomorrow.

SELECTING THE CORRECT TROUBLESOME VERB

Following are numerous sample sentences that demonstrate the selection of the correct troublesome verbs:

He spent the summer just (*laying, lying*) about the house.
lying

Someone (*lay, laid*) the dictionary on my glasses.
laid

Jackie (*lay, laid*) down across the bench.
lay

I saw your hat (*laying, lying*) on the hall table.
lying

Did you (*bring, take*) your sister to the party last night?
take

Mother said I (*can, may*) go to the river to swim.
may

I (*should, would*) like to propose a toast to the happy couple.
should

She had just (*laid, lain*) down when the telephone rang.
lain

Have the workers (*laid, lain*) the cornerstone yet?
laid

The children were (*laying, lying*) on an old army blanket.
> **lying**

(*Set, Sit*) the box in a place where we'll find it again.
> **Set**

Don't leave any money (*laying, lying*) in plain sight.
> **lying**

The shipwreck (*lay, laid*) in 20 feet of water.
> **lay**

I am determined that I (*shall, will*) ground you for misbehaving.
> **will**

The chairman insists that all members (*shall, will*) vote this time.
> **shall**

My cat loves to (*lay, lie*) on the windowsill.
> **lie**

The old shirt was (*laying, lying*) in a corner of the closet.
> **lying**

(*Shall, Will*) you be ready to go to the game on time?
> **Shall**

The cat (*shall, will*) catch the mouse sooner or later.
> **will**

Do you remember where you (*laid, lay*) my pen?
> **laid**

Did you (*bring, take*) your report to class when you came today?
> **bring**

You shouldn't have (*laid, lain*) in the sun so long.
> **lain**

I could see Jack (*laying, lying*) on the deck.
> **lying**

The general said they (*shall, will*) attack at dawn.
> **shall**

(*Can, May*) I help you build this table?
> **May**

If you are good, we (*shall, will*) sing to you.
> **shall**

I'm so tired I can't (*raise, rise*) myself from this bed.
   raise

Did you (*bring, take*) some apples to your sister when you went to visit her?
   take

Maria has been (*setting, sitting*) by the telephone all evening.
   sitting

Bill just (*sat, set*) still and didn't say a word.
   sat

Extra chairs were (*sat, set*) in the aisles by the ushers.
   set

Had you (*sat, set*) there awhile, you would have caught a fish.
   sat

Some careless person had (*sat, set*) in the fresh paint.
   sat

The river has been (raising, rising) all night.
   rising

When you come to work on your car, (*bring, take*) your new tools.
   bring

The new tax would (*raise, rise*) prices again.
   raise

The (*raise, rise*) in prices would affect us all.
   rise

Our hopes (*raised, rose*) and fell at the same instant.
   rose

(*Can, May*) I do this task with only one uninjured hand?
   Can

Do you think you (*shall, will*) finish this quiz before noon?
   shall

(*Bring, Take*) me to your leader!
   Take

I (*may, might*) go to the gym if I have enough time.
   may

The witness (*may, might*) have seen the defendant in her home.
   might

The old hen (*sat, set*) on the nest for two weeks.
    sat

We saw smoke (*raising, rising*) behind the barn.
    rising

The moon (*raises, rises*) about 7 P.M. and (*sets, sits*) about 8 A.M.
    rises
    sets

Because of its heavy load, the plane could not (*raise, rise*).
    rise

The glue we used on the shelf would not (*set, sit*) right.
    set

The doll has (*laid, lain*) in the yard for two days.
    lain

You (*shall, will*) follow instructions or be punished!
    shall

All of us (*may, might*) go to the beach next week.
    may

I (*shall, will*) not be able to attend class tomorrow.
    shall

We all hope that the band (*shall, will*) appear on stage.
    will

Rents are (*raising, rising*) too rapidly.
    rising

The weather (*may, might*) be too hot for us to go camping.
    may

A thick film of oil (*laid, lay*) on the water.
    lay

Can't you (*set, sit*) still a while longer?
    sit

If his temperature (*raises, rises*), call a doctor.
    rises

The dog has been (*laying, lying*) on my bed.
    lying

Shall I (*bring, take*) my things to your room right now?
    take

You should have tried harder; you (*may, might*) have won.
>**might**

Were the logs (*setting, sitting*) near the fireplace?
>**sitting**

Leslie forgot where she had (*laid, lain*) her gloves.
>**laid**

Last night Carl (*laid, lay*) awake, worrying about the storm.
>**lay**

Kate (*laid, lay*) the sleeping child in her crib.
>**laid**

The old dog (*laid, lay*) down in the cool sand.
>**lay**

We (*shall, will*) respond when we are requested to do so.
>**shall**

If you plan to be there, I'll (*bring, take*) the money to your room tonight.
>**take**

(*Can, May*) I help you correct these tests?
>**May**

Regardless of his instructions, I (*shall, will*) do as I wish!
>**will**

If you wish, you (*can, may*) take my bicycle for a short ride.
>**may**

Books were (*laying, lying*) on tables and chairs.
>**lying**

Elizabeth said she (*shall, will*) ask her boss for a (*raise, rise*).
>**shall**
>**raise**

The stragglers (*may, might*) experience an unpleasant surprise.
>**may**

Carl (*can't, couldn't*) have done that; he was with me today.
>**couldn't**

Can you (*raise, rise*) yourself to a sitting position?
>**raise**

My favorite hen (*lays, lies*) three eggs a day.
>**lays**

The exotic food did not (*set, sit*) very well with the hungry travelers.
sit

The twins have (*laid, lain*) in bed since dawn.
lain

Try to (*set, sit*) a good example for children to follow.
set

Are the scouts (*setting, sitting*) out those young trees?
setting

We should try to (*lay, lie*) aside our prejudices.
lay

The farm hands (*sat, set*) the posts in concrete.
set

If the weather is nice tomorrow, I (*shall, will*) go sailing.
shall

I insist: You (*shall, will*) defend yourself.
shall

I could see the old dog (*laying, lying*) in the sun.
lying

I (*shall, will*) sing that song this evening.
shall

(*Bring, Take*) these tools to the barn when you go.
Take

We (*may, might*) go swimming if the water is warm enough.
may

Peter found a young hen (*setting, sitting*) on some old eggs.
sitting

Latecomers (*may, might*) not find seats that they like.
may

Mabel said that she (*shall, will*) be willing to help.
shall

(*Shall, Will*) you take me to the picnic tomorrow?
Shall

General Observations About Verbs

- A *verb* expresses an act, an occurrence, or a state of being.
- Verbs may be classified in a number of ways, but for the purposes of this text, they are classified as follows:
  - Transitive verbs: *Transitive verbs* are verbs that pattern with direct objects— that is, they express an action that directly affects a grammatical unit (usually a noun or pronoun) elsewhere in a clause or sentence.
  - Intransitive verbs: If a sentence has a verb that shows action of some sort but does not have a direct object, it has a verb known as an *intransitive verb*.
  - To be: The verb *to be* is a copulative verb, which means that it usually patterns with a modifier or noun (or noun substitute) that is necessary to complete the meaning of the sentence.
  - Linking verbs: *Linking verbs* are copulative verbs because they require a subject complement to complete the meaning of the sentence.
  - Auxiliaries: An *auxiliary* is one of a small set of verbs that combine with a main verb to express various shades of meaning, usually of time or voice. The three primary auxiliaries are *be, have,* and *do.*

- In sentences with verbs in the *active voice,* the subject of the verb is the *doer* of the action, or the *actor.* Sentences with verbs in the *passive voice* usually pattern with the actor-action-patient elements in a reverse order.
- *Tense* refers to the time of a situation.
- Unlike tense, which indicates a verb's location in time in absolute terms (past or present), a verb's *aspect* refers to the way the time of the situation is regarded. Aspects are expressed using a combination of an auxiliary and a main verb.
- Although the vast majority of verbs in the English language have a predictable pattern when it comes to indicating tense, a number of verbs differ in this regard.
- In English, writers employ three *moods* or *modes* to indicate various relationships or conditions:
  - The indicative mood: The *indicative mood* is employed to state a fact or to ask a question and is the form common to most sentences, whether declarative or question.
  - The imperative mood: The *imperative mood* is employed when a sentence states a request, command, or suggestion.
  - The subjunctive mood: The *subjunctive mood* is employed to express a condition contrary to fact, a wish, a supposition, a prayer, or a doubt, as well as in *that* clauses. The subjunctive mood is most commonly employed in contrary-to-fact statements.

- One fundamental requirement for every sentence you write or speak is that the subject and verb of the sentence agree. Following various rules ensures that subjects and verbs agree.
- Three sets of verbs are troublesome even to native speakers of English: *sit/set, lay/lie,* and *raise/rise. May/can, shall/will, should/would, may/might,* and *bring/ take* are other verb sets that cause difficulties.

Chapter 4

Modifiers

A *modifier* is a word that describes or limits another word, such as a noun, a pronoun, or a verb or, in the case of some modifiers, a preposition, a conjunction, a verbal, or even another modifier.

There are two types of modifiers:

- Adjectives
- Adverbs

Adjectives

An *adjective* is a word that describes or limits a noun or pronoun, meaning that an adjective places restrictions on any noun with which it is associated. For example, the adjective *small* in the phrase "the small boy" not only describes the boy but also limits the focus to a certain boy, not just any boy—specifically, to the *small* boy.

Usually, an adjective answers one or more of the following questions:

- Which?
- What kind of?
- How many?

For example, examine the following sentences:

The small boy is my brother.
(The adjective *small* both describes and tells which boy.)

A new car is a valuable possession.
(The adjective *new* describes the noun *car* and tells what kind of car.)

The girl had four apples.
(The adjective *four* limits the plural noun *apples* to a certain number by telling how many—in this case, four.)

Although numerals and word numbers (*six, 44,* and so on) are sometimes considered to be adjectives, some teachers of grammar consider them to be members of a special class of prenominal modifiers—*postdeterminers*—which pattern between determiners and adjectives in noun phrases. For our purposes, it seems more practical to consider numerals to be adjectives.

See the section titled "The Hyphen" in Chapter 8, "Punctuation," for the correct way to punctuate two or more words used as single adjectives before nouns, as in this example:

> Roger had a down-in-the-mouth look about him this morning.

Types of Adjectives

Three major types of adjectives are generally recognized:

- Attributive
- Appositive
- Predicate

Attributive Adjectives

Attributive adjectives are those that are found immediately before the word(s) that they modify. Each of the adjectives in italics in the following sentences is an attributive adjective:

> He was reading a *boring* book.
> The *young* man stood by himself in the rain.
> We saw an *old, dark, wooden* house in the woods.

Appositive Adjectives

Appositive adjectives follow the words that they modify. These adjectives are usually used in pairs and employ the conjunction *and* or *but* between them:

> The tree, *tall* and *straight,* stood in the yard.
> The doctor, *young* but *experienced,* remained calm.
> We all knew the cat, *tired* and *wet,* would come home.
> The players, *cold* but *happy,* smiled at the photographer.

Predicate Adjectives

Predicate adjectives are adjectives that occur after linking verbs or after a form of the verb *to be* and that modify the subjects of those verbs. As the name implies, these adjectives occur in the predicate of a sentence or clause, but they must modify the subject of the sentence or clause to be considered predicate adjectives. The adjectives in italics in the following sentences are predicate adjectives:

That girl is *adorable*.
My new car looked *dirty*.
The baby's forehead felt *hot*.
The night was *sultry*.

The adjectives in the following sentence are not predicate adjectives because although they appear in the predicate, they do not modify the subject of the sentence:

The explorer's only company was a huge, white polar bear.

Most predicate adjectives are located after linking verbs such as the following:

ɔoom
appear
look
taste
feel
smell
become

Note that a few verbs not usually considered linking verbs until they are closely examined are verbs such as *work, run,* and *stand:*

The boards covering the old well *worked* loose.
Be sure the keg does not *run* dry before the party begins.
The defendant *stood* mute before his accusers.

Linking verbs are covered in more detail in Chapter 3, "Verbs," in the section titled "Linking Verbs."

Proper Adjectives

A fourth classification, *proper adjective,* should be recognized, although it is semantically different from the other classifications, and members of this group are also members of the other three groups. *Proper adjectives* are adjectives derived from proper nouns or are proper nouns used as adjectives. The first letter of a proper adjective is generally capitalized. The proper adjectives in the following sentences are in italics:

The *American* flag is red, white, and blue.
Although he is an *African* tourist, he enjoys the *Colorado* climate.
We enjoyed seeing *Kentucky* bluegrass again.

DEGREES OF COMPARISON

Adjectives have three degrees of comparison. These three degrees of comparison show relationships between or among the words they modify:

- Positive
- Comparative
- Superlative

Positive Degree

The *positive degree* expresses a quality without a comparison; a statement is made concerning only one entity:

The tree is *tall*.
The grass is *green*.
The water is *cold*.
The twins are *enormous*.

Although *twins* in the last sentence is plural, the entity (*twins*) is not being compared to anything or anyone else.

Comparative Degree

The *comparative degree* expresses a higher or lower degree than the positive. It is used to compare two things, and the inflectional suffix is usually *er:*

Roger is *shorter* than Bill.
Mary seems *taller* than Betty.
She is the *younger* of the two sisters.
Of the two wrestlers, John is the *stronger*.
She sings *better* than anyone else in the choir.

Else or *Other* in Comparative Situations

Else or *other* is required when comparing a person or thing with a class of which it is a part:
Calvin is taller than *anyone* in this class. (Calvin is not in the class. If he were, he would, apparently, be taller than himself.)
Calvin is taller than *anyone else* in this class. (The word *else* indicates that Calvin is in the class.)

Jane is more intelligent than *any* person in the group. (Jane is not in the group.)
Jane is more intelligent than *any other* person in the group. (Jane is a member of the group.)

Superlative Degree

The *superlative degree* is the highest or lowest degree when comparing more than two persons or things. The inflectional suffix for the superlative degree is usually *est.* Adjectives of three or more syllables usually take *most* instead of *est:*

Susan is the *brightest* of all the students in class.
Carl is the *nimblest* player on the team.
That was the *most beautiful* sunset I have ever seen.

Use the *comparative degree* of an adjective or an adverb when speaking of two things and the *superlative degree* when speaking of three or more:

This is the *smaller* of the *two* puppies.
The black one is the *smallest* of the *three* puppies.

More and *Most* with *All, Any,* and *Any Other*

More and *most* are used in special ways with *all, any,* and *any other* to indicate comparisons, especially class (group) and unit (individual) comparisons:

Jeremy is *more* energetic than *any* worker in the group. (Jeremy is obviously not in the group, because he cannot be more energetic than himself.)

Jeremy is *more* energetic than *any other* worker in the group. (Jeremy is a member of the group and is being compared to the other workers in the same group.)

Jeremy is the *most* energetic of *all* workers in the group. (Jeremy is one of the workers, and of all workers in the group, Jeremy is the most energetic.)

Jeremy is *more* energetic than *all* the workers in the group. (The combined energy of all the workers in the group is less than Jeremy's energy. Jeremy is not in the group.)

Jeremy is *more* energetic than *all other* workers in the group. (Jeremy is a member of the group and has more energy than the combined energy of the other workers.)

Adjectives Expressing Absolute Qualities

Adjectives that express within themselves the highest degree of comparison will not submit to further comparison. They express *absolute qualities*. Examples of such words are the following:

    unique
    perfect
    round
    square
    honest
    vertical
    horizontal
    perpendicular
    exact
    endless
    frozen
    dead
    full
    empty
    straight

You compare such words as these by using *more nearly* and *most nearly*. Here are some examples:

> My picture is *more nearly perfect* than your picture.
> That figure seems *more nearly round* than this one.
> Roger's glass is the *most nearly empty* of the three.

The logic reflected by the preceding observation is readily apparent: If something is empty or square or perfect, something else cannot be any emptier or "squarer" or perfect to an even greater extent. A number of writers and authors of textbooks, however, recognize a legitimacy in comparing some of the absolutes. For instance, "more perfect" means something similar to "nearer to a state of perfection," a meaning clearly intended by the writers of the Constitution of the United States of America when they wrote this famous preamble:

> We the people of the United States, in Order to form a *more perfect Union*, establish Justice, insure domestic Tranquility, provide for the common defence, promote the general Welfare, and secure the Blessings of Liberty to ourselves and our Posterity, do ordain and establish this Constitution for the United States of America.

You may often find examples of fine writing that employ such constructions as "more perfect," "sincerest form [of flattery]," and "more honest." In general, you should avoid calling attention to your writing style by employing such constructions.

This same meaning of "nearer to" may be applied to such words as *complete* and *unique*. Consider a sentence such as the following:

> The addition of the various stage directions makes this the most complete edition of Shakespeare's works I have ever read.

"Most nearly complete" does not, logically, fit into the context of the sentence. How can anyone really know when an edition of Shakespeare's works will ever be complete? Although you could argue for a better sentence (perhaps by replacing *complete* with *inclusive*), writers feel less hesitant now than in previous years to use the comparative form with *perfect* and *unique*. However, you should employ such constructions judiciously. In a formal situation—writing or speaking—you should probably consider alternate constructions; and you surely would want to avoid using the comparative suffix *er* or the comparative *more* with such words as *dead, empty, full, infinite,* and *equal*.

NOUNS THAT ACT LIKE ADJECTIVES

Possessive nouns pattern in sentences in nearly the same manner as adjectives:

> I found *John's* book in the garage.
> The *cat's* claws were really sharp.

Some nouns pattern before other nouns and function as adjectives. These nouns cannot be inflected with *er* or *est* and may themselves take modifiers:

> The company developed *puppy* chow.

In this sentence, *puppy* modifies *chow* and has its own modifier, *small*. How we treat *puppy* is somewhat a matter of choice, depending mostly on how technical our discussion becomes. What is important at this point is that we recognize that some words have the qualities of nouns but function as adjectives.

Some linguistically oriented texts treat words by establishing a three-part classification for words: *form, function,* and *position*. In this way, a word may be a noun in form, an adjective by position, and a modifier by function. A word could likewise be an adjective in form, a nominal by position, and a subject of a verb by function, as in this sentence:

> The *destitute* were determined to persevere.

Adjectives may be located in sentence constructions that you may easily overlook—for example, in object-complement constructions, as in this sentence:

All of us considered the singer *talented*.

For more information about object complements, see the section titled "Object Complements" in Chapter 9, "Sentence Parts."

Although nouns and adjectives sometimes pattern and function in similar ways (and you should use care not to confuse the two), adjectives can usually be distinguished from nouns by determining whether a restrictor can be placed before the word in question:

The sun was *really* bright yesterday.
The crew planned to demolish the *very* tall building.

Nouns do not admit this construction. You would be unlikely to say the following:

We rode to town in the *really* school bus.
We had a picnic in a *very* park.

RECOGNIZING THE VARIOUS TYPES OF ADJECTIVES

The following sentences contain examples of various types of adjectives:

The furry animal was identified as a Chinese panda.

furry: attributive, positive
Chinese: proper, positive

The audience found the speaker witty and humorous.

witty: predicate, positive
humorous: predicate, positive

The factory, old and abandoned, was scheduled for demolition.

old: appositive, positive
abandoned: appositive, positive

The work was very difficult, but the eager students enjoyed it.

difficult: predicate, positive
eager: attributive, positive

The frightened child tripped over the twisted root.

> **frightened:** attributive, positive
> **twisted:** attributive, positive

My brother won the second prize in the composition competition.

> **second:** attributive, positive
> **composition:** attributive, positive

The shy, timid child would not participate in the various activities.

> **shy:** attributive, positive
> **timid:** attributive, positive
> **various:** attributive, positive

Your dog is certainly very fluffy.

> **fluffy:** predicate, positive

The cowardly lion delighted the laughing children.

> **cowardly:** attributive, positive
> **laughing:** attributive, positive (*laughing* is a verb form known as a *participle,* not really an adjective; however, participles can function as adjectives in sentences)

The poor often have educational disadvantages.

> **educational:** attributive, positive

The biggest berries are those on the very edge of the patch.

> **biggest:** attributive, superlative
> **very:** attributive, positive

My neighbor's house is much larger than mine.

> **neighbor's:** attributive, positive (this is an example of a possessive noun patterning in the same way as an adjective)
> **larger:** predicate, comparative

Driving a large truck through city traffic is not easy.

> **large:** attributive, positive
> **city:** attributive, positive
> **easy:** predicate, positive

When the snow is deep, we know winter is here.
   deep: predicate, positive

All the hikers felt tired from the steep climb.

   tired: predicate, positive
   steep: attributive, positive

The state police drove the stranded motorist to a motel.

   state: attributive, positive
   stranded: attributive, positive

My laptop computer is very portable.

   laptop: attributive, positive
   portable: predicate, positive

The young of most species need parental protection.

   most: attributive, positive
   parental: attributive, positive

I made my wife happy by giving her a diamond ring.

   happy: attributive, positive (*happy* is an adjective modifying the direct object in this sentence, thus it is called an "object complement")
   diamond: attributive, positive

He laced his boots tight to keep out the swamp water.

   tight: attributive, positive
   swamp: attributive, positive

I made a complete fool of myself at the party last night.

   complete: attributive, positive
   last: attributive, positive

The State Museum attracts many regular visitors each year.

   many: attributive, positive
   regular: attributive, positive
   each: attributive, positive

Even a very short speech can be extremely boring.

   short: attributive, positive
   boring: predicate, positive

The milk tasted sour to the fussy child.

> **sour:** predicate, positive
> **fussy:** attributive, positive

Adverbs

An *adverb* is a word that modifies a verb, an adjective, or another adverb. In certain constructions, an adverb may also modify a preposition, a conjunction, a verbal, a noun, or a pronoun. As a general rule, adverbs tell *how, when, where, why, under what conditions,* and *to what extent.*

CLASSES OF ADVERBS

According to their functions in sentences, adverbs are divided into three classes:

- Simple
- Interrogative
- Conjunctive

Simple Adverbs

Simple adverbs are usually one-word adverbs that modify a word or phrase appearing next to them. In the following sentences, the entity modified is in bold print; the type of entity is in parentheses. The adverbs are in italics.

The horse **runs** *swiftly*. (verb)

The *softly* **falling** snow made no noise. (*falling*, a participle, functions as an adjective)

He found the *bright* **red** shirt at a garage sale. (adjective)

He was standing *just* **around the corner.** (prepositional phrase)

Alberto liked **to ski** *rapidly* down the mountains. (the verbal *to ski* is an infinitive)

By **saving** *faithfully*, he had accumulated a small fortune. (the verbal *saving* is a gerund)

Sally arrived *just* **before you did.** (adverb clause)

The *newly* **rich** are sometimes considered inferior by members of that country club. (adjective serving as subject of verb)

Sometimes an adverb appears to modify an entire sentence and is therefore called a *sentence adverb* or *sentence modifier,* as in this example:

> *Unfortunately*, the book you seek is not in stock.

Sentence modifiers are discussed in more detail in Chapter 9 in the section titled "Sentence Modifiers."

Simple adverbs are divided into five classes:

- **Manner:** Adverbs of manner indicate *how* the action takes place:

  The little girl read *silently*.

- **Time:** Adverbs of time indicate *when* the action takes place:

  We worked in the garden *yesterday*.

- **Place:** Adverbs of place indicate *where* the action takes place:

  The package was *there* when we returned.

- **Number:** Adverbs of number indicate *order* or *how many times:*

  Bill arrived *first*.
  He spoke *twice*.

- **Degree:** Adverbs of degree indicate *how much:*

  We were *really* surprised.

Very and *too* with past participles require intervening words such as *much, greatly, highly, little,* and the like. To omit such an intervening word causes the intended past participle to function as part of a passive verb phrase:

> The patient was *very much satisfied* with the results of her surgery.
> We were *too highly motivated* to stop as we should have.

Interrogative Adverbs

Interrogative adverbs are used in asking questions, as in the following examples:

> *Where* have you been?
> *When* were you in Paris?
> *Why* did you tear that picture in half?

Conjunctive Adverbs

Conjunctive adverbs are used to connect dependent clauses to the remainder of the sentence. The most widely used conjunctive adverbs are the following:

> where
> when
> whenever
> while
> as
> why
> before
> after
> until
> since

These words are commonly referred to as *subordinating conjunctions* because they join dependent clauses to main clauses.

A *dependent clause* (also called a *subordinate clause*) is a clause that cannot stand alone. You'll learn more about this and other types of clauses in Chapter 9 in the section titled "Clauses."

Note the following examples:

> He arrived at the party *before* I did.
> Nearly a decade has passed *since* I last saw him.
> I visit my sister *whenever* I'm in the neighborhood.

ADVERBIAL FORMS

An adverb may be a *word*, a *phrase*, or a *clause*. In the following two sentences, the adverb is a word:

> The little boy walked *slowly*.
> We all completed the exam *quickly*.

In the following two sentences, the adverb is a phrase:

> The children ran *to the playground*.
> My brother found the ball *in our neighbor's yard*.

In the following two sentences, the adverb is a clause:

> *After I arrived at school,* I talked with my professor.
> The girls played tennis *until the rain began to fall*.

COMPARISON AND USAGE

Adverbs, like adjectives, have three degrees of comparison:

- Positive
- Comparative
- Superlative

Positive Degree

The *positive degree* expresses a quality without a comparison. That is, a statement is made concerning only one entity:

> Jessica rode the horse *masterfully*.
> Heidi sings *beautifully*.

Comparative and Superlative Degree

The comparative and superlative forms of comparison show a relationship between or among two or more actions or things. The comparative degree expresses a higher or lower degree than the positive. It is used to compare two things. The superlative degree is the highest or lowest degree when comparing more than two persons or things. These degrees of comparison are formed by adding *er* (comparative) or *est* (superlative) to the positive degree or by using the word *more* or *most,* as in the following examples:

> Jim works *hard*. (positive)
> Sally works *harder*. (comparative)
> Stella works *hardest*. (superlative)
>
> My neighbor plays football *skillfully*. (positive)
> I play football *more skillfully*. (comparative)
> My friend plays football *most skillfully*. (superlative)

Adverbs that end in *ly* and adverbs of more than two syllables usually form the comparative and superlative by using *more* and *most:*

> Betty finished the test *more rapidly* than Bill.

Use the *comparative degree* of an adjective or an adverb when speaking of two things and the *superlative degree* when speaking of three or more:

> This is the *prettier* of the *two* dresses.
> The pink one is the *prettiest* of the *three* dresses.

You must choose the comparative form carefully and not confuse the comparative of an adverb with the comparative of an adjective:

> **Incorrect:** He learns things *easier* than Frances.
> **Correct:** He learns things *more easily* than Frances.

Adjectives are often erroneously employed in place of adverbs:

> **Incorrect:** That person runs *good*.
> **Correct:** That person runs *well*.

Some adverbs are compared irregularly, as in these examples:

> well ➪ better ➪ best
> much ➪ more ➪ most

RECOGNIZING THE VARIOUS TYPES OF ADVERBS

The following sentences contain examples of various types of adverbs. Listed below each sentence are the adverbs themselves (adverbial phrases and clauses notwithstanding), the word or construction modified, and the type of word or construction modified.

> You must move quietly if you wish to observe wildlife.
>
> > **quietly:** move (verb)

> I shall study really hard to pass my examinations.
>
> > **really:** hard (adverb)
> > **hard:** study (verb)

> We thought the team played unusually well yesterday.
>
> > **unusually:** well (adverb)
> > **well:** played (verb)
> > **yesterday:** played (verb) (*yesterday,* a noun by form, functions as an adverb in this instance by telling *when*)

> The paleontologist found an extremely rare specimen.
>
> > **extremely:** rare (adjective)

> The spectators clapped enthusiastically for the performers.
> > **enthusiastically:** clapped (verb)

To play well, you must practice daily.

> **well:** to play (infinitive)
> **daily:** practice (verb)

A teacher is always happy to see her students succeed.

> **always:** is (verb)

He had too many bricks to carry at one time.

> **too:** many (adjective) (*too,* in this case, is an intensifier meaning "more than enough")

An *intensifier* is an adverb that adds emphasis to or amplifies an adjective. The term *intensifier* is also used to describe an adjective that creates an emphasizing or amplifying effect.

Her cloak was found in the very back of the closet today.

> **very:** back (noun) (*very* functions much as *too* earlier in this list)
> **today:** found (verb)

The truck stopped briefly before proceeding farther.

> **briefly:** stopped (verb)
> **farther:** proceeding (verb)

I certainly believe that my neighbor is completely honest.

> **certainly:** believe (verb)
> **completely:** honest (adjective)

You will surely be penalized if you don't do your work correctly.

> **surely:** penalized (verb)
> **correctly:** do (verb)

The officer walked slowly and cautiously down the street.

> **slowly:** walked (verb)
> **cautiously:** walked (verb)

Students are now required to spend more money for education.

> **now:** required (verb)

I did well on my tests, but I received very low marks on my homework assignments.

well: did (verb)
very: low (adjective)

We walked northward to the clearing.

northward: walked (verb)

I have serious reservations about your totally unbelievable tale.

totally: unbelievable (adjective)

The hikers wandered aimlessly through the deep woods.

aimlessly: wandered (verb)

The philanthropist spoke sincerely about the joys of giving.

sincerely: spoke (verb)

We argued enthusiastically for the new gymnasium.

enthusiastically: argued (verb)

We were more confident than we had reason to be.

more: confident (adjective) (*more,* too, is an intensifier)

It finally happened: That really old tree was blown down.

finally: happened (verb)
really: old (adjective)
down: blown (verb)

He called to us twice, but we hardly heard him.

twice: called (verb)
hardly: heard (verb)

We all worked long and hard, but we had barely begun the task.

long: worked (verb)
hard: worked (verb)
barely: begun (verb)

We left early, but we truly intended to return later.

early: left (verb)
truly: intended (verb)
later: return (verb)

Common Pitfalls with Adverbs and Adjectives

Many writers and speakers of the English language commonly encounter certain pitfalls when employing adverbs and adjectives:

- Misplaced modifiers
- Squinting modifiers
- Hedge words

MISPLACED MODIFIERS

Misplaced modifiers are those located in places other than near the words they modify and that seem to modify words other than those they are intended to modify. For example, note the placement of *nearly* in this sentence:

> I *nearly* won a million dollars in the lottery.

Does this sentence mean what it says—that someone nearly won that money but actually did not win any money? Or does it mean this:

> I won *nearly* a million dollars in the lottery.

This type of error causes confusion on the part of the reader or listener. The clause in italic type in the following sentence presents the same problem: What, exactly, does the sentence mean?

> Carl purchased a new fishing pole from the store *that he liked*.

Did Carl like the new fishing pole, or did he like the store? One of the following revised sentences would be more appropriate, depending on the intended meaning:

> Carl purchased a new fishing pole that he liked from the store.
> Carl purchased from the store that he liked a new fishing pole.

SQUINTING MODIFIERS

Squinting modifiers are, in a way, misplaced modifiers, except that they are placed in a sentence in such a manner that they may modify either of two nouns in the sentence. In the following sentence, the word *quickly* could modify either *eating* or *caused:*

> Seeing the children eating quickly caused Mother to lose her temper.

One of the following revised sentences would be more appropriate, depending on the intended meaning:

> Mother quickly lost her temper upon seeing the children eating.
> Mother lost her temper upon seeing the children eating quickly.

Serious writers try to avoid these kinds of errors. Although the errors may seem harmless enough, they cause a reader to focus on the manner of composition rather than on the thought the writer is attempting to convey to the reader.

HEDGE WORDS

Writers and reporters for various media are increasingly sensitive to possible legal repercussions regarding the things they report. As a result, many of them, seemingly to protect themselves and their organizations, tend to overuse *hedge words*—that is, words that allow the speaker or writer to hedge on the meaning of his or her statement. As such, readers and listeners are subjected to such statements as the following:

> The *alleged* burglary occurred last night.
> The diplomat died of an *apparent* heart attack.

Such hedge words are unnecessary if the police report indeed shows that a burglary occurred and if the medical report lists a heart attack as the cause of the diplomat's death. In any case, the second sentence above would certainly make more sense if it were written another way. (Besides, what is an "apparent heart attack"?)

> Apparently, the diplomat died of a heart attack.
> The diplomat died, apparently of a heart attack.

General Observations About Modifiers

- An *adjective* is a word that describes or "limits" a noun or pronoun, meaning that an adjective identifies by placing restrictions on any noun with which it is associated.
- Usually, an adjective answers one or more of the following questions:
  - Which?
  - What kind of?
  - How many?

- Three major types of adjectives are generally recognized:

  - **Attributive:** *Attributive adjectives* are those that are found immediately before the word(s) that they modify.
  - **Appositive:** *Appositive adjectives* follow the words that they modify. These adjectives are usually used in pairs and employ the conjunction *and* or *but* between them.
  - **Predicate:** *Predicate adjectives* are adjectives that occur after linking verbs or after a form of the verb *to be* and that modify the subjects of those verbs.

- *Proper adjectives* are adjectives derived from proper nouns or are proper nouns used as adjectives.
- Adjectives have three degrees of comparison. These three degrees of comparison show relationships between or among the words they modify:

  - **Positive:** The *positive degree* expresses a quality without a comparison; a statement is made concerning only one entity.
  - **Comparative:** The *comparative degree* expresses a higher or lower degree than the positive. It is used to compare two things, and the inflectional suffix is usually *er*.
  - **Superlative:** The *superlative degree* is the highest or lowest degree when comparing more than two persons or things. The inflectional suffix for the superlative degree is usually *est*, although adjectives of three or more syllables typically take *most* instead of *est*.

- Certain adjectives usually do not admit comparison. They express absolute qualities. Examples of such words are *unique, perfect, round, square, perpendicular, endless, dead, full, empty,* and *straight*.
- Some nouns pattern before other nouns and function as adjectives. These nouns cannot be inflected with *er* or *est* and may themselves take modifiers.
- An *adverb* is a word that modifies a verb, an adjective, or another adverb. In certain constructions, an adverb may also modify a preposition, a conjunction, a verbal, a noun, or a pronoun.
- As a general rule, adverbs tell *how, when, where, why, under what conditions,* and *to what extent*.
- According to their functions in sentences, adverbs are divided into three classes:

  - **Simple adverbs:** *Simple adverbs* are usually one-word adverbs modifying the word or phrase appearing next to them.
  - **Interrogative adverbs:** *Interrogative adverbs* are used in asking questions.

- **Conjunctive adverbs:** *Conjunctive adverbs* are used to connect dependent clauses to the remainder of the sentence. The most widely used conjunctive adverbs are *where, when, whenever, while, as, why, before, after, until,* and *since*.

- An adverb may be a *word,* a *phrase,* or a *clause*.
- Adverbs, like adjectives, have three degrees of comparison:

  - Positive
  - Comparative
  - Superlative

CHAPTER 5

Function Words

Unlike content words, such as nouns, verbs, adjectives, and adverbs, *function words*, also called *structure words*, arc words that have a grammatical (or syntactic) role in a sentence or clause as opposed to a lexical (or semantic) meaning. Function words include the following:

- Determiners
- Prepositions
- Conjunctions
- Interjections
- Auxiliary verbs

Auxiliary verbs are discussed in this book in the context of verbs rather than function words; refer to the section titled "Auxiliary Verbs" in Chapter 3, "Verbs."

Determiners

A *determiner* is a word that limits the potential referent of a noun phrase. There are various types of determiners:

- Definite and indefinite articles
- Demonstratives
- Quantifiers
- Possessives

Possessives are discussed in Chapter 1, "Nouns," in the section titled "Making Nouns Possessive" and thus are not covered here.

DEFINITE AND INDEFINITE ARTICLES

The presence of a *definite article* (there is only one: *the*) typically denotes a definite noun phrase, as in *the woman*. That is, the speaker or writer refers to a specific woman (*the woman*), not just any woman (*a woman*). *A woman* illustrates the use of an *indefinite article*—that is, no specific woman is being discussed. There are two singular indefinite articles: *a* and *an*. *Some* operates as a plural indefinite article.

Many grammarians consider the words *a, an,* and *the* to be adjectives rather than determiners.

The decision to use either *a* or *an* is based upon the initial sound of the word following the article and not on the spelling. For instance, a word beginning with a silent *h* actually begins with a vowel sound. Examine these examples:

> We discovered *an* old, abandoned house in the woods.
> I had never seen *a* wooden ship before.
> Please remain in this room for *an* hour.
> Should we adopt *an* honor system?
> Jane wore *a* uniform of blue. (*Uniform,* of course, begins with a *y* sound, as in the word *you*.)

Using *a*, *an*, and *the* before Separate Items

Repeat the article *a, an,* or *the* before separate items if it is otherwise not clear that the items are indeed separate. For example, the following sentence does not easily reveal the number of cows that the farmer had:

> The farmer had *a* black and white cow.

If the farmer had only one cow, the sentence is acceptable; but a better sentence, perhaps, would be one of the following:

> The farmer had a cow that was black and white.
> The farmer had *a* black and *a* white cow. (In this sentence, of course, the farmer had two cows.)

You should also use a, an, and the before separate items if some items take one determiner and other items take a different one:

> Janet ate an apple, a pear, a banana, and the grapes.

DEMONSTRATIVES

A *demonstrative* is a word whose role is to locate a referent in relation to a speaker, an addressee, or some other person. Examples of demonstratives are the following:

> this
> these
> that
> those

This and *these* should be used when the referent is physically closer to the speaker; *that* and *those* should be used when the referent is physically more remote from the speaker.

This, that, these, and *those* must agree in quantity with the words that they modify. *This* and *that* refer to singular words, while *these* and *those* refer to plural words:

> *These* books are mine.
> *Those* kids are loud.
> *That* boutique sells beautiful jewelry.
> *This* chair is broken.

QUANTIFIERS

A *quantifier* indicates a relative or indefinite quantity, such as the following words:

> all
> many
> several
> few

Quantifiers are distinguished from numerals, which provide an absolute indication of quantity (*nine* ladies dancing). Examine the following examples:

> *All* the king's men wore breeches and tunics.
> *Many* of the rabbits had spots.
> I find I can read for *several* hours at a time.
> *Few* children enjoy lima beans.

Prepositions

A *preposition* is a word or, in some instances, a word group that relates one sentence element (the *object of the preposition*) to another sentence element. Because a preposition must have an object, the preposition and the object of the preposition and any modifiers that pattern with them constitute a *prepositional phrase.*

Prepositional phrases are discussed in more detail in Chapter 9, "Sentence Parts," in the section titled "Prepositional Phrases."

Prepositions show certain relationships. One popular way of remembering these relationships is by remembering this statement: Anywhere a mouse can go, a preposition can go. For example, a mouse can go *in* a hole, *along* the wall, *inside* the cupboard, etc. There are more than 100 prepositions; following are a few of the most common ones:

about
above
across
after
against
along
among
around
at
before
behind
below
beneath
beside
between
beyond
by
down
from
in
into
near
off
on
over
past
round
through
throughout
to
toward
under
up
upon
within
without

Of course, other relationships exist, such as the following prepositions:

but
during
except
for
like

of
since
than
until
with

Of, in, and *to,* in that order, are the most frequently used prepositions in English.

Only one preposition in the English language—*near*—can be inflected: *near, nearer, nearest.*

In each of the following sentences, the preposition is in boldfaced italics and the object of the preposition is in bold. The word to which each prepositional phrase relates is in italics:

> The *canoe* **with** its **passengers** negotiated the rapids.
> The *book* **with** the torn **pages** is Mitzi's.
> Not a cloud could be *seen* **in** the **sky.**
> The yellow duckling *jumped* quickly **into** the **water.**

Prepositions often have the same form as adverbs. Adverbs can be distinguished from prepositions, however, by the fact that adverbs do not pattern with objects. In the first sentence below, *up* is an adverb; in the second sentence below, *up* is a preposition, while *up the tree* is a prepositional phrase:

> The little girl looked *up.*
> The squirrel ran *up* the tree.

Here's another example: In the first sentence below, the word *down* obviously modifies the verb (and is therefore an adverb) and is not a part of a separate grammatical unit, whereas in the second sentence, the word *down* is a part of the prepositional phrase, *down the street.*

> The prisoner looked *down* as he entered the courtroom.
> We looked *down* the street before entering the building.

TYPES OF PREPOSITIONS

For the purposes of this book, only three types of propositions need be identified:

- Simple
- Participial
- Phrasal

Simple Prepositions

A *simple preposition* is made up of either a simple or a compound word, as in the following:

up
down
in
into
from
to
with
inside
around
before
upon
along
without

Sometimes prepositions formed from two words, such as *inside* and *before,* are called *complex prepositions* because they have the form of complex words.

Participial Prepositions

Participial prepositions look like verbs (the *ing* form) but function as prepositions. They include the following:

assuming
barring
beginning
considering
following
including
involving
regarding

Note in the following sentences how these *ing* words function as prepositions:

The professor presented his plans *involving the students*.
She talked with her parents *regarding her violin lessons*.
The witness *recalling the details* was quite specific.
The quotation *including the error* was stricken from the record.
All of the animals *seeking shelter* walked to the barn.
The project *involving drilling for oil* was terminated.

Phrasal Prepositions

A *phrasal preposition* is, as its name suggests, a unit of two or more words serving as a single preposition (these types of prepositions are also called *compound prepositions*). Often a phrasal preposition is itself a prepositional phrase. These prepositional phrases usually pattern together and are seldom modified in any way—that is, very seldom do speakers or writers change their constructions or add modifiers within the word groups. The following are a few of these word groups:

> by way of
> in place of
> in spite of
> in case of
> on behalf of
> in addition to
> in lieu of
> in front of
> by means of
> in contrast to
> in comparison with
> with regard to

The following examples use phrasal prepositions:

> Use the rear stairs *in case of* fire.
> We drove to Las Vegas *by way of* Zion National Park.

Verb-Adverbial Composites

Words that are used as prepositions or as single-word adverbs are sometimes linked to verbs to form *verb-adverbial composites* (VACs). The words in italics in the following sentence comprise a VAC:

> Mother *called up* the doctor as soon as his office opened.

In sentences containing phrases such as *called up, fell out, give in,* and *run into,* the VAC is recognizable by the fact that it substitutes for a single word. In the preceding sentence, for example, the VAC may be replaced by the single word *telephoned*. When such a replacement is made, the possibility of a prepositional phrase employing the adverbial is eliminated:

> Mother *telephoned* the doctor as soon as his office opened.

The other examples of VACs in the preceding paragraph may be replaced with the single words *quarreled, surrender,* and *meet.*

TWO- OR THREE-PART PREPOSITIONS

Another type of preposition found in English is the *two-* or *three-part preposition.* These types of prepositions consist of words such as *together, due,* and *as,* followed by a word that is easily recognized as a preposition. Such prepositions include the following:

> ahead of
> out of
> apart from
> due to
> as for
> instead of
> because of
> aside from
> contrary to
> up to
> together with

Analyzing a sentence with these constructions in it as adverb plus prepositional phrase would require stretching logic to its extreme. For example, examine the following sentence:

> Fritz is up to his neck in trouble again.

In this sentence, the phrase *up to his neck* clearly indicates the amount of trouble that Fritz is in: Fritz is in trouble again. How badly? Up to his neck.

Now try analyzing the sentence this way:

> Fritz is up in trouble again.

The basic sentence parts *Fritz is up* do not reflect sound "sentence sense," even though this is the same basic sentence pattern as *Fritz is in trouble,* which does make sentence sense. The missing words *up to his neck* clearly pattern as a single unit—that is, as a prepositional phrase. Thus, calling *up to* a two-part preposition seems to reflect sound judgment.

Sentence patterns are discussed in detail in Chapter 6, "Types of Sentences."

Many times, people use two prepositions when one is sufficient—for example, *off of* or *inside of.* This should be avoided.

PREPOSITIONS AND GUIDE WORDS

The English language employs many expressions that require certain prepositions to show proper relationships. These expressions are, in a sense, peculiar to themselves because of the sometimes seemingly elusive meaning of the preposition. Nevertheless, standard English requires the showing of the proper relationships in all instances. If you have doubt about the correct preposition, you should consult a standard dictionary, looking up the guide word (the key word that controls the preposition).

Following is a list of guide words and prepositions. Although it is fairly up to date, language is always in a state of change; therefore, some entries may one day become obsolete. For now, however, it reflects general desired standards of usage. You should note that not all uses of any guide word or preposition are listed. If you recall a particular usage of a preposition and that usage is not listed, check a dictionary to determine the appropriateness of that usage.

abhorrent of (repulsion): We are all *abhorrent of* greed.

abhorrent to (opposed): His ideas are *abhorrent to* decency.

absolve of (to free from penalty or obligation): His excuses do not *absolve* him *of* his responsibility.

abstain from (to refrain): Please *abstain from* talking during the film.

accede to (to consent or agree): I *accede to* your demands for an inspection.

accompanied by (with a person): The starlet was *accompanied by* her manager.

accompanied with (to have things): The professor, *accompanied with* all his books, entered the room.

accord with (to agree with): His views are in *accord with* ours.

accordance with (agreement): His plans were in *accordance with* our plans.

according to (in accordance with): He did the work *according to* our instructions.

accused by (a person): He was *accused by* his brothers of disrupting the family reunion.

accused of (a deed): We were *accused of* misbehaving in class.

acquiesce to (to consent, assent): We *acquiesced* to the governor's wishes.

acquit of (to free, exonerate): He was *acquitted of* the charge of murder.

adapt from (take from): The movie was *adapted from* Hemingway's first novel.

adapt to (make to fit): I *adapted* a Harley Davidson engine *to* my custom chopper.

addicted to (given over to habit): I am *addicted to* soy vanilla lattes.

adept in (skilled): Eric was quite *adept in* hunting.

adhere to (follow, adhere, devoted): He *adhered* closely *to* the instructions when assembling the table.

admit of (to afford possibility or opportunity): This plan *admits of* numerous errors.

admit to (confess): He should *admit to* his part in the prank.

adverse to (opposed, antagonistic): No one should be *adverse to* cleaning up the environment.

afraid of (frightened): Everyone knows that Indiana Jones is *afraid of* snakes.

agree in (an opinion): They *agreed in* their selection of candidates for president.

agree on (a matter): We all *agreed on* the next course of action.

agree to (a proposal): The boys seemed to *agree to* my suggestion.

agree with (a person): They *agreed with* Jane that they should file a report.

agreeable to (in accordance, conformity): We are certainly *agreeable to* reasonable proposals.

aim to (try): I *aim to* consider every facet of the plan.

amenable to (in accordance, conformity): Ellen was *amenable to* the idea of moving to Seattle.

ambition for (desire for): It was Lady Macbeth's *ambition for* her husband's success that led to their downfall.

ambitious of (extensive, elaborate): The most *ambitious* recounting *of* the Battle of the Bulge has just been published.

angry at (a situation): I'm certainly *angry at* the way the test turned out.

angry about (a situation): Edgar is *angry about* the theft of his wallet.

angry at (a thing): I was *angry at* my car because it wouldn't start.

angry with (a person): I was very *angry with* Ian for not doing his part of the project.

apprehensive for (fearful): We were all *apprehensive for* our lives.

apprehensive of (fearful): I was *apprehensive of* the bear, but fortunately he didn't attack.

argue about (a situation): We *argued about* dividing the lost treasure.

argue for (a cause or position): Carl *argued for* an end to tests.

argue with (a person): I *argued with* my father over use of the car.

arrive in (a large city): They *arrived in* Denver at midnight.

arrive at (a small place): The group *arrived at* the park at the scheduled time.

authority of (actions or acting): We understood the *authority of* the security guard over the food court.

authority on (a subject): My lawyer is an *authority on* taxes.

beside (by the side): The spider sat *beside* Miss Muffet.

capable of (able): I'm sure he is not *capable of* such a thing.

careless of (neglectful): You should not be *careless of* your appearance.

center in (focus upon): Our studies *centered in* Asian culture.

Avoid the usually illogical *center around*.

characteristic of (attribute): It was *characteristic of* John to try to outrun Tom.

collide with (crash): Sam *collided with* Chris on the football field.

compare to (to liken): Shall I *compare* thee *to* a summer's day?

compare with (to examine for similarities): *Compare* the size of your feet *with* mine; there's no way my shoes will fit you.

comply with (consent, obey): We must *comply with* all requirements before graduation.

concentrate on (to focus): Please *concentrate* your attention *on* the chalkboard.

concern for (troubled): He is really *concerned for* his old dog.

concern in (interest): He showed no *concern in* that matter.

concern with (involved): We are not *concerned with* that project.

concur in (an opinion): We all *concurred in* the decision to go to the theater.

concur with (a person): If you all *concur*, we'll begin.

confide in (a person): I *confided in* Mitzi that I was in love with Erik.

confide to (a person about something): John *confided to* Bill that he had cheated on the examination.

conform to (to be in accordance): Our plans *conform to* the latest specifications.

conformity with (agreement, harmony): Our spending is in *conformity with* our earnings.

connect by (join): The two rooms are *connected by* a short hall.

connect with (associate): We could *connect* his success *with* his hard work and diligent study.

contend against (an obstacle): We had to *contend against* a strong tide to land our small boat.

contend for (a prize or principle): Greta *contended for* the gold medal in the giant-slalom event.

contend with (a person): The store manager was forced to *contend with* an irate customer.

contrast (*noun*) between (difference): The *contrast between* Sara and her sister is nearly unbelievable.

contrast (*verb*) to (to differ): His methods *contrast* sharply *to* mine.

correspond to (things): The claws of a bird *correspond to* a person's fingers.

correspond with (a person): We did not *correspond with* each other until I left for California.

desire for (wish, craving): I have a sincere *desire for* ice cream.

desire of (longing): It is the *desire of* most students to avoid tests.

desirous of (adjective form): Cecil was *desirous of* the award.

desist from (refrain, stop): *Desist from* your abhorrent behavior!

devoid of (without): Cindy's kitchen was completely *devoid of* mess.

die by (violence): He *died by* hanging.

die from (exposure): He *died from* the iciness of the water.

die of (disease, injury): He *died of* smallpox last year.

differ about (a situation): Jay and I *differed about* the best route from Pacific Palisades to West Hollywood.

differ from/different from (something else): Of course my report is quite *different from* yours; my ideas *differ from* yours.

differ with (disagree): You may *differ with* me if you wish.

disagree with: We all *disagree with* your view of the matter.

disappointed by (what happened): The farmer was *disappointed by* the failure of his crops.

disappointed in (a thing obtained): My brother was *disappointed in* the new bicycle he received for Christmas.

disappointed with (a thing not obtained): We were *disappointed with* the results of the election.

disdain for (contempt): He has *disdain for* the paperwork required to do his job.

dissent from (withhold consent or approval): He always *dissents from* the group's thinking.

distaste for (aversion): I have a *distaste for* sushi.

empty of (without): My mind is *empty of* any original thoughts.

enamored of (charmed or fascinated by): He is *enamored of* the star of that movie.

Avoid use of *enamored by* in place of *enamored of*.

engage in (be involved in): Do not *engage in* idle chatter.

enter into (plan or program): We *entered into* a plan to save money for Mother's birthday.

envious of: You should not be *envious of* others.

expert in: Oz is an *expert in* repairing motorcycles.

focus on (to concentrate): *Focus on* the positive.

foreign to: His way of thinking is utterly *foreign to* me.

free from (independent): She tries to be *free from* all responsibility.

free of (void): As far as we know, the moon is *free of* any life forms.

frightened at (a thought): He was *frightened at* the prospect of having heart surgery.

frightened by (a thing): As he tramped through the woods, he *was frightened* by an enormous, hairy spider.

glad of (pleased): All his friends were *glad of* his company.

graduate (*verb*) from: It's no small feat to *graduate from* medical school!

graduate (*noun*) of: The new chairman is a *graduate of* Yale.

guard against: We must all *guard against* hazardous waste.

hatred for: My daughter seems to have a *hatred for* vegetables.

hint at: Josephine *hinted at* her intentions.

identical to: It seems like the symptoms of mononucleosis are nearly *identical to* those of simple boredom.

ill from (an action): The children became *ill from* eating the cookie dough.

ill with (ailing): My brother is *ill with* a high fever.

impatient for (thing desired): We were all *impatient for* the opening of the new ice cream parlor.

impatient with (a person): Genevieve was often *impatient with* her friends.

implicit in: His expectations were *implicit in* his discussions with the group.

in accordance with: You must act *in accordance with* the law.

independent of (free from): Edward is so good at billiards, he seems to play *independent of* thought.

infer from (conclude): I *infer from* your statement that you have resigned.

inferior to: My report is obviously *inferior to* yours.

initiate into (to originate): The police *initiated* an investigation *into* the jay-walking incident.

in search of: The expedition left *in search of* the abominable snowman.

inseparable from: The twins were *inseparable from* each other.

jealous of: Don't be *jealous of* Jessica; her life may seem perfect, but even she has problems.

kind of (not *kind of a*): He had a *kind of* makeshift airplane.

join in (participate): Everyone wanted to *join in* the singing.

join to (connect): *Join* the wire *to* the terminal.

join with (associate): You may *join with* us if you wish to protest this legislation.

listen to: For greater insight, *listen to* your elders.

live at (an address): I wonder who *lives at* 1703 Parklane Drive.

live in (house, geographic location): The former president now *lives in* Georgia.

live on (a street or road): My sister *lives on* Oxford Street.

martyr for (a cause): He was one of the *martyrs for* freedom in South Africa.

martyr to (a disease): My father was a *martyr to* rheumatism.

mastery of: Alexander the Great gained *mastery of* the entire known world.

meddle in: Try not to *meddle in* someone else's business.

monopoly of: The company gained *monopoly of* the entire cereal business.

necessity for (followed by an infinitive): We felt the *necessity for* all of us *to fight* for our rights.

necessity of (followed by a gerund): He knew the *necessity of getting* good grades in his classes.

need for (followed by an infinitive): There is a *need for* Bill *to improve*.

need of (followed by a gerund): The *need of finding* a cure for cancer is more pressing than ever.

obedient to: Like it or not, mankind must be *obedient to* the laws of nature.

object to: How can anyone *object to* that proposal?

oblivious to: The children were *oblivious* to the danger nearby.

overcome by (an element): The firemen were nearly *overcome by* smoke.

overcome with (an emotion): When Janet's father walked her down the aisle, he was nearly *overcome with* emotion.

parallel between (two similar objects): We all could understand the *parallel between* a river and life itself.

parallel to/with (two or more lines): The railroad tracks ran *parallel to* the highway.

part from (a person or place): Many college graduates are eager to *part from* their home towns.

part with (a possession): A miser does not wish to *part with* his money.

peculiar to (belonging exclusively): The giant panda is *peculiar to* China.

plan to (followed by a verb): Let's *plan to* meet at the Odeon.

prefer (one) to (another): I really *prefer* peaches *to* apples.

preferable to: Do you find failing *preferable to* passing this course?

preparatory to: You should complete a course in typing *preparatory to* taking a computer course.

prerequisite for (something required before an allowance): A valid license is a *prerequisite for* driving.

prerequisite of (a constant requirement): Steady hands are a *prerequisite of* all good surgeons.

prerequisite to (a requirement prior to transaction): Knowing the rules of safety is a *prerequisite to* surfing.

prior to (beforehand): We wanted to leave *prior to* the storm.

privilege of (with a gerund): He wanted the *privilege of sitting* in the front seat.

prodigal with (extravagant): The treasurer was too *prodigal with* the club's funds.

proficient in: My sister is really *proficient in* first aid.

profit by (receive benefit): We could all *profit by* studying harder.

profit from (gain materially): We should *profit from* the sale of the jewelry.

prohibit from: The government tried to *prohibit* us *from* seeing the report.

protest against: The NCAA would not hear our *protest against* the referee's call.

reason for (an action): The *reason for* your failing grade is obvious.

reason with (a person): Parents sometimes simply cannot *reason with* teenagers.

reconcile to: No one could *reconcile* the cost *to* the quality of the new building.

regret for: We all had a keen *regret for* our thoughtless actions.

repent of: Criminals seldom *repent of* their misdeeds.

repugnant to: Your actions were *repugnant to* your classmates.

rewarded by (a person): We were *rewarded by* the president for cleaning the streets.

rewarded for (something done): Joseph was *rewarded for* returning the money he found.

rewarded with (a gift): Bernice was *rewarded with* a silver bowl for her performance.

sensitive to: I am highly *sensitive to* changes in barometric pressure.

separate from: No one could *separate* fact *from* fiction.

speak to (communicate a fact): Does anyone here wish to *speak to* the other issue?

speak with (converse): I'd like to *speak with* Jaime before I leave.

stay at: We were so tired, we all wanted to *stay at* home.

subscribe to: I don't *subscribe to* the notion that girls can't play baseball.

substitute for: Soda pop is no *substitute for* wholesome, fresh milk.

superior to: Metal gears are *superior to* plastic ones.

sympathize with: No one would *sympathize with* the complaining boy.

talk to (lecture): The lobbyist *talked to* the senator about the proposed tax.

talk with (converse): Joanie wanted to *talk with* Stephanie about the baby shower.

tamper with: It is not wise to *tamper with* recognized success.

try to (attempt): Stephen *tried to* best Al, but youth trumped experience.

> *Try and* is never correct, unless *to try* is being used in conjunction with an unrelated verb, as in the sentence *He tried and failed to run a four-minute mile*.

unequal to: We were all *unequal to* the task.

unmindful of: He was *unmindful of* the weather when he went hunting geese.

variance with: Your story is at *variance with* the police report.

vary from (one object to another): Most people's left foot *varies from* their right one.

vary in (qualities): These homes *vary in* color and design.

vary with (tastes): Preferences for paintings *vary with* the individuals surveyed.

vexed with (perturbed): She was *vexed with* her son for tracking in mud on the clean floor.

vie with (compete): Politicians often *vie with* one another for publicity.

void of (free of): The room was *void of* light.

wait at/on/in (a place): *Wait at* the bus station for your parents to arrive. *Wait on* the corner for the bus. *Wait in* the lobby of the hotel.

wait for (delay): Please *wait for* me to finish reading the paper before you go for your walk; I'd like to join you.

wait on (serve): The clerk will *wait on* you when she gets an opportunity.

> Do not use *wait on* in place of *wait for*.

worthy of: His performance was *worthy of* an award.

SELECTING THE CORRECT PREPOSITION

Following are numerous sample sentences that demonstrate the correct selection of the preposition:

The cuckoo is peculiar (*to, in*) the northern part of that country.
to

This year he was initiated (*into, within*) the fraternity.
into

The child was frightened (*by, at*) the idea of walking home alone.
at

Everyone must adhere (*with, to*) the regulations.
to

The winner was rewarded (*with, by*) a silver cup.
with

Study the script preparatory (*of, to*) entering the tryouts.
to

What kind (*of, of a*) car do you have?
of

It is best to guard (*from, against*) driving when you are sleepy.
against

(*With, To*) which other Byron poem does this selection compare?
To

The mother was concerned (*with, for*) the injured child.
for

He acquiesced (*about, in*) the disputed matter.
in

The clerk would wait (*for, on*) only one customer at a time.
on

Many people subscribe (*to, for*) more than one daily paper.
to

Martha lives (*in, on*) Chicago (*in, on*) Michigan Avenue.
in
on

The character Eloise lives (*at, in*) a hotel.
in

A library should be free (*from, of*) noise.
   of

(*From, Of*) what illness did he die?
   Of

The automobile collided (*against, with*) a fast-moving train.
   with

He did the work in accordance (*to, with*) the suggestion.
   with

This portion is unequal (*to, with*) the one on the left.
   to

Yesterday I spoke (*to, with*) the chairman of the committee for an entire hour.
   with

What is the necessity (*for, of*) going to court at this time?
   of

At a lecture everyone should listen attentively (*with, to*) the speaker.
   to

The clerk expressed disdain (*about, for*) complaining customers.
   for

The group must desist (*from, of*) further activity of this kind.
   from

The tenant was accused (*by, of*) his landlord of failing to pay the rent.
   by

Do not wait (*for, on*) me because I shall be very late.
   for

Draw a line parallel (*with, against*) the first one on the page.
   with (or to)

One country must not meddle (*in, with*) the affairs of another.
   in

This method is totally foreign (*to, with*) those with my training.
   to

Dr. Jones was disappointed (*by, with*) your not passing the test.
   with

That attitude is characteristic (*of, to*) one who has been defeated.
   of

Did the delegate abstain (*against, from*) voting?
from

The chairman delivered a protest (*about, against*) the proposal that was offered.
against

A senior usually prefers living off campus (*over, to*) living on campus.
to

The squad leader became impatient (*toward, with*) the malingerer.
with

Everyone should be glad (*for, of*) the opportunity to improve himself or herself.
of

Please confide (*in, to*) me.
in

Everyone should concentrate (*on, with*) the assignment.
on

The entire group agrees (*about, in*) its beliefs.
in

The cause is worthy (*for, of*) your support.
of

Many people are sensitive (*of, to*) certain kinds of pollen.
to

Most people are reluctant to part (*from, with*) their favorite books.
with

Everyone should join (*in, into*) the games.
in

His composition is almost completely free (*from, of*) spelling errors.
of

Mrs. Wilson corresponds regularly (*to, with*) her son via e-mail.
with

Your work compares favorably (*to, with*) the work of that artist.
to

The witness' testimony acquitted him (*from, of*) the charge.
of

It is better to try (*and, to*) complete the work than to stop now.
to

Is there a necessity (*for, of*) you to be present tomorrow?
for

The child was disappointed (*by, with*) not getting a bicycle.
with

His interests eventually centered (*around, in*) politics.
in

The elderly woman was accompanied (*by, with*) her granddaughter.
by

Susan is careless (*of, with*) her appearance.
of

Did he contrast my plan (*against, to*) yours?
to

John is totally independent (*from, of*) his father.
of

What should we infer (*from, with*) her statements?
from

I don't wish to part (*from, with*) my old car.
with

This snake is peculiar (*of, to*) that region.
to

This generic medicine is a substitute (*for, of*) the name-brand one.
for

He is quite capable (*of, to*) doing the work.
of

The college will prohibit him (*against, from*) taking that class until he completes the prerequisites.
from

Can the committee agree (*on, to*) an agenda?
on

Is he a person (*in, to*) whom you can confide?
in

I am frightened (*at, by*) the idea of your going home alone.
at

Does he live (*at, in*) Brooklyn?
in

These boxes vary (*in, with*) size and shape.
> **in**

Will you wait (*for, on*) me (*at, on*) the office?
> **for**
> **at (or in)**

We have the privilege (*by, of*) attending the opening ceremonies.
> **of**

We issued a protest (*against, of*) the ruling.
> **against**

Terri must reconcile herself (*to, with*) the latest changes.
> **to**

Dr. Allen will speak (*to, with*) the assembled students.
> **to**

I can sympathize (*toward, with*) a person who has suffered such a loss.
> **with**

Too many citizens are unmindful (*about, of*) their responsibilities.
> **of**

The professor became vexed (*about, with*) the unruly students.
> **with**

The salesperson will wait (*for, on*) you next.
> **on**

The two plans are at variance (*against, with*) each other.
> **with**

The group arrived prior (*of, to*) the first address.
> **to**

No one can reason (*on, with*) Anthony (*about, on*) the best route.
> **with**
> **about**

Does he have a reason (*by, for*) objecting?
> **for**

The student was rewarded (*by, from*) the dean.
> **by**

Many delegates abstained (*from, on*) voting.
> **from**

You must separate the good (*and, from*) the bad.
> **from**

If you are ill, you must stay (*at, in*) home.
at

The thief tampered (*on, with*) the lock.
with

What do you infer (*by, from*) his comment?
from

The secretary is in search (*for, of*) an eraser.
of

What kind (*of, of a*) story is this one?
of

He lives (*at, on*) Broadway Street.
on

His firm has a monopoly (*of, on*) sales in that territory.
of

Mary was overcome (*by, with*) the heat.
by

I prefer the red one (*over, to*) the blue one.
to

The student is proficient (*at, in*) music.
in

The soldier was rewarded (*about, for*) his bravery.
for

He spoke (*to, with*) me about the problem.
with

The new product is superior (*over, to*) the old one.
to

The student will vie (*against, with*) his classmates for honors.
with

This act is worthy (*for, of*) praise.
of

He studied Shakespeare preparatory (*of, to*) seeing *Hamlet*.
to

One should profit (*by, from*) his mistakes.
from

Red hair is peculiar (*in, to*) that family.
> **to**

He is unmindful (*about, of*) all risk.
> **of**

Did you comply (*to, with*) his request?
> **with**

The evidence will absolve him (*from, of*) suspicion.
> **of**

Do the work in accordance (*to, with*) the instructions.
> **with**

Was he accused (*of, with*) the crime?
> **of**

Jane is adept (*at, in*) music.
> **in**

A politician is usually averse (*of, to*) criticism.
> **to**

Mother was apprehensive (*about, of*) the danger.
> **of**

The professor is a supposed authority (*about, on*) linguistics.
> **on**

This book is different (*from, than*) the other one.
> **from**

Should he be acquitted (*from, of*) the charge?
> **of**

Everyone was disappointed (*in, with*) the quality of the new material.
> **in**

We were glad (*for, of*) the opportunity to hear him speak.
> **of**

The students showed their hatred (*for, of*) their rivals.
> **for**

The race-car driver died (*from, of*) his injuries.
> **of**

Was he impatient (*at, with*) me?
> **with**

Two new members were initiated (*in, into*) the club.
    into

POSTPONED PREPOSITIONS

A *postponed preposition* is one that patterns *after* its object. In the following sentences, the postponed preposition is in italics, and its object is in bold:

> The **danger** that I was warning you *about* is very real.
> The **situation** he has got himself *into* is very embarrassing.
> **What** do you suppose he's *up to?*

Up to may be construed as a two-part preposition, discussed earlier in this section.

Many speakers and writers frown upon postponed prepositions, and you should exercise caution in using them. However, in informal English and in general speaking situations, postponed prepositions can be appropriate. For example, the first sentence below is acceptable in informal situations, while the second sentence seems somewhat inappropriate in informal settings. In formal situations, however, the reverse is true, as shown in the third and fourth sentences:

> **Informal:** She is the person I told you about.
> **Formal:** She is the person about whom I told you.
> **Informal:** From now on, ending a sentence with a preposition is something I will not put up with.
> **Formal:** From now on, ending a sentence with a preposition is something up with which I will not put.

In some sentence constructions, the object of the preposition may be absent, as in the following:

> She is nearly impossible to get along *with*.

This, of course, is a perfectly acceptable sentence. Recasting it to provide an object of the preposition would result in a sentence similar to this:

> To get along *with* **her** is nearly impossible.

But this sentence does not convey the same message the one before it conveys. Postponed prepositions such as in the preceding should be used without fear of censure, despite the strong prejudice that has developed against such uses in formal English. That said, patterns such as those in the following sentences should be avoided, even in most informal situations, because the preposition is superfluous:

> Where is the book *at?*
> Where is that group going *to?*
> The game is over *with*.

In situations involving postponed prepositions, a writer or speaker must choose between strictly formal English—and thus sounding awkward or stilted (or even affected)—and less-formal English—and thus sounding somewhat more natural. In these and many other instances, the situations must dictate the standards.

PREPOSITIONS AND COMPOUND OBJECTS

A real problem for many people is the use of compound objects of the preposition. Basically, the matter is quite simple: Both objects are in the objective case. In the following sentence, the pronouns used as objects of the preposition are in the proper case—the objective case:

> We knew the dean was referring to *him* and *me*.

Difficulties seem to arise, however, when the first object of the preposition is a noun and the second is a pronoun, as in this sentence:

> We knew the dean was referring to *Jake* and *me*.

The tendency in this case is to use the nominative case for the second object of the preposition:

> **Incorrect:** The judge awarded the prize to Sally and *I*.

To avoid this pesky error, you need only to make two sentences of the one, each having a different object of the preposition:

> The judge awarded the prize to *Sally*.
> The judge awarded the prize to *me*.

Now that the correct forms are obvious, the two objects can be used together in one prepositional phrase:

> **Correct:** The judge awarded the prize to *Sally* and *me*.

RECOGNIZING PREPOSITIONS AND OBJECTS OF PREPOSITIONS

After each of the following sentences, you'll find listed prepositions in that sentence, the object of each preposition, and the word modified by each prepositional phrase:

> We looked into the garage and saw a car with stainless-steel wheels.
>
> > **into:** garage, looked
> > **with:** wheels, car

In this class, you cannot pass a test without studying.

> **in:** class, pass
> **without:** studying, pass

Rianne found a ruler in the desk at which she was sitting today.

> **in:** desk, found (this prepositional phrase extends from *in* to the end of the sentence)
> **at:** which, desk

The cardinal in the tree was calling to its mate.

> **in:** tree, cardinal
> **to:** mate, calling

In the back of this text, you will find answers to the problems.

> **in:** back, find (this prepositional phrase is actually a combination of all the words from *in* to *text*)
> **of:** text, back
> **to:** problems, answers

The shirt with the green trim appeals to me.

> **with:** trim, shirt
> **to:** me, appeals

When you go to the store, try to find some fresh asparagus.

> **to:** store, go (*to find* is an infinitive phrase, not a prepositional phrase)

"Elegy for Jane" by Theodore Roethke is a poignant poem.

> **for:** Jane, elegy
> **by:** Theodore Roethke, "Elegy for Jane"

For Whom the Bell Tolls is one of Hemingway's best novels.

> **for:** whom, tolls
> **of:** novels, one

Ashley was walking to the store when the rain began to fall.

> **to:** store, walking (*to fall* is an infinitive phrase, not a prepositional phrase)

Ben bought a new truck for hauling his farm produce.

    for: hauling, truck

The dog with the white paws is named Jake.

    with: paws, dog

Felix is the person about whom I was complaining.

    about: whom, person

Conjunctions

Conjunctions, like prepositions, are "connectives," joining word groups to the rest of the sentence. Although prepositions have a rather restricted distribution in that they exist solely in a phrase and usually connect the object of the preposition (typically a noun or pronoun) to the sentence, conjunctions may join single words, phrases, or clauses to the rest of the sentence. Several types of conjunctions and their uses are shown in the following sentences:

Carlos *and* James went fishing yesterday.
    (The conjunction joins single words.)

We invited the neighbors *and* their friends to the party.
    (The conjunction joins groups of words.)

Sally did her assignment, *but* Carl went fishing.
    (The conjunction joins independent clauses.)

An *independent clause* is, essentially, a sentence; that is, although it may lack the capitalization and punctuation of a sentence, it can stand alone, grammatically speaking. You will learn more about this and other types of clauses in Chapter 9, in the section titled "Clauses."

We didn't go to the picnic *because* we were tired.
    (The conjunction joins a dependent clause to the sentence.)
Neither the parents *nor* the students expected school to be dismissed early today.
    (The two-part conjunction joins word groups.)

A few *adverbial conjunctions* such as the following serve to connect independent clauses:

> however
> nevertheless
> moreover
> then
> therefore
> thus
> consequently

Here are two examples of adverbial conjunctions in use:

> The rain fell all day; *therefore*, the picnic was canceled.
> We lost our money; *consequently*, we had to return home.

CATEGORIES OF CONJUNCTIONS

Although conjunctions can be classified in a number of categories and subcategories, we need to examine only three major categories:

- Coordinating conjunctions
- Subordinating conjunctions
- Correlative conjunctions

Coordinating Conjunctions

Coordinating conjunctions connect elements of equal rank in the sentence. The sentence elements may be single words, phrases, or clauses. The seven coordinating conjunctions can be remembered by forming the words *boy fans* with each first letter:

> but
> or
> yet
> for
> and
> nor
> so

The coordinating conjunctions are in italics in the sentences that follow. The elements joined by the conjunctions are identified within the parentheses after the sentence:

The dog *and* cat were sleeping peacefully. (words)
She enjoys jogging *but* not swimming. (words)
We were lost, *for* we had never been on this trail before. (independent clauses)
Hoping to earn money *and* to save for school, Henry searched for a summer job. (infinitive phrases)
He knew I was right, *yet* he continued to argue. (independent clauses)

If coordinating conjunctions join pronouns being used as the same part of the sentence, the pronouns must be in the same case:

Incorrect: Sue *and* **me** went to the concert.
Correct: Sue *and* **I** went to the concert.

The word *but* is often used as both coordinating conjunction and preposition. If the meaning of *but* is "except," it is used as a preposition:

Conjunction: Mike went to the game, *but* I did not.
Preposition: Everyone *but* me went to the game. (*But* means "except" in this sentence.)

Use coordinating conjunctions to join grammatical units that are parallel in form. For instance, do not mix words and phrases or different kinds of phrases:

Incorrect: He liked *skiing, swimming,* and *to hike*.
Correct: He liked *skiing, swimming,* and *hiking*.

Incorrect: He liked *to hike* and *swimming* in the lake.
Correct: He liked *to hike* in the forest and *to swim* in the lake.

Subordinating Conjunctions

Subordinating conjunctions connect two *clauses* of unequal rank. They begin dependent clauses (usually adverb clauses) and show the relationship of those dependent clauses to the independent clauses of which they are a part. Some of the subordinating conjunctions are the following:

if
because
after
since
when
while
until
unless
although
for (meaning "because")

wherever
than
as

Some relative pronouns also function as subordinating conjunctions:

who
whom
whose
which
what
that

In the following sentences, the dependent clauses are in italics, with the subordinating conjunctions in bold:

While *I was in Texas,* my motorcycle was stolen.
You'll regret it later **if** *you waste your money at the fair.*
The audience waited for the speaker **until** *it grew weary.*
I avoided Jack, **whose** *presence upset me.* (In this sentence, the dependent clause is also a relative clause.)
Because *few students elected to take them,* the courses were canceled.

Correlative Conjunctions

Correlative conjunctions function like the other conjunctions. They are distinct from the others, however, in that they pattern in pairs (hence *co,* as in "co-captains," plus *relative,* meaning "related"). The correlative conjunctions are the following:

as . . . as
either . . . or
neither . . . nor
whether . . . or
both . . . and
not only . . . but also

Notice how the correlative conjunctions are used in the following two sentences:

Either you'll clean your room *or* you'll be punished.
Both Nancy *and* John were eager for the play to begin.

Repeat the second *as* when using the correlative conjunction in making comparisons:

Incorrect: Marjorie is *as* tall, if not taller than, Nicole.
Correct: Marjorie is *as* tall *as,* if not taller than, Nicole.

Use *nor,* not *or,* after negative words in conjunctions showing comparisons:

> **Incorrect:** The apartment was *neither* clean *or* furnished.
> **Correct:** The apartment was *neither* clean *nor* furnished.

RECOGNIZING THE VARIOUS TYPES OF CONJUNCTIONS

The following sentences contain examples of various types of conjunctions:

> I really wish that I could help you, but I simply cannot.

> **but:** coordinating

The store was closed because the fire destroyed the building.

> **because:** subordinating

If you care to help, I'll assign a task to you.

> **if:** subordinating

Friends and neighbors should respect one another.

> **and:** coordinating

Neither Rae nor Sue had finished the assignment by midnight.

> **neither . . . nor:** correlative

We drank lemonade while we waited for the eclipse.

> **while:** subordinating

Do not leave the building until I give the signal.

> **until:** subordinating

Both Pete and Phil graduated with honors.

> **both . . . and:** correlative

They complained when they had good reason for doing so.

> **when:** subordinating

The teachers as well as the students enjoyed the demonstration.

> **as . . . as:** correlative

The chairman was reinstated; therefore, it will be business as usual when we meet on Monday.

> **therefore:** adverbial
> **when:** subordinating

I think I know whose house this is.

> **whose:** subordinating (*Whose* is a relative pronoun serving as a subordinating conjunction.)

You may not leave until the bell rings.

> **until:** subordinating

Whether we win or lose, we'll have played an exciting game.

> **whether . . . or:** correlative

Because you are leaving anyway, take these books to the library.

> **because:** subordinating

CONJUNCTIONS AND USAGE

A few rules govern the use of conjunctions:

- *Like* should be used as a preposition and not as a conjunction in formal writing:

  > **Incorrect:** We feel *like* we belong here.
  > **Correct:** We feel *as if* we belong here.
  > **Correct:** We feel *that* we belong here.

- Use *that* before a clause that follows a verb expressing *saying, thinking,* or *feeling:*

  > **Incorrect:** I think we should read something by John Steinbeck.
  > **Correct:** I think *that* we should read something by John Steinbeck.

- Use *when* after constructions employing *hardly* or *scarcely:*

  > We had hardly arrived *when* the rain began falling.

- In sentences expressing reason or purpose, use *so that* rather than *so* alone:

  > **Incorrect:** We walked *so* we could get some exercise.
  > **Correct:** We walked *so that* we could get some exercise.

- In formal writing or speaking, use *whether,* not *if,* to express uncertainty:

  > **Incorrect:** We did not know *if* the professor was coming.
  > **Correct:** We did not know *whether* the professor was coming.

Although some writers and speakers maintain that *or not* should always be used after *whether,* it is this author's belief that the *or not* is superfluous.

Incorrect: We did not know *whether or not* the professor was coming to class today.
Correct: We did not know *whether* the professor was coming to class today.

Although opinions are divided on this matter,

- Use *where* to refer to location. Do not use *where* to mean *that:*

    Incorrect: I saw on the news *where* Congress passed a new law.
    Correct: I saw on the news *that* Congress passed a new law.

Interjections

An *interjection* is a word or phrase "injected" into a sentence to express strong feeling or sudden emotion. Because the interjection is not grammatically related to the sentence or any word in a sentence, it is not a true part of speech. In fact, interjections are sometimes used as complete sentences, and often a complete sentence is implied when an interjection is an element attached to independent clauses. The words in italics in the following sentences are interjections:

Ouch! I cut my finger.
Oh! This water is too hot.
Drat! The tire is flat again.
Fine—then I'll do it myself!
Well, what do you have to say for yourself?
Duck! They're throwing snowballs at us again.

The interjection *duck* has the meaning of the sentence "(You) duck your head."

O Versus Oh

O is an interjection. It is used in very formal direct address, is always capitalized, and is never followed by a mark of punctuation:

O Great Spirit, hear now our prayers.
O wild West Wind, thou breath of Autumn's being….

Oh expresses a wish, grief, pain, or surprise and is always followed by a comma or an exclamation point:

Oh! How I wish this semester would end.
Oh, I suppose I'll just stay home tonight.

RECOGNIZING INTERJECTIONS

The following sentences contain examples of interjections:

"Help! I've been robbed," cried the tourist.
> **Help**

Oh, I suppose I could give you the money, since I owe it to you.
> **Oh**

Fine! Just fine! You've ruined my painting.
> **Fine**
> **Just fine**

Work and sleep, sleep and work—shucks, that's all we ever do.
> **shucks**

Hey, where are the apples and oranges I brought?
> **Hey**

Well, nobody's perfect, but I'm nearly so.
> **Well**

Wow, did you see that crater where the meteor hit the earth?
> **Wow**

So! You've been sneaking around behind my back, have you?
> **So**
> **have you** (*Have you* is an idiomatic expression used as a means of converting a preceding statement into a question. As you can see, however, it does not have a direct grammatical relationship to the independent clause that precedes it.)

GENERAL OBSERVATIONS ABOUT FUNCTION WORDS

- Unlike content words, such as nouns, verbs, adjectives, and adverbs, *function words*, also called *structure words*, are words that have a grammatical (syntactic) role in a sentence or clause as opposed to a lexical (semantic) meaning. Function words include the following:

  - Determiners
  - Prepositions
  - Conjunctions
  - Interjections
  - Auxiliary verbs

- A *determiner* is a word that limits the potential referent of a noun phrase.

- A *preposition* is a word or, in some instances, a word group that relates one sentence element (the *object of the preposition*) to another sentence element. One popular way of remembering these prepositional relationships is by remembering this statement: Anywhere a mouse can go, a preposition can go.
- A preposition must have an object. A preposition and the object of the preposition and any modifiers that pattern with them constitute a *prepositional phrase*.
- Prepositions often have the same form as adverbs; however, adverbs can be distinguished from prepositions by the fact that adverbs do not pattern with objects.
- For the purposes of this text, only three types of prepositions need be identified:
  - **Simple:** A *simple preposition* is made up of either a simple or a compound word: up, down, in, into, from, to, with, inside, around, before, upon, along, without, and so on.
  - **Participial:** *Participial prepositions* look like verbs (the *ing* form) but function as prepositions. They include assuming, barring, beginning, considering, following, including, involving, and regarding.
  - **Phrasal:** A *phrasal preposition* is a unit of two or more words serving as a single preposition (these types of prepositions are also called *compound prepositions*). Often, a phrasal preposition is itself a prepositional phrase.
- Words that are used as prepositions or as single-word adverbs are sometimes linked to verbs to form *verb-adverbial composites* (VACs).
- *Two-* or *three-part preposition*s consist of words such as *together, due, as,* and other words followed by a word that is easily recognized as a preposition.
- The English language employs many expressions that require certain prepositions to show proper relationships. These expressions are, in a sense, peculiar to themselves because of the sometimes seemingly elusive meaning of the preposition.
- A *postponed preposition* is one that patterns after its object.
- When compound objects of the preposition are used, both objects are in the objective case.
- *Conjunctions*, like prepositions, are "connectives," joining word groups to the rest of the sentence.
- Although prepositions have a rather restricted distribution in that they exist solely in a phrase and usually connect the object of the preposition (usually a noun or pronoun) to the sentence, conjunctions may join single words, phrases, or clauses to the rest of the sentence.
- Although conjunctions may be classified in a number of categories and subcategories, we need to examine only three major categories:

- **Coordinating conjunctions:** *Coordinating conjunctions* connect elements of equal rank in the sentence. The sentence elements may be single words, phrases, or clauses.
- **Subordinating conjunctions:** *Subordinating conjunctions* connect two clauses of unequal rank. They begin dependent clauses (usually adverb clauses) and show the relationship of those dependent clauses to the independent clauses of which they are a part.
- **Correlative conjunctions:** *Correlative conjunctions* function like other conjunctions. They are distinct from the others, however, in that they pattern in pairs.

- An *interjection* is a word or phrase "injected" into a sentence to express strong feeling or sudden emotion.
- Because an interjection is not grammatically related to the sentence or any word in a sentence, it is not a true part of speech. In fact, interjections are sometimes used as complete sentences, and often a complete sentence is implied when an interjection is an element attached to an independent.

PART II

SENTENCE ELEMENTS

The word *grammar* is often used synonymously with the word *syntax*—that is, the way in which words are put together to form phrases, clauses, and sentences. The relationship among words, phrases, clauses, and sentences is a hierarchical one:

- One or more clauses comprise a sentence.
- One or more phrases comprise a clause.
- One or more words comprise a phrase.

Phrases and clauses are relatively easy to define. A *phrase* is a group of words that, together, function as a part of speech (noun, verb, adjective, adverb, preposition, and so on). A *clause* is a sentence or sentence-like construction within another sentence.

You'll learn more about phrases and clauses in Chapter 9, "Sentence Parts," in the sections titled "Phrases" and "Clauses," respectively.

Sentences are a little more difficult to define; indeed, various texts define sentence in different ways. The usual definition identifies a sentence as a group of words containing a subject and predicate and expressing a complete thought.

A *subject* is a sentence element that represents a person or thing of which something is said. For example, in the sentence, "Alexia began taking ballet lessons at age five," *Alexia* is the subject of the sentence; it is being said of her that she "began taking ballet lessons at age five." A subject may be a noun, pronoun, or noun phrase and normally appears before the verb in a sentence. Subjects are covered in more detail in Chapter 9, in the section titled "Subjects and Predicates."

The *predicate* of a sentence makes an assertion or a denial about the subject of that sentence; that is, it represents what is said about the sentence's subject. For example, in the sentence, "Cammy gave up skiing to become a champion snowboarder," *Cammy* is the subject, and "gave up skiing to become a champion snowboarder" is the predicate. Predicates are covered in more detail in Chapter 9, in the section titled "Subjects and Predicates."

A standard definition of *sentence* may also include statements about "understood" subjects and predicates. This type of definition is often followed by further explanations of how such constructions as the following are sentences, even though one or more elements seem to be missing:

Stop!
Yes.
John.

The explanation usually given is that parts of the sentence that appear to be missing are really present and "understood"; for example, we can read the preceding sentences as something similar to the following:

> (You must) stop!
> Yes, (I agree with you).
> John (is the person).

Readings of these sentences, then, demonstrate that all of them have both subjects and predicates, elements that nearly all grammarians agree that sentences must have. Likewise, nearly all grammarians and others would agree that the following word groups are sentences:

> She is in the backyard.
> The dog dragged it away.
> That color is my favorite color.

These three sentences, however, present problems: Something is obviously missing from each one. Who is "she" in the first sentence? What is "it" in the second sentence? What color is "my favorite color" in the third sentence? In other words, how can one logically declare that these three sentences express complete thoughts? Logically, of course, one can't, which seems to nullify the definition of *sentence* given earlier.

Ironically, we all know what a sentence is; we just have trouble verbalizing what we know. Here's a definition. See how this relates to what you know about sentences:

> A *sentence* is a grammatical unit of language that is recognized by speakers
> as having relative independence of meaning, that conveys a complete idea or
> question, and that has a definite beginning and ending.

Much of this definition is, of course, similar to the earlier one; however, *sentence* is defined as a grammatical unit of language, which it certainly is, and as having "relative independence," a phrase meaning that it is moveable—perhaps within the paragraph—without sacrificing its meaning. Further, native speakers of a language recognize the boundaries of a sentence by voice patterns (*intonation contours*), which are represented in writing (*orthography*) by capital letters and periods or other end marks.

This leaves the matter of a sentence's expressing a "complete idea" still unresolved. As long as a sentence has only "relative independence," however, the definition will suffice. Total independence cannot be achieved by any sentence employing pronouns or other words that depend on other words for meaning. If the listener understands the antecedent of the word "she" in the sentence "She is in the backyard" and knows the meaning of the phrase "in the backyard," he or she should have little difficulty comprehending the meaning of the sentence. Any sentence can be seen, then, to be related to other sentences in some way; or, as the definition suggests, they are units of language, not entities existing in isolation.

Chapter 6

Types of Sentences

A *sentence* is classified as being of one of the following basic types:

- Simple
- Complex
- Compound

In addition to being called simple, complex, or compound, sentences are categorized according to their primary function:

- Declarative
- Interrogative
- Imperative
- Exclamatory

Simple Sentences

A *simple sentence* is a sentence that consists of one independent clause with no coordinate or subordinate clause:

> Lloyd and Evelyn went to the World's Fair.
> Sue is an avid knitter.
> Jay practices well.
> Will you sing?
> Javier skis.
> Caitlin teaches at a private school.

The various types of clauses are discussed in more detail in Chapter 9 under the heading "Clauses."

Complex Sentences

A *complex sentence* contains an independent clause and one or more dependent clauses. When the dependent clause is placed before the independent clause, the two clauses are separated by a comma; otherwise, no punctuation is necessary:

> After you finish your homework, you can have a snack.
> > (*You can have a snack* is the independent clause. *After you finish your homework* is dependent.)

Compound Sentences

A *compound sentence* contains multiple independent clauses, which are often linked by a coordinating conjunction (*but, and,* and so on). These clauses should always be separated by a comma or a semicolon. Clauses may also be linked with a conjunction, such as *however, therefore,* and the like.

> Cindy cut grass, and Kitty raked the leaves.
> Betsy writes the letters; Chelsea licks the envelopes.
> I paid a fortune to furnish my condo; however, I did not like the results.

In addition to simple compound sentences, such as the preceding examples, there are complex-compound sentences, which have at least two independent clauses and one or more dependent clauses (shown in italics below):

> Cycling in Boulder is fantastic; *since I started living there five years ago*, I've logged thousands of miles.
> *Although I wanted to stay home and read*, I went to the game, and I had a good time.
> Anil forgot to take his lunch, so he bought pizza from the cafeteria *when he got to school*.

Declarative Sentences

A *declarative sentence* (also called a *declarative*) is one whose primary role is to make a statement. The following sentences are examples of declaratives:

Edwina drives race cars for a living.
Dogs dislike fleas.
My favorite movie is *Rocky*.

Interrogative Sentences

The role of the *interrogative sentence* is to ask a question:

Will we arrive soon?
Has Victor ever visited Las Vegas?
Do you prefer wine or beer?

Imperative Sentences

An imperative sentence is one that gives an order or issues a command:

Stand up.
Walk this way.
Stop talking.

Exclamatory Sentences

An *exclamatory sentence* conveys strong emotion. These types of sentences, which often contain no verb, sometimes consist of the word *what* or *how* followed by a noun phrase:

How wonderful you look!
Please go!
What big eyes you have!

General Observations about Types of Sentences

- A sentence is classified as being of one of the following types:

  - **Simple:** A *simple sentence* is a sentence that consists of one independent clause with no coordinate or dependent clause.
  - **Complex:** A *complex sentence* contains an independent clause and one or more dependent clauses.
  - **Compound:** A *compound sentence* contains multiple independent clauses, which are often linked by a coordinating conjunction (*but, and,* and so on). These clauses should always be separated by a comma or a semicolon. Clauses may also be linked with a conjunction, such as *however, therefore,* and the like.
  - **Complex-compound:** In addition to simple compound sentences, there are complex-compound sentences, which have at least two independent clauses and one or more dependent clauses.

- In addition to being called simple, complex, or compound, sentences are categorized according to their primary function:

  - **Declarative:** A *declarative sentence* (also called a *declarative*) is one whose primary role is to make a statement.
  - **Interrogative:** An *interrogative sentence* asks a question.
  - **Imperative:** An *imperative sentence* is one that gives an order or issues a command.
  - **Exclamatory:** An *exclamatory sentence* conveys strong emotion. These types of sentences, which often contain no verb, sometimes consist of the word *what* or *how* followed by a noun phrase.

Chapter 7

Sentence Patterns

One approach to understanding English sentences involves recognizing the various patterns upon which English sentences are based. Fortunately, you must concern yourself with only nine basic patterns. These basic sentence patterns are combined in various ways to generate (or construct) longer sentences. But no matter how long a sentence is, it is still based on one pattern, or a combination of two or more basic patterns. It follows, then, that if you learn to recognize these patterns (you already know them; you use them in your speech), you will more easily and quickly grasp the basics of the English sentence. Here, in simplified form, are the nine basic patterns of the English sentence:

- **Pattern 1:** Noun + Verb (to be) + Adjective

    The grass is green.

- **Pattern 2:** Noun + Verb (to be) + Adverb

    My bedroom was upstairs.

    The single-word adverb in this sentence pattern may be replaced by a prepositional phrase with a "there" or "then" meaning, as in this sentence:

    Mother was *in the garden.*

- **Pattern 3:** Noun 1 + Verb (to be) + Noun 1

    Some dogs are good hunters.

- **Pattern 4:** Noun + Intransitive Verb

    The shadows deepened.

- **Pattern 5:** Noun 1 + Transitive Verb + Noun 2

    The cat caught the mouse.

- **Pattern 6:** Noun 1 + Transitive Verb + Noun 2 + Noun 3

    My brother gave his wife some flowers.

    or Noun 1 + Transitive Verb + Noun 2 + to + Noun 3

    My brother gave some flowers to his wife.

- **Pattern 7:** Noun 1 + Transitive Verb + Noun 2 + X, wherein X equals any one of several possibilities:

- ○ Another noun or a pronoun
  We elected Mabel president.

- ○ An adjective
  They considered Sam handsome.

- ○ A pronoun
  The FBI thought Jerry me.

- ○ An adverb of place
  We imagined him downstairs.

- ○ Verb, present participle
  We discovered the child crying.

- ○ Verb, past participle
  The boys found their clothes pressed.

- ○ Prepositional phrase
  They considered him in their way.

- ○ Infinitive phrase with *to be*
  Everyone considered Ella to be a friend.

In the Pattern 7 sentence (Noun 1 + Transitive Verb + Noun 2 + X), the X may also represent a combination of sentence elements, such as a verb *and* a prepositional phrase.

- **Pattern 8:** Noun + Linking Verb + Adjective

  The milk smells bad.

- **Pattern 9:** Noun 1 + Linking Verb + Noun 2

  Marie remained interim president until the special election.

Patterns 1, 2, and 3: Sentences with the Verb *To Be*

You must be familiar with the various forms of the verb *to be*. They are the following:

be
been
am
are
is
was
were

Most basic grammar books describe how these forms of the verb work with *has* and *have*—in other words, these books show the conjugation of the verb *to be*. But for purposes of this book, you need only to recognize sentences with *to be* as the main predicate (verb). Here are examples of sentences with patterns 1, 2, and 3, discussed earlier in this part:

> These apples are delicious. (Noun + Verb [to be] + Adjective)
> The dog is outside. (Noun + Verb [to be] + Adverb)
> That woman is a senator. (Noun 1 + Verb [to be] + Noun 1)
> > (The nouns *woman* and *senator* refer to the same entity—in this case, the woman who is the senator; hence they are both Noun 1.)

Of course, more elements may be added to the sentences; but no matter how many elements are added, the basic pattern remains the same. Note this sentence:

> The old bull with the crooked horn was really mean.
> > The pattern is still Noun (*bull*) + Verb [to be] (*was*) + Adjective (*mean*).

To determine whether a confusing sentence is a Pattern 1 or a Pattern 2, insert the word *very* before the third element. If the sentence seems natural, it is probably a Pattern 1 sentence. If it seems unnatural, it is probably a Pattern 2 sentence:

> The sky is (very) blue today. (Pattern 1: Noun + Verb [to be] + Adjective)
> The baby is (very) outside this afternoon. (Pattern 2: Noun + Verb [to be] + Adverb)

Sometimes a sentence may have a "there" or "then" phrase that takes the place of the single-word adverb; however, the sentence pattern remains Noun 1 + Verb [to be] + Adverb:

> The old books were *in the attic*. (there)
> The meeting will be *at 6 o'clock*. (then)

Patterns 8 and 9: Sentences with Linking Verbs

Linking verbs are similar to the verb *to be* in that they show a relationship between an element in the predicate and the subject of the sentence. They do not, however, convey action from one to the other as transitive verbs do, nor do they show a subject in action as intransitive verbs do. Many of the linking verbs relate to the senses, such as the following:

> smell

> look
> taste
> appear

Refer to the section titled "Linking Verbs" in Chapter 3, "Verbs," for more information about linking verbs.

Examine the linking verbs in these sentences:

> This food *smells* bad. (Noun + Linking Verb + Adjective)
> The small sapling *became* a towering oak. (Noun 1 + Linking Verb + Noun 1)
> The workers *look* tired. (Noun + Linking Verb + Adjective)

Notice that these verbs, unlike the verb *to be,* do not make the same type of positive assertions about the subjects of the sentences. Whereas the verb *to be* states that the subject is in a certain state or condition, linking verbs suggest that relationship but affirm another—appearance, odor, taste, sound, and so on. Compare these pairs of sentences, the first with the verb *to be* and the second with a linking verb:

> The stew *was* good. (Noun + Verb [to be] + Adjective)
> The stew *looked* good. (Noun + Linking Verb + Adjective)
>
> The child *is* a good helper. (Noun 1 + Verb [to be] + Noun 1)
> The child *seems* a good helper. (Noun 1 + Linking Verb + Noun 1)

Obviously, you can easily detect whether a sentence has the verb *to be* as its main predicate. Likewise, you can quickly determine whether a sentence has a linking verb as its predicate. If the verb in question can be replaced by a form of the verb *to be* (albeit with a change in meaning), it is probably a linking verb. Similarly, any verb that can be substituted for *seems* in a sentence, such as "These boards seem rotten," without varying the meaning of the sentence is probably a linking verb.

A variety of other linking verbs exists in English. Some common ones are the following:

> grow
> remain
> get
> continue
> become
> go

Other linking verbs sometimes not understood to be linking verbs are these:

> work
> stand
> run
> prove

Here are examples of sentences that employ these linking verbs:

The knot in my shoelace *worked* loose.
The well *ran* dry from the lack of rain this spring.
The gunman *proved* true to the code of the West.

You should be careful when working with sentences containing these kinds of linking verbs so that you don't confuse them with Pattern 4 sentences (Noun + Intransitive Verb), as in these sentences:

The carpenter *worked* slowly and carefully.
The children *grew* quickly.
The dog *went* into the woods.

These three sentences do not have an adjective following the verb, unlike the preceding five sentences, which do. Note, too, that the verbs in these sentences can't be replaced by a form of the verb *to be* and still make sense.

In all the preceding sentences containing linking verbs, the linking verbs relate the subject to a predicate adjective (an adjective in the predicate that modifies the subject of the verb). A few linking verbs may relate a predicate noun to the subject of the verb in the same way, as in these sentences:

My uncle *remained* coach for the season. (Noun 1 + Linking Verb + Noun 1)
Elizabeth *became* an ambassador to Iceland.
The boys *stayed* close friends until graduation.
Books *make* fine gifts for college students.

Again, you should not mistake sentences of this pattern with sentences of a different pattern:

The governor *stayed* the execution until midnight.
Don't *make* a mess on the clean floor.

Understanding Sentence Patterns

Each sentence in this section is followed by its associated sentence pattern:

That sideboard is certainly an antique.
    Pattern 3 (Noun 1 + Verb [to be] + Noun 1)

Bake those cookies a nice golden brown.
    Pattern 7 (Noun 1 + Transitive Verb + Noun 2 + Adjective)

The sailor gave the scouts a lesson in knot tying.
> Pattern 6 (Noun 1 + Transitive Verb + Noun 2 + Noun 3)

The puppy played outside nearly all day.
> Pattern 4 (Noun + Intransitive Verb)

The crew paved the road all the way to Elm Street.
> Pattern 5 (Noun 1 + Transitive Verb + Noun 2)

The senator declared the charges totally false.
> Pattern 7 (Noun 1 + Transitive Verb + Noun 2 + Adjective)

Some birds are excellent fishers.
> Pattern 3 (Noun 1 + Verb [to be] + Noun 1)

That board is too long to be of any use.
> Pattern 1 (Noun + Verb [to be] + Adjective)

The bridge appeared too weak to hold us all.
> Pattern 8 (Noun + Linking Verb + Adjective)

The rescuers found the survivors disoriented.
> Pattern 7 (Noun 1 + Transitive Verb + Noun 2 + Adjective)

The door was open.
> Pattern 1 (Noun + Verb [to be] + Adjective)

We found the kite torn by the branches of the tree.
> Pattern 7 (Noun 1 + Transitive Verb + Noun 2 + Verb + Prepositional Phrase)

From a distance, we thought Kerry him.
> Pattern 7 (Noun 1 + Transitive Verb + Noun 2 + Pronoun)

Give the point guard the ball.
> Pattern 6 (Noun 1 + Transitive Verb + Noun 2 + Noun 3)

We are the world.
> Pattern 3 (Noun 1 + Verb [to be] + Noun 1)

We found the rabbit under the back porch.
> Pattern 5 (Noun 1 + Transitive Verb + Noun 2)

The cat's basket is in the cellar.
> Pattern 2 (Noun + Verb [to be] + Adverb)

We found Marie an apartment for the semester.
> Pattern 6 (Noun 1 + Transitive Verb + Noun 2 + Noun 3)

They discovered the visitors to be charlatans.
> Pattern 7 (Noun 1 + Transitive Verb + Noun 2 + Infinitive Phrase with *to be*)

The minister gave the congregation a stern sermon.
> Pattern 6 (Noun 1 + Transitive Verb + Noun 2 + Noun 3)

The milk in the carton smells sour to me.
> Pattern 8 (Noun + Linking Verb + Adjective)

The flowers seemed a virtual rainbow of colors.
> Pattern 9 (Noun 1 + Linking Verb + Noun 2)

My neighbor gave my little brother a summer job.
> Pattern 6 (Noun 1 + Transitive Verb + Noun 2 + Noun 3)

We found the president unresponsive to our request.
> Pattern 7 (Noun 1 + Transitive Verb + Noun 2 + Adjective)

The babysitter heard the child giggling.
Pattern 7 (Noun 1 + Transitive Verb + Noun 2 + Present Participle)

The chairman was the only dissenting speaker.
> Pattern 3 (Noun 1 + Verb [to be] + Noun 1)

The club members made Richard treasurer.
> Pattern 7 (Noun 1 + Transitive Verb + Noun 2 + X [Noun])

They thought him sufficiently competent.
> Pattern 7 (Noun 1 + Transitive Verb + Noun 2 + Adjective)

The coach found the team members depressed about the loss.
> Pattern 7 (Noun 1 + Transitive Verb + Noun 2 + Past Participle)

Fortunately, we saved some money for the trip home.
> Pattern 7 (Noun 1 + Transitive Verb + Noun 2 + Prepositional Phrase)

The witness appeared frightened of the jury.
> Pattern 8 (Noun + Linking Verb + Adjective)

Jim lied.
> Pattern 4 (Noun + Intransitive Verb)

Some books are really difficult to read.
> Pattern 1 (Noun + Verb [to be] + Adjective)

Generally, students are people who are intellectually curious.
> Pattern 3 (Noun 1 + Verb [to be] + Noun 1)

All the wedding guests were downstairs.
  Pattern 2 (Noun + Verb [to be] + Adverb)

Few people are natural leaders.
  Pattern 3 (Noun 1 + Verb [to be] + Noun 1)

All the horses were in the barn.
  Pattern 2 (Noun + Verb [to be] + Adverb)

General Observations about Sentence Patterns

- One recent approach to understanding English sentences is to recognize the various patterns, of which there are nine, upon which English sentences are based. These basic sentence patterns are combined in various ways to generate (or construct) longer sentences.
- Sentences containing the verb *to be* display one of the following patterns:

  - Noun + Verb [to be] + Adjective
  - Noun + Verb [to be] + Adverb
  - Noun 1 + Verb [to be] + Noun 1

- *Linking verbs* are similar to the verb *to be* in that they show a relationship between an element in the predicate and the subject of the sentence. They do not, however, convey action from one to the other as transitive verbs do, nor do they show a subject in action as intransitive verbs do.
- Many linking verbs relate to the senses, such as *smell, look, taste,* and *appear*.
- You can quickly determine whether a sentence has a linking verb as its predicate. If the verb in question can be replaced by a form of the verb *to be*, it is probably a linking verb. Likewise, any verb that can be replaced with *seems* without varying the meaning of the sentence is probably a linking verb.

Chapter 8

Punctuation

P unctuation is a mechanical aid to accurate written communication and exists in its present form for two reasons:

- The need for clarity of thought and expression
- Custom

Although custom is a fine reason for the perpetuation of a linguistic standard, the most important reason for the existence of punctuation is clarity of expression. For example, examine the following two letters, created by Gloria Rosenthal for *Games Magazine* (© Games Magazine 1984. Reprinted with permission.). Both letters use exactly the same words in exactly the same order but punctuate those words differently:

> Dear John,
> I want a man who knows what love is. All about you are generous, kind, thoughtful people who are not like you. Admit to being useless and inferior, John. You have ruined me. For other men, I yearn. For you, I have no feelings whatsoever. When we're apart, I can be forever happy. Will you please let me be?
> Yours,
> Marcia
>
> Dear John,
> I want a man who knows what love is all about. You are generous, kind, thoughtful. People who are not like you admit to being useless and inferior, John. You have ruined me for other men. I yearn for you. I have no feelings whatsoever when we're apart. I can be forever happy. Will you please let me be yours?
> Marcia

As you can see, the message in the first letter is exactly the opposite of that in the second letter—simply because the punctuation is different.

Bear in mind that a number of punctuation *styles* exist:

- Closed (formal)
- Open (informal)
- Newspaper (generally a variety of the open style)

For example, when punctuating items in a series, a writer may elect to omit the comma between the last two items if no lack of clarity results:

Closed: The three brothers were named Tim, Jim, and Kim.
Open: The three brothers were named Tim, Jim and Kim.

The punctuation guide presented in this chapter uses closed punctuation, meaning that when options exist, the rules reflect a more formal approach to style.

Various publications employ different styles, some of which are unique to a single journal or newspaper. In general, though, most publications subscribe to a common set of conventions relative to punctuation. You should check a style guide or several editions of a publication if you intend to submit material to a particular journal or magazine to be certain your punctuation style conforms to the style employed by the journal.

This chapter covers the two basic types of punctuation:

- Terminal punctuation
- Internal punctuation

Terminal Punctuation

Terminal punctuation is punctuation that brings something, such as a sentence or an abbreviation, to an end. The various types of terminal punctuation include the following:

The period (.)
The question mark (?)
The exclamation point(!)

THE PERIOD (.)

A *period* is used in the following circumstances:

- After a declarative sentence:

    John Kennedy was elected president in the fall of 1960.

- After an imperative sentence that is a polite request:

    Please close the door as you leave.

- After an indirect question:

    He asked whether I had called.

- After a polite request that is put in the form of a question:

    Will you please sign this contract and return it to me.

    In many circumstances, such as in business letters, either a period or a question mark may be used as end punctuation with a polite request.

- After each initial in a proper name and after most abbreviations:

    S. I. Hayakawa
    Dr.
    M.A.
    Ph.D.
    LL.D.
    P.S.
    etc.
    i.e.
    Ms.
    U.S.A.
    A.M.
    B.S.
    D.Litt.
    Mr.
    Jr.
    B.C.E.

    Abbreviations occur without spaces between letters except for initials in proper names—for example, George H. W. Bush.

    Use no periods after the initials of radio or television call letters, network call letters, government agencies, and the terms *SOS* and *IOU*.

    If an abbreviation ends a sentence, no extra termination period is required.

- As a decimal point:

    His temperature is 98.6 degrees.
    This book costs $32.95.
    The answer to the problem is 88.5 percent.

- After each numeral or letter division in an outline except those enclosed in parentheses

THE QUESTION MARK (?)

A *question mark* is used in the following circumstances:

- After a direct question:

    Did the committee really agree to the proposal?

- After each incomplete question in a series:

    What have you done with your books? Your papers? Your pen?

- In parentheses to indicate historical doubt or uncertainty:

    William Kidd (Captain Kidd) lived from 1645(?) to 1701.

THE EXCLAMATION MARK (!)

An *exclamation mark* is used in the following circumstances:

- After a strong interjection:

    Help! The boat is sinking!

- After phrases or sentences that show strong emotions:

    What a beautiful view!
    Call the guards!

Avoid using the exclamation mark for emphasis, irony, or humor.

Internal Punctuation

Internal punctuation separates, divides, and points out elements within an expression, thereby developing clarity and specific identity. Internal punctuation includes such marks as the following:

The comma (,)
The semicolon (;)
The colon (:)
The hyphen (-)
The em dash (—)
The en dash (–)
Parentheses (( ))
Brackets ([ ])
The ellipsis (... or ... .)
Quotation marks (" " and ' ')
The apostrophe (')
Italics

Although italics are not punctuation per se, they are a related concept.

THE COMMA (,)

Use *commas* to separate words, phrases, and clauses written in a series. The comma should appear before the conjunction that connects the last two items—unless all the items in a series are joined by conjunctions, in which case no commas should be used. Following are several examples of the correct use of commas, as well as sentences for which no commas are required:

> Marian has visited Seattle, Tacoma, and Walla Walla.
> The police officer searched under the house, in the attic, and in the garage.
> The president is in his office, the dean is out of town, and the registrar is in the auditorium.
>
> He asked for coats and hats and shoes.
> Tiffany and Amber and Tallulah visited Nana.
> We prefer apples or peaches or pears.

Within a series of independent clauses separated by semicolons, use commas to indicate the omission of verbs:

> The president is in his office; the dean, out of town; and the registrar, in the auditorium.

Use commas to set off expressions that interrupt a sentence:

- Some appositives with their modifiers are set off with commas:

  > Cronk, the captain of the team, played a good game.
  > We visited Rosemary, my favorite cousin.

  See the section titled "Appositives" in Chapter 9, "Sentence Parts," for more information about them.

- Words of direct address are set off by commas:

  > Jean, please help me wash the car.
  > I do believe, Lynne, that you are right.

- Parenthetical expressions are set off by commas:

  > You are, on the contrary, not studying seriously.
  > On the other hand, we shall continue to strive for success.

- Certain words, such as *well, yes, no, why,* and so on, when used at the beginning of a sentence as a *starter* or to indicate *stammering,* are followed by a comma.

  > Yes, well, I could have sworn I saw Edgar at the theater.

- In dates and addresses, every item after the first is enclosed by commas:

    Is 261 Parklane Drive, Murray, Kentucky, the correct address?
    Yes, August 3, 1964, was the date of his arrival.

When the month appears *immediately before* the year, no comma is used:

    During April 2008, he revealed his invention.
    The discovery was made on 22 June 1936.

- A nonrestrictive clause is set off by commas:

    Dr. Miller, who is retiring soon, was honored at the banquet.
    Miss Allen's car, which is quite old, is a conversation piece around campus.

Restrictive and nonrestrictive clauses are covered in more detail in Chapter 9 in the section titled "Restrictive Versus Nonrestrictive Clauses."

- A nonrestrictive participial phrase is set off by commas:

    The players, tired from many rehearsals, left early.

In addition, commas should be used in the following circumstances:

- Before *and, or, for, but,* and *nor* when these words join independent clauses unless the comma has been used for another purpose within one or more of the independent clauses:

    The employees asked for an increase in salary, but the manager did not grant it.
    Babies require constant attention, love, and nurturing but this doesn't mean that caring for them is a hardship.

- Before *for, as,* and *because* when these words introduce clauses of reason; before *though* and *although* when these words introduce clauses and mean "in spite of"; and before *while* when it means "but":

    We chose to remain at home, because we could not get good seats.
    Mr. Williams climbed the stairs, although the doctor had warned him not to do so.
    He was rewarded, while his teammates were not.

- After conjunctions such as the following when they join independent clauses:

    hence
    thus
    then
    still
    accordingly
    also
    besides

however
moreover
otherwise
therefore

In this use, these words are often preceded by a comma or a semicolon:

Dr. Copps has taught for more than forty years; however, she has no plans to retire.
We thought, therefore, that we might as well stay home.

- After an introductory adverb clause, an introductory participial phrase, a succession of introductory prepositional phrases, or an introductory infinitive phrase not used as the subject of the sentence:

While the weather was warm, we went swimming every day.
Standing quietly in the corner, the child waited for his mother.
On top of the mountain in that country, we found some relics.
To win easily in this contest, you must have a special talent.

- After the salutation of a friendly letter and after the complimentary close of any letter:

Dear Mother,
Yours sincerely,
Very truly yours,

- Between coordinate adjectives—that is, adjectives alike in usage, between which the word *and* can be used as a sensible alternative:

The student was a quick, savvy young man.
(*And* would fit between quick and savvy but not between savvy and young.)

Adjectives indicating size, shape, color, age, material, religion, or national origin are not separated by commas:

The hermit lived in a little old wooden shack near the river.
The gigantic rectangular American flag was a sight to behold.

- To set off a direct quotation, except when the sense of the sentence requires a question mark or an exclamation mark:

"Yes, this is the assignment," replied Dr. Jones.
"What was your reply to that question?" asked Fred.

- To separate proper nouns that refer to different persons, places, or things:

To Tom, Jim was always very kind.
In January, Russia called for the meeting.
To Francine, England was paradise.

- After *etc., viz., i.e.,* and *namely:*

  The patient asked for three things; namely, a television set, several magazines, and a radio.

- To separate two identical or closely similar words, even if the sense or grammatical structure does not require such separation:

  Whatever it was, was not what we asked for.

- To separate two unrelated numbers:

  In 2009, 3,245 professors attended the convention.

- Before *of* in connection with residence:

  We visited Mr. and Mrs. Cousins, of Louisville.

- To set off words, phrases, or other modifiers that are out of their natural order in the sentence:

  The young child, ill and sleepy, whimpered as he sat with his mother.

- To set off a clause that changes a statement into a question or an exclamation:

  The morning paper did arrive already, didn't it?
  Those explosions were surely loud, weren't they?

- After digits indicating thousands:

  1,254
  115,589
  22,674
  4,789,654

- To set off a title or a degree following a proper name:

  William Darnton, Jr., was the first speaker.
  Joseph N. Colley, Ph.D., is the dean.

  No comma is employed between a name and Roman numeral designating generations:

  Henry Ford III became president of the Ford Motor Company.

- After a surname when it precedes a first name (if the reversed name is within a sentence, two commas are required):

  The book is listed under the name of Grise, G. C.
  Write the name Grise, G. C., at the top of the card.

- To separate contrasted coordinate elements:

  The child's name is Mary, not Susan.
  The bandit struck wildly, but forcefully.

- To separate an absolute phrase from the rest of the sentence:

  > Winter having come, we lit a fire in the fireplace.
  > On the porch, the storm having passed, he saw the rain-soaked decorations from the celebration.

- Wherever necessary to prevent misreading:

  > Ever since, she has prepared her assignments well.
  > Inside, the workers were holding a meeting.

THE SEMICOLON (;)

Semicolons are used in the following circumstances:

- Between *independent clauses* that are not joined by *and, or, for, nor, but, so,* or *yet:*

  > You have presented a valid reason for your request; nevertheless, we find that we are unable to honor it.

- Between the *items in a series* if any one of the items contains commas:

  > Mr. Snyder, owner of the store; Mr. Henry, an eminent attorney; and Miss Wilson, a retired nurse, were elected to the board.

THE COLON (:)

Colons are used in the following circumstances:

- After the salutation of a business letter:

  > Dear Dr. Tucker:
  > Gentlemen:
  > Madam:

- Before a list of any kind that is introduced formally by such words as *the following* or *as follows,* by a number, or by any other "pointing out" expression:

  > Dr. Standard made the following observation: "The time has come when a general college education is almost as common as a high-school education was 20 years ago."
  > In his pockets, the little boy had four things: a pocket knife, a piece of string, a rusty washer, and a large marble.

  Do not use a colon after a linking verb or the verb *to be,* even if it introduces a list:

> **Incorrect:** The things we took with us were: a tent, a camp stove, some food, and sleeping bags.
> **Correct:** The things we took with us were a tent, a camp stove, some food, and sleeping bags.

Do not use a colon after a preposition, even if it introduces a list:

> **Incorrect:** These books are for: Mary, James, and Frankie.
> **Correct:** These books are for Mary, James, and Frankie.

- Before a long and formal statement:

  > To the witches, Banquo said: "If you can look into the seeds of time and tell which grain will grow and which will not. . . . "

- Between independent clauses when the second clause explains or restates the first:

  > This coat is the most durable kind: It is reinforced with double stitching and has a nylon lining.

The first word of the second clause should begin with an uppercase letter if it is preceded by a colon and the clause is an independent clause.

- Between numbers expressing the time, between the volume and page number of a magazine, between chapter and verses of a Bible passage, and between the title and subtitle of a book when the subtitle explains the title:

  > 5:30 A.M.
  > *Harper's* 198:56–64
  > John 3:16 is a very famous Bible passage.
  > Her book, *Rubbish: Reuse Your Refuse,* contains some great craft ideas.

THE HYPHEN (-)

Hyphens should be used in the following situations:

- Between words that act as a single adjective modifier preceding the word being modified:

  > 40-yard line
  > poverty-stricken children
  > holier-than-thou attitude
  > up-to-date accounts

Similar words used in the predicate to modify the subject are not hyphenated.

The hyphen should be omitted from compounds when the first word is an adverb form ending in *ly:*

He ran 40 yards.
The accounts were up to date.
He jumped from the slowly moving train.

- In two-word fractions, when the fraction is a single adjective that appears directly before the noun it modifies:

    He was elected by a two-thirds majority.
    Two thirds of the food has been eaten already.

- In numbers from *twenty-one* through *ninety-nine*.

- After a prefix that has been attached to a proper noun:

    un-American
    pro-British
    pre-Cambrian

- After *self* and *all* when these words are prefixed to nouns:

    self-control
    all-American

- In compound titles containing *vice, ex,* and *elect:*

    President-elect Smith
    Vice-President Adams
    ex-President Carter

- In words when there may be doubt as to meaning:

    They re-acted the entire ceremony.
    I plan to re-tire my car soon.
    She re-sent her paper to the professor.
    The re-creation of the crime scene swayed the jury.

- When the joining of a prefix with the root causes an awkward combination of letters:

    co-op
    de-emphasize

Consolidate a prefix and a root word unless the root word begins with the last letter of the prefix or with *w:*

    coeducational
    nonessential
    semi-invalid
    postgraduate
    co-worker

- To show the *omission* of a connecting word:

    the Anglo-Saxon people (*and* is omitted)

In addition, a hyphen should be used to divide a word at the end of a line. When you use a hyphen in this way, however, observe the following rules:

- Divide a word between pronounceable parts only. One-syllable words should never be divided.
- A word having double consonants should be divided between the consonants.
- Do not divide proper names, or divide a title, initials, or a first name from a last name.
- Do not divide a word so that a single letter stands alone. If possible, do not divide a word so that only two letters are carried over to the next line.
- Words having prefixes and suffixes should be divided between the prefix and the root of the word or between the root of the word and the suffix.

When in doubt about whether a word should be broken with a hyphen, consult a good dictionary.

THE EM DASH (—)

Em dashes should be used in the following situations:

- To indicate an important break in thought or in sentence structure:

    The title—if it has a title—cannot be found on this page.
    Books, paper, pens—these are essential materials.

- To set off an appositive that is a series:

    The winners—Allen, Susan, and Dan—have entered the finals.

- To mean *namely, in other words, that is,* and similar expressions that precede explanations:

    The umpire had it in his power to prevent the trouble—he could have stopped the game.

- To indicate speech that is broken or faltering:

    "I—I'm not sure exactly where—where they went," he stammered.

- After an incomplete sentence (the em dash should be used without a period):

    She murmured, "When I saw the giant mushroom cloud in the sky—"

Four spaced periods may be used in place of the em dash in this situation. See the section titled "The Ellipsis (. . . or . . . .)" later in this part.

THE EN DASH (–)

En dashes should be used in the following situations:

- To connect continuing (that is, inclusive) numbers, as in dates, time, or reference numbers:

    1997–2007
    13 May 2006–1 August 2009
    8:00 A.M.–5:00 P.M.
    pp. 11–40

    If a preposition, such as *from* or *between,* is used to introduce the range of numbers, an en dash should not be used. Instead, *to* should be used with *from,* and *and* should be used with *between:*

    Incorrect: from 11:00 A.M.–2:00 P.M.
    Correct: from 11:00 A.M. to 2:00 P.M.
    Correct: 11:00 A.M.–2:00 P.M.

    Incorrect: between May–August
    Correct: between May and August
    Correct: May–August

    When the concluding date of a range denoting duration of time has not yet been determined, as in the case of dates denoting the life span of a person who is still living, a single en dash is used after the first date in the range:

    Adelina Plaisance (1947–)

- To indicate a single period or season spanning parts of two successive calendar years:

    fiscal year 2008–2009
    winter 1942–1943

- In cases of a compound adjective that precedes the word it modifies, an en dash is used in place of a hyphen when one element of the adjective is an open compound or when multiple elements are hyphenated compounds:

    post–World War II
    New York–based company
    half-chocolate–half-vanilla milkshake

PARENTHESES (( ))

Parentheses should be used under the following conditions:

- To enclose material that is only remotely connected with the content:

  This punctuation (I am convinced it is important) should be studied carefully.

- To enclose references, directions, and incidental explanatory matter:

  Communism (see Book I) was the second topic.
  Senator Morton (R., Ky.) was the chair of the committee.

- To enclose numerals repeated to ensure accuracy:

  He paid sixty dollars ($60) for those shoes.

- To enclose numerals or letters used to mark divisions or enumerations that run into the text:

  There were three reasons for his resignation: (1) advanced age, (2) failing health, and (3) a desire to see more of the world.

In addition, you can use a question mark within parentheses after a word or a statement of which the accuracy is questionable:

Chaucer was born in 1340 (?) and died in 1400.

BRACKETS ([ ])

Brackets should be used under the following conditions:

- To enclose explanations within parentheses or in quoted material when the explanation is not part of the quotation:

  When I broke my arm halfway through the second semester (the injury being a result of a field test, conducted by me, to determine whether a downhill suit is, in fact, faster than regular ski gear [conclusion: It is]), I was thrilled; having to wear a cast meant I could legitimately drop out of typing class.
  This is an excerpt from Dr. Swanson's address of acceptance: "I am honored by [the appointment], but I am also keenly aware of the many responsibilities that I shall assume today."

- To rectify a mistake such as may appear in a book or other manuscript when quoting it:

  "The [English] dramatist Shakespeare will live forever."

Alternatively, use a bracketed [sic] to show that an error in a quotation is not an error in quoting:

Mr. Laurence wrote as follows: "I am enclosing the monie [sic] that I promised you when you were here."

THE ELLIPSIS (. . . OR . . . .)

An *ellipsis* should be used to indicate an omission from a quotation. To indicate an omission within a sentence, use three periods. To indicate an omission at the end of a sentence, employ the original mark of punctuation and then three periods:

> Sharon wrote that she had met "an unusually brilliant young man . . . whose ancestors came over on the *Mayflower.* . . ."

Do not use ellipsis marks before or after quoted words or word groups incorporated into your sentence:

> Juan said he had an "unfortunate incident" as he traveled in Spain.

If internal punctuation occurs where an ellipsis begins, include that mark of punctuation before the ellipsis mark. If the omitted words occur at the beginning of a quotation, do not employ the ellipsis mark:

> He clearly stated that he "would never, . . . consent to the agreement; but who would even request such an action?"

Some authors prefer to put the end punctuation after the ellipsis mark if the omitted material carries to the end of the sentence:

> Lady Macbeth asked, "Why did you bring these daggers. . . ?"

QUOTATION MARKS (" " AND ' ')

Quotation marks are used only for quotations that employ the exact words from some source (either spoken or written) but not for indirect quotations in which a source's ideas are used but not the exact words. Here are a few guidelines to remember when using quotation marks:

- Use double quotation marks to enclose a direct quotation:

  > He said, "I shall never be able to do this work."

- Use double quotation marks to enclose slang expressions, epithets, and nicknames employed in formal writing:

  > The professor said that our idea is "far out."
  > Lou Gehrig is often referred to as the "Iron Horse."
  > His younger brothers have always called him "Pat."

- Use double quotation marks to enclose borrowed material:

  > It grieved Charles much to think "what man has made of man."

- Use double quotation marks to enclose words or expressions used in a particular way. Such expressions may be coined, technical, or ironic:

  > We must develop more "stick-to-it-iveness."
  > Did you say that you wish to "up" the bid?

- Use double quotation marks to enclose the titles of songs, short stories, chapters, articles, poems, booklets, and radio and television programs that are single episodes in a series:

  > Have you read Poe's "The Raven"?
  > He enjoyed today's episode of *The Twilight Zone*, entitled "It's a Good Life."

See the section titled "Italics" later in this part for information about punctuating television episodes and programs.

- Use single quotation marks to enclose a quotation within a quotation:

  > Beulah told us, "He began by saying, 'I shall always remember this day.'"

Other marks of punctuation, when used with quotation marks, are placed according to the following principles:

- Commas and periods are always placed inside the closing quotation mark, with one exception: When citing a reference, the quotation is enclosed in quotation marks, the source is enclosed in parentheses, and then a period is placed at the end of the sentence, outside the closing quotation mark:

  > After reviewing, he stated, "The data are quite clear" (Carlane 141).

- Semicolons and colons are always placed outside the closing quotation mark.

- Question marks and exclamation marks are placed inside the closing quotation mark if they belong with the quotation; otherwise, they are placed outside:

  > Quietly she asked, "May l go along with you?"
  > Was it she who said, "I have no desire to quit"?

Only one mark of end (terminal) punctuation is used at the end of a sentence.

- When a quoted passage consists of more than one paragraph, place quotation marks at the beginning of each paragraph and at the end of the entire passage, not at the end of each paragraph.

  For dialogue (two or more persons carrying on a conversation), begin a new paragraph with each change of speaker.

THE APOSTROPHE (')

The *apostrophe* is used in forming most possessives. To form the possessive case of a singular noun, write the noun and add an apostrophe and an *s:*

Father's opinion
Mr. Smith's car
a man's coat
Olivier's hat
Elly's travels

To form the possessive case of a plural noun, first write the plural form of the noun; next, add an apostrophe if the plural form ends in *s;* otherwise, add an apostrophe and an *s:*

the dogs' trainers
children's games
women's fashions
mice's tails
the two Charleses' cars

In certain "tongue-twister" words, acceptable shortcuts may be taken. For instance, the possessive form of Jesus (Jesus's) may be written Jesus' and then pronounced "Jesus":

In Jesus' name we pray.

To determine whether this shortcut is appropriate, examine the word in question. If the word is one syllable, add the *'s* inflection; if a word is of more than one syllable or ends with a "z" sound, add an apostrophe only:

The boss's husband answered the phone.
Ms. Lopez' daughter won the highest prize.
My nieces' kittens were fluffy and white. (*Nieces* is plural in this sentence.)

Do not use an apostrophe on signs or plaques to indicate a family's residence:

Incorrect: The Smidgeon's
Correct: The Smidgeon Family

The indefinite pronouns—*one, everyone, everybody,* and the like—form their possessive case in the same way as do nouns:

one's chances
everybody's opportunity

Personal, interrogative, and relative pronouns in the possessive case (*his, its, ours, hers, yours, whose, theirs*) do not include an apostrophe.

In compound words, words followed by *else*, names of business firms, and words showing joint possession, only the last word is made possessive in form:

> his mother-in-law's address
> Dun and Bradstreet's publication
> Jack and Tom's responsibility
> someone else's book

When two or more persons possess something individually, each of the names is possessive in form:

> Fred's and Sam's sweaters
> Barry's and Barbara's eyes

The words *minute, hour, day, week, month,* and *year,* when used as possessive adjectives, require an apostrophe. Words indicating amount in dollars and cents, when used as adjectives, also require apostrophes:

> a minute's work
> five minutes' work
> a day's rest
> three days' rest
> one cent's worth
> five cents' worth
> a dollar's worth
> ten dollars' worth

Besides possession, various semantic relationships exist between one noun and a following noun that are expressed through the use of the apostrophe:

- Characterization or description

  > horse's gait
  > sailor's walk
  > boys' sneakers
  > women's garments
  > bird's flight
  > master's degree (but Master of Arts degree)

- Origin

  > Hemingway's novels
  > Joyce's short stories
  > Poe's poems

- Measure

    Time: a day's journey; a night's work
    Value: a dime's worth; a quarter's worth
    Distance: a hair's breadth; a stone's throw

- Subject of an act

    athlete's leap
    umpire's decision
    bird's flight

- Object of an act

    team's penalty
    child's scolding
    author's critics

Additionally, apostrophes are used in the following circumstances:

- To indicate where letters have been omitted in a contraction (a *contraction* is made up of two words combined into one by omitting one or more letters):

Two Words	Contraction
they have	they've
does not	doesn't
is not	isn't
would not	wouldn't
we have	we've
he is	he's
I have	I've
they are	they're
I am	I'm
will not	won't
you are	you're
are not	aren't

- To indicate the omission of letters in words in dialect and to indicate missing numbers in a date:

    I'm goin' to see 'im now.
    It all happened in '63.

An apostrophe with an *s* should be used to form the plurals of lowercase letters; just an *s* is used with uppercase letters, numbers, and symbols:

> Why aren't there two *m*'s on an M&M?
> Jennifer has a collection of 732 CDs.
> Kendra received all *10*s on her routine.

ITALICS

Use italics for names of books, magazines, newspapers, long plays, long poems (book length), motion pictures, musical productions, works of art, ships, aircraft, and trains. The words *A*, *An*, and *The* written before a title are italicized only when they are part of the title. Before the names of magazines and newspapers, these three words are not italicized within a sentence:

> He is reading *The Catcher in the Rye*.
> Do you subscribe to the *Saturday Review*?
> President Truman's plane was *The Sacred Cow*.
> He has a miniature of *Venus de Milo*.
> Did you see the motion-picture version of *Gone with the Wind*?
> Indeed, it was Shakespeare who wrote *Twelfth Night*.

The matter of using quotation marks when punctuating the titles of television series and the titles of episodes within those series has created confusion at times. A logical manner in which to proceed is to put the titles of weekly, titled episodes within quotation marks and then italicize the name of the series. This is becoming more and more common:

> Did you see the *Star Trek* episode "The City on the Edge of Forever"?

Italics should also be used for words, letters, figures, and symbols referred to by name:

> The word *Mississippi* has four *s*'s.
> Doesn't his license plate have a 7 in it?
> The entire composition has only one *and* in it.
> E-mail addresses always contain an @ symbol.

Use italics for foreign words and phrases, but note that many words and phrases of foreign origin have been absorbed into the English language and are no longer italicized. When you are in doubt about the acceptability of a word, consult a recent dictionary. If the word appears in the main section and is not set off in any way, it should not be italicized. If, however, the word appears in a special section that deals with foreign words and phrases or if it is set off in the main section, it should be italicized.

Finally, you should use italics to lend emphasis:

> Unfortunately, this was indeed *not* the correct answer to the question.

Common Punctuation Mistakes

Punctuation is a mechanical aid to accurate written communication, meant to ensure clarity of expression. As such, it is imperative to use punctuation correctly; otherwise, the meaning of your writing may be obscured. The following list presents some common punctuation mistakes, which you would do well to avoid:

- Using an apostrophe to indicate a plural. Although apostrophes are used to form contractions (e.g., "We're thrilled with our new home") and to indicate possession (e.g., "Helen's motorcycle would not start"), they are never used to indicate a plural:

  > **Incorrect:** Sheila bought four *steak's* from the butcher.

- Using an apostrophe to show possession with *it*. Although an apostrophe is typically used to indicate possession, this rule does not apply to personal, interrogative, and relative pronouns in the possessive case (*his, its, ours, hers, yours, whose, theirs*). An apostrophe is used with *it*, however, when forming a contraction:

  > **Correct:** While Joel was riding the bicycle, its front tire went flat.
  > **Correct:** It's time for us to go.

- The comma splice. A comma used to separate two independent clauses must be followed by a conjunction. If no conjunction is present, the comma should be replaced by a period or by a semicolon:

  > **Incorrect:** Luke was gardening, Anna was sleeping.
  > **Correct:** Luke was gardening, and Anna was sleeping.
  > **Correct:** Luke was gardening; Anna was sleeping.
  > **Correct:** Luke was gardening. Anna was sleeping.

- Omitting a comma after an introductory element. As you learned in Chapter 7, "Sentence Patterns," most sentences begin with a subject, which is followed by a verb and perhaps a direct object or other element. Some sentences, however, begin with an *introductory element*—a single word, a phrase, or a clause—

which typically serves as an adverb that modifies the rest of the sentence. This introductory element must be followed by a comma:

> **Incorrect:** After spending the day with her grandmother Hannah returned home.
> **Correct:** After spending the day with her grandmother, Hannah returned home.

- Omitting the serial comma in a series of three or more terms. In a series of three or more terms, each term—including the last one—should be separated from the preceding one by a comma:

> **Incorrect:** The main ingredients in my black bean chili recipe are ground turkey, black beans, chicken broth and salsa.
> **Correct:** The main ingredients in my black bean chili recipe are ground turkey, black beans, chicken broth, and salsa.

No commas are necessary, however, if all the terms in the series are joined by conjunctions:

> **Correct:** Was that movie directed by Spielberg or Lucas or Bruckheimer?

- Adding quotation marks for emphasis. In addition to being used to indicate spoken words or to indicate a quotation, quotation marks can be used to indicate irony. They should not, however, be used to emphasize a word, phrase, clause, or sentence. Instead, bold or italic type should be used.

- Overuse of exclamation points. Exclamation points, used to convey excitement, should be used sparingly—that is, when their omission would look strange. For example, the following sentence merits the use of an exclamation point due to its subject matter:

> **Correct:** When the lottery official placed the check for $43 million in Samantha's hands, she jumped up and down, screaming "This is the best day of my life!"
> **Incorrect:** These pretzels are making me thirsty!

Note, too, that exclamation marks should not be used to indicate emphasis, irony, or humor. In addition, you should avoid using multiple exclamation marks in a row at the end of a sentence.

- Incorrect placement of punctuation with closing quotation mark. Unless citing a reference, commas and periods should always be placed inside the closing quotation mark. Semicolons and colons, on the other hand, should be placed outside the closing quotation mark. Question marks and exclamation marks should be placed inside the closing quotation mark if they are part of the quotation; otherwise, they are placed outside.

Correct: Mary asked, "Who is responsible for this mess?"
Correct: Who was it who said, "I do not wish to run"?

Examples of Correctly Punctuated Sentences

Following are several sentences that contain correct punctuation:

Our instructor is Dr. J. L. Jerome, Ph.D., associate professor of English.

His address—at least as far as it is known—is 1703 Parklane Drive, Murray, Kentucky.

Help! I'm drowning!

Send your letter to 1000 Oak Street, Tulsa, Oklahoma, if you want a reply.

Jane has lived in Yuma, Arizona; Ingalls, Michigan; Nome, Alaska; and Austin, Texas.

As I told you yesterday, six cows, three hogs, and two chickens are for sale—cheap.

"No," she said. "Let's go see St. Nick." (Alternatively: "No." She said, "Let's go see St. Nick.")

The runners, suffering from the heat, decided not to finish the race. (No commas are needed if some of the other runners finished the race.)

Did Mother say, "Let's go on a picnic"?

He said, "Can you hear me?"

I arrived late; therefore, I did not receive a handout for the presentation.

The dog, hungry and wet, scratched at my door.

I was really ill: I had a bad case of the flu.

He had a choice: He could have chosen red or green.

He, Graham Fulton, swore never to ride a horse again.

There are four *s*'s in *Mississippi*.

She stated that she was "perturbed" about the results of the test.

The usher did not know what to do with the women's coats.

Mother told us the following: "Dad said you can go to the fair 'over my dead body.'"

Joan stammered, "Well, I'll be. . . ."

"I'll receive the report tomorrow," said Janet.

Queen Elizabeth reigned from A.D. 1558 to A.D. 1603.

Our neighbors are—to use Father's word—"idiots."

That soon-to-be-painted lighthouse is a true landmark.

Melville's *Moby-Dick* is one of the great books of American literature.

General Observations About Punctuation

- Terminal punctuation is punctuation that brings something, such as a sentence or an abbreviation, to an end. The various types of terminal punctuation include the following:
  - The period (.)
  - The question mark (?)
  - The exclamation mark (!)

- Internal punctuation separates, divides, and points out elements within an expression, thereby developing clarity and specific identity. Internal punctuation includes such marks as the following:
  - The comma (,)
  - The semicolon (;)
  - The colon (:)
  - The hyphen (-)

○ The em dash (—)
○ The en dash (–)
○ Parentheses (( ))
○ Brackets ([ ])
○ The ellipsis (… or ….)
○ Quotation marks (" " and ' ')
○ The apostrophe (')
○ Italics

Chapter 9

Sentence Parts

A sentence may be composed of many parts. Some of these parts, such as the following, are required:

- Subjects and predicates
- Punctuation (covered in Chapter 8, "Punctuation")

Others are not required but frequently appear in sentences nonetheless:

- Direct objects
- Indirect objects
- Complements
- Appositives
- Sentence modifiers
- Phrases
- Clauses

These sentence parts may be in the form of single words (nouns, verbs, adjectives, adverbs, or any of the other parts of speech discussed in earlier chapters) or may be phrases or clauses.

Subjects and Predicates

Most students of English have been told that a sentence is composed of two parts: a *subject* and a *predicate*. Although it seems it would be simple to identify these basic parts of a sentence, sometimes identifying the subject and predicate can be confusing.

IDENTIFYING THE SUBJECT OF A SENTENCE

With some sentences, answering a simple "who" or "what" question identifies the subject of the sentence:

> Richard finished the examination.
>> (Who finished the examination? *Richard. Richard* is the subject of this sentence.)
> The current was too strong for us to go swimming.
>> (What was too strong? The *current. Current* is the subject.)

The big dogs that were in the barnyard seemed friendly.
(What seemed friendly? The *dogs*. *Dogs* is the subject.)

The single most important word in the group of words in which the subject is located is the *simple subject*. The *complete subject* is the simple subject along with all the words that pattern with it—that is, are grammatically tied to the subject rather than to the predicate. These related words may be single words, phrases, or clauses. For example, in the third sentence above, the complete subject is *the big dogs that were in the barnyard*.

You can also determine the subject in some sentences by noting which word or group of words alternates positions with another part of the sentence when a sentence that is a statement is converted to a sentence that is a question:

Betty has answered all the questions on the examination.
Has Betty answered all the questions on the examination?

Because no words pattern with *Betty,* that word alone is the subject of the sentence, and all the other words are the predicate. To test this theory, try the phrase *My friend Betty* instead of just *Betty* in the sentences above.

IDENTIFYING THE PREDICATE OF A SENTENCE

The *predicate* of a sentence is all the words that do not pattern with the subject, as long as the entire sentence (or clause, as you'll see later in this chapter, in the section titled "Clauses") fits into one of the patterns discussed in Chapter 7, "Sentence Patterns." If a pattern is inverted, you can still ask the "who" or "what" question, but you will not find the subject located at the beginning of the sentence string:

Out in the field stood the horse and cow.

Who or *what* stood out in the field? The horse and cow. The phrase *the horse and cow* is, then, the subject of the sentence. Note, too, the inverted position of *stood* and *the horse and cow* when the statement is converted to a question. (In this example, the form of the verb is changed from *stood* to the basic verb form *stand,* and an auxiliary verb, or "helping verb," is added, as is often done in questions.)

Out in the field *stood* the horse and cow.
Did the horse and cow *stand* out in the field?
Had the horse and cow *stood* out in the field?

Direct Objects

A major sentence element contained in many predicates is the *direct object,* which occurs in sentences that have transitive verbs. A *transitive verb* is a verb that requires a direct object to give the sentence a sense of completeness.

Refer to the section titled "Transitive Verbs" in Chapter 3, "Verbs," for more information about them.

Note these word groups:

> The small boy found
> The old mule could not carry

Neither "sentence" conveys a sense of completeness. But if certain nouns were to be added, the sentences would seem normal:

> The small boy found *a silver coin.*
> The old mule could not carry *the heavy load of wood.*

The nouns that have been added are *direct objects.*

IDENTIFYING DIRECT OBJECTS

To identify direct objects, you may ask the "what" question (or the "who" question) in conjunction with the verb. In the first sentence above, *what* did the small boy find? *A silver coin. A silver coin* is the complete direct object, while *coin* is the simple direct object. In the second sentence above, *what* couldn't the old mule carry? *The heavy load of wood. The heavy load of wood* is the complete direct object, and *load* is the simple direct object. (*Load,* not *wood,* is the simple direct object, as prepositional phrases are seldom subjects or direct objects.)

For the following sentences, various sentence elements are identified: the complete subject, the simple subject, the predicate, and, within the predicate, the verb, the complete direct object, and the simple direct object:

> The boy and his companion found a buried treasure.
>
> > **Complete subject:** the boy and his companion
> > **Simple subject:** boy, companion
> > **Predicate:** found a buried treasure
> > **Transitive verb:** found
> > **Complete direct object:** a buried treasure
> > **Simple direct object:** treasure

The little kitten quietly drank the warm milk.

> **Complete subject:** the little kitten
> **Simple subject:** kitten
> **Predicate:** quietly drank the warm milk
> **Transitive verb:** drank
> **Complete direct object:** the warm milk
> **Simple direct object:** milk

The senator read the speech to his audience.

> **Complete subject:** the senator
> **Simple subject:** senator
> **Predicate:** read the speech to his audience
> **Transitive verb:** read
> **Complete direct object:** the speech
> **Simple direct object:** speech

The black bears ate the berries out of the wooden crate.

> **Complete subject:** the black bears
> **Simple subject:** bears
> **Predicate:** ate the berries out of the wooden crate
> **Transitive verb:** ate
> **Complete direct object:** the berries out of the wooden crate
> **Simple direct object:** berries

She wrote the letter on her computer.

> **Complete subject:** she
> **Simple subject:** she
> **Predicate:** wrote the letter on her computer
> **Transitive verb:** wrote
> **Complete direct object:** the letter
> **Simple direct object:** letter

Every student in the class did the first three exercises.

> **Complete subject:** every student in the class
> **Simple subject:** student
> **Predicate:** did the first three exercises
> **Transitive verb:** did
> **Complete direct object:** the first three exercises
> **Simple direct object:** exercises

The hawk caught the mouse in its strong talons.

> **Complete subject:** the hawk
> **Simple subject:** hawk
> **Predicate:** caught the mouse in its strong talons
> **Transitive verb:** caught
> **Complete direct object:** the mouse
> **Simple direct object:** mouse

The students found the buses in the parking lot.

> **Complete subject:** The students
> **Simple subject:** students
> **Predicate:** found the buses in the parking lot
> **Transitive verb:** found
> **Complete direct object:** the buses in the parking lot
> **Simple direct object:** buses

The old cow chewed its cud contentedly.

> **Complete subject:** The old cow
> **Simple subject:** cow
> **Predicate:** chewed its cud contentedly
> **Transitive verb:** chewed
> **Complete direct object:** its cud
> **Simple direct object:** cud

Indirect Objects

Indirect objects are those parts of the predicate that occur in sentences containing direct objects and that are closely related to the direct objects by identifying the person/thing to whom or for whom something is done or given or of whom a question is asked. Indirect objects are usually nouns or pronouns.

In a sentence containing an indirect object, you can use only certain verbs, such as the following:

> give
> tell
> buy
> send
> write

teach
get
bring

Notice that all these verbs suggest giving or communicating. The sentences that follow contain indirect objects, which are italicized. Note that indirect objects occur before the direct objects:

The boy gave the thirsty *puppy* a drink.
The scout leader told the young *scouts* a frightening story.
Don't tell *me* your troubles!

Notice how the direct object and indirect object are related in each of the sentences. In the first sentence, you determine what was given—a drink. *Drink* is the direct object. To determine the indirect object, you determine to whom that drink was given—in this case, the thirsty puppy. Therefore, *puppy* is the simple indirect object. Each of the other sentences may be analyzed in much the same way. In the second sentence, the leader told a story. To whom did he or she tell the story? To the young scouts. *The young scouts* is the indirect object, while *scouts* is the simple indirect object. In the third sentence, *you* is the understood subject of the verb *tell*. *Troubles* is the direct object. To whom were the troubles told? To me. Thus, *me* is the indirect object.

Sentences such as the preceding ones that express requests, commands, or instructions and that begin with a verb and have no apparent subject, are called *imperative sentences*. The subject of such sentences is an understood *you*. For more information, refer to the section titled "Imperative Sentences" in Chapter 6, "Types of Sentences."

Another way to locate the indirect object in a sentence is to recast the sentence to include a prepositional phrase starting with *to* or *for*. For example, when "Don't tell me your troubles!" becomes "Don't tell your troubles to me!" you can see that *me* is the indirect object.

The following sentences further illustrate subjects, verbs, direct objects, and indirect objects:

The children brought their mother some wildflowers.

Complete subject: the children
Simple subject: children
Predicate: brought their mother some wildflowers
Transitive verb: brought
Complete direct object: some wildflowers
Simple direct object: wildflowers
Complete indirect object: their mother
Simple indirect object: mother

Can you give me directions to the stadium?

> **Complete subject:** you
> **Simple subject:** you
> **Predicate:** can give me directions to the stadium
> **Transitive verb:** give
> **Complete direct object:** directions to the stadium
> **Simple direct object:** directions
> **Complete indirect object:** me
> **Simple indirect object:** me

The class got Professor Allen a book and a card.

> **Complete subject:** the class
> **Simple subject:** class
> **Predicate:** got Professor Allen a book and a card
> **Transitive verb:** got
> **Complete indirect object:** a book and a card
> **Simple direct object:** book, card
> **Complete indirect object:** Professor Allen
> **Simple indirect object:** Professor Allen

The postman gave me Mother's package.

> **Complete subject:** the postman
> **Simple subject:** postman
> **Predicate:** gave me Mother's package
> **Transitive verb:** gave
> **Complete direct object:** Mother's package
> **Simple direct object:** package
> **Complete indirect object:** me
> **Simple indirect object:** me

The musician taught us the words to the song.

> **Complete subject:** the musician
> **Simple subject:** musician
> **Predicate:** taught us the words to the song
> **Transitive verb:** taught
> **Complete direct object:** the words to the song
> **Simple direct object:** words
> **Complete indirect object:** us
> **Indirect object:** us

We bought our father a book for his birthday.

> **Complete subject:** we
> **Simple subject:** we
> **Predicate:** bought our father a book for his birthday
> **Transitive verb:** bought
> **Complete indirect object:** a book for his birthday
> **Simple direct object:** book
> **Complete indirect object:** our father
> **Simple indirect object:** father

Complements

A *complement,* which can be a noun, an adjective, a pronoun, or a phrase, is added to a verb to complete the predicate of a sentence. The complement provides information about a clause's subject or object.

There are four main types of complements:

- Object complement
- Subject complement
- Adverbial complement
- Adjectival complement

OBJECT COMPLEMENT

Sentences that correspond to the following pattern have a sentence element known as an *object complement:* In effect, an object complement describes, or "completes," the direct object, usually by adding a noun or an adjective immediately after the direct object.

The words in bold in the following sentences are direct objects; the words in italics are object complements. Note how the object complements relate to the direct objects and complete the idea of the action of the verb:

> Our neighbors painted their **house** *green*.
> The student council elected **me** *president*.

When a sentence containing an object complement is made passive, only the direct object can become the subject of the verb in the passive voice, as in this passive form of the second sentence:

> I was elected president by the student council.

Only a limited number of verbs can be used in sentences containing an object complement, including the following:

> appoint
> believe
> call
> choose
> consider
> declare
> elect
> feel
> find
> get
> imagine
> keep
> make
> nominate
> prove
> suppose
> think

These verbs suggest a "to be" meaning after the direct object, but bear in mind that the verb *to be* is not stated:

> We all thought George [was] honest.

Understanding object complements helps you correctly choose modifiers and pronouns because both relate to the object. The following sentences exemplify a common problem: Which is the correct form?

> Shut the door (*tight, tightly*).
> The dean thought Fred (*me, I*).

Because the word in parentheses in the first sentence modifies door—a noun—the adjective form, *tight,* is correct. Consider a similar sentence:

> Paint the door (*white, whitely*).

Obviously, *whitely* is incorrect. We know the door will be white.

In the second sentence, the pronoun that relates to Fred is in the same case as Fred—the objective case—because Fred is the direct object. The correct choice, therefore, is *me.*

Some speakers, thinking *I* sounds more "elegant" than *me* in such constructions, mistakenly employ the nominative case in these and similar constructions. Avoid this.

SUBJECT COMPLEMENT

A *subject complement* is an adjective, a noun, or a noun phrase that is linked to a subject by the verb *to be* or by other copulative verbs such as the following:

> become
> turn
> look
> appear
> seem
> feel
> sound

Refer to the section titled "Copulative Verbs" in Chapter 3 for more information about *them*.

The words in bold in the following sentences are subjects; the words in italics are subject complements. Notice how the subject complements relate to the subjects:

> **Benedict Arnold** turned *traitor* during the Revolutionary War.
> **Susan** was *upset* about her grade.
> **Julie** is my close *friend*.

In the relatively few instances where the subject complement is a pronoun, the pronoun must be in the nominative case, just as it is after a form of the verb *to be*:

> The **treasurer** was *she* whom we elected.
> The **treasurer** remained *she* whom we elected.

ADVERBIAL COMPLEMENT

An adverbial complement functions as an adverb and is necessary to complete the meaning of the sentence that contains it. It is similar to a subject complement but usually conveys the meaning of location, direction, progression, duration, condition, circumstance, or purpose.

Several examples of these meanings are demonstrated in the following sentences:

> These flowers are *for Roweena*. (purpose)
> My race is *in its final stage*. (condition)
> The entire project is *on schedule*. (progression)

The warranty is *for thirty days*. (duration)
The entire delegation is *under surveillance*. (circumstances)

Adverbial complements differ from simple adverbs and adverb phrases in that simple adverbs and adverb phrases are usually not essential elements of a sentence. The following sentences demonstrate the differences between adverb phrases and adverbial complements:

The new recruits were *in their barracks*. (adverbial complement)
The new recruits were standing *in the rain*. (adverb phrase)

I have a package *in my car*. (adverb phrase)
The package is *in my car*. (adverbial complement)

To distinguish between the two types of constructions, simply reread the preceding sentences, omitting the phrases in italics. In the first and fourth sentences, the italicized phrases are essential elements of the sentences.

Although adverbial complements are usually short prepositional phrases, single-word adverbs may function as adverbial complements:

The book is *there*.
The money is *here*.
Our final examination is *tomorrow*.

ADJECTIVE COMPLEMENT

In some sentences, a construction identified as an *adjective complement* can occur. This type of complement restricts or completes the meaning of an adjective in a sentence.

Notice the adjective complements in the sentences below. The adjective complements are italicized:

I am happy *that you won the game*.
The gardener was reluctant *to plant roses in that area*.
The boys grew tired *of waiting*.
I am afraid *that we are lost*.

IDENTIFYING THE VARIOUS TYPES OF COMPLEMENTS

Following are some sample sentences that make use of complements:

Seeing is believing.

> **Subject:** Seeing
> **Verb:** is
> **Complement:** believing (subject complement)

The wanderers looked exhausted from their experience.

> **Subject:** wanderers
> **Verb:** looked
> **Complement:** exhausted (subject complement)
> **Complement:** from their experience (adjective complement)

The rain remained steady all night.

> **Subject:** rain
> **Verb:** remained
> **Complement:** steady (subject complement)
> **Complement:** all night (adjective complement)

Many students are concerned about the environment.

> **Subject:** students
> **Verb:** are
> **Complement:** concerned (subject complement)
> **Complement:** about the environment (adjective complement)

Jealousy is a foolish emotion.

> **Subject:** jealousy
> **Verb:** is
> **Complement:** emotion (subject complement)

All the cargo was in the ship's hold.

> **Subject:** cargo
> **Verb:** was
> **Complement:** in the ship's hold (adverbial complement)

The tenant painted his room yellow.

> **Subject:** tenant
> **Verb:** painted
> **Direct Object:** room
> **Complement:** yellow (object complement)

Our club elected Mary president.

> **Subject:** club

Verb: elected
Direct Object: Mary
Complement: president (object complement)

I have made Ronald the captain.

Subject: I
Verb: have made
Direct Object: Ronald
Complement: captain (object complement)

Renee is a very fine singer.

Subject: Renee
Verb: is
Complement: singer (subject complement)

Appositives

An *appositive* is a word, a phrase, or a clause usually located near a nominal (a noun, a noun phrase, or a noun substitute) to identify, explain, or describe the nominal. Although adjectives can be used as appositives, appositives are usually nouns and pronouns. The following sentences contain appositives, which are often set off within commas and appear here in italics:

The editor of the paper, *Mr. Parker*, spoke to our group, *the senior English class*.
We chatted with the curator, the man responsible for the exhibit.
Your friend Pascal is quite funny.
A friendly cat, Whiskers was my first pet.
Sally gave the dog, *a family pet*, a good home.

To determine whether an appositive should be set off by commas, consider whether the appositive contains information that is essential to the reader's understanding of the sentence. Appositives containing non-essential information require commas; appositives containing essential information should not be set off by commas. Consider these examples:

The talented race-car driver *Helio Castroneves* has won several important races.
     (Here, the appositive does not take commas because it is essential to the reader's understanding of the sentence. Without the appositive, the sentence would read "The talented race-car driver has won several important races." Readers would not know which race-car driver was being discussed.)

Helio Castroneves, *the talented race-car driver*, has won several important races.
(Here, the appositive does take commas because it is not essential to the reader's understanding of the sentence. Without the appositive, the sentence would read "Helio Castroneves has won several important races." Readers would know who the subject of the sentence is even without the appositive.)

Helio Castroneves *performer on Dancing on the Stars* is almost as famous as Helio Castroneves *race-car driver*.
(Here, neither appositive takes commas because both are essential to the reader's understanding of the sentence. Without the appositives, the sentence would read "Helio Castroneves is almost as famous as Helio Castroneves.")

Appositives especially cause speakers or writers problems when pronouns are involved. In such instances, you must remember that the case (or form) of the pronoun is determined by the use of the nominal with which the pronoun is in apposition, as in these sentences:

The swimmers, John and *he*, were ready for the competition.
(*He* patterns with the subject of the sentence and is, therefore, in the nominative case.)

The winners were the two seniors, Mary and *she*.
She patterns with a subject complement [seniors] and is, therefore, in the nominative case.)

They watched the two cyclists, Carlos and *me*.
(*Me* patterns with the direct object and is thus in the objective case.)

The professor gave the two students, Peggy and *him*, some extra problems to work.
(*Him* patterns with the indirect object and is, therefore, in the objective case.)

Sentence Modifiers

Certain types of adverbials can be employed as *sentence modifiers*. Usually set off by a comma, a sentence modifier relates to an entire sentence, not to any separate element within the sentence.

Adverbials, which are optional elements in sentence or clause structure, come in three forms: *adjuncts*, *conjuncts*, and *disjuncts*.

- *Adjuncts* are integrated to some degree in the sentence or clause structure and typically inform as to space, time, process, or focus:

> in my neighborhood
> next week
> easily
> primarily

- *Conjuncts*, which are mainly adverbs or prepositional phrases, indicate logical relationships between sentences or clauses:

> therefore
> however
> nonetheless
> on the other hand

- *Disjuncts* are one of two styles: style or content.
  - *Style disjuncts*—which can be adverbs, prepositional phrases, finite clauses, and non-finite clauses—comment on the act of speaking or writing:

  > truthfully
  > in short
  > frankly speaking
  > since you mentioned it

  - *Content disjuncts* evaluate or comment on the truth of what is said:

  > probably
  > unfortunately

For the purposes of comparison, examine the sentence that follows. This sentence employs the adverbs *naturally* and *gracefully* as modifiers of the verb *ran:*

> The boy ran naturally and gracefully.

In the next sentence, however, *naturally* cannot be associated with *ran* and still have the sentence retain the meaning that seems to be intended:

> *Naturally*, my sister won the election.

In this sentence, the word *naturally* modifies the entire sentence. As another example, consider this sentence:

> Because the door was locked, the thief crawled through the window.

The introductory adverbial clause, *Because the door was locked,* does not tell why the thief crawled. Rather, it tells why the thief crawled through the window. The thief crawled, presumably, because the window was too low and too small to have enabled the thief to walk through. He crawled through the window because the door was locked.

Various types of sentence modifiers exist:

- Single-word adverbials

    Strangely, the moon seemed to rise in the west.
      (The moon did not *rise* strangely.)

- Clause adverbials

    Because the table was dirty, we ate at the counter.

- Prepositional phrases

    In fact, we made some serious errors.
      (The errors were not errors of fact.)

- Absolute phrases

    The rain having stopped, we went on our picnic.

- Infinitive phrases

    To summarize, we need a new committee.

- Participial phrases

    Knowing the dog's temper, we circled the barn at a respectable distance.

- "-ever" clauses

    Whoever she is, I will catch her.

Sentence modifiers such as those previously shown may also be placed after or within the sentences they modify. For example, examine the following:

    We need, to summarize, a new committee.

Notice the essential commas. If the commas are omitted, the "We" of the sentence would be summarizing a new committee, whatever that means. On the other hand, if the sentence modifier is placed after the sentence without being separated by a comma, the sentence takes on still another meaning:

    We need a new committee to summarize.

The following sentences contain sentence modifiers, which are italicized:

    My uncle was, *understandably*, upset about the damage to his car.
    As I was saying, not enough people vote in our elections.
    Because the mail was not delivered, we didn't receive the invitation.
    We can, *in retrospect*, see where we made the greatest errors.
    We missed the concert *because of the flat tire*.
    The boat did not sail, *the crew having gone on strike*.

Before we know it, the vacation will be over.
We need new officers, *to put the matter briefly.*
Knowing where the fish were, we caught many nice bass.

Phrases

The traditional definition of a *phrase* is somewhat as follows: A phrase is a group of words not containing a subject and predicate and used as a single part of speech. While certain aspects of this definition may be subject to some dispute, the definition is functional and adequate for the purposes of this book; but we must remember that phrases (the groups of words) may contain modifying *clauses,* which, by definition, contain subjects and verbs. The various types of phrases include the following:

- Noun phrases
- Prepositional phrases
- Verbals

NOUN PHRASES

Noun phrases (which, for the purposes of this book, may be a noun without any other words patterning with it) can be used in a sentence just as a noun is used. That is, a noun phrase can be used in a sentence as the subject, direct object, indirect object, subject complement, object complement, object of a preposition, object of an infinitive, subject of an infinitive, and so on.

Notice the two noun phrases in the following sentence:

The boy who was here is my nephew.

On the most superficial level, the sentence contains two noun phrases, one (*the boy*) with a modifying clause (*who was here*) and one (*my nephew*) without such a clause. To determine the extent of the first noun phrase, you must identify the head word of the phrase (usually called the *noun head*) and then include all the modifiers of the noun head—all the single words, phrases, and clauses that pattern with that head word. The noun head of the first noun phrase in the preceding example is *boy.* The words that pattern with *boy* are *the* and *who was here.* In the second phrase, *nephew* is the noun head, and *my* is the only other word in the phrase.

Examine the noun phrases in italics in the following sentences. The noun heads of the target phrases are in bold:

Try to find *the little **boy** with the wet feet.*
We do our shopping at *the convenience **store*** on *the corner.*
*The **students** who were absent* missed *the final **examination.***

Other noun phrases in the preceding examples are *the wet feet*, *the corner*, *the final examination*, and pronouns.

PREPOSITIONAL PHRASES

A *preposition* is a word that functions as a connector between sentence elements. The element that it connects and patterns with is usually a noun and is identified as the *object of the preposition*. The preposition itself is "pre-positioned" (thus the term "preposition") between the object and the word to which the object is related. Take the following sentence as an example:

The kitten *with the white paws* is named Fluffy.

In this sentence, the preposition *with* shows a relationship between *kitten* and *paws*. The prepositional phrase serves as an adjective indicating which kitten is named Fluffy.

Prepositional phrases may also serve as adverbs, as in this sentence:

The scouts hurried *to their campsite*.

Because adverbs indicate where, when, why, under what conditions, and to what extent, and because *to their campsite* tells where the scouts hurried, the prepositional phrase is an adverbial prepositional phrase—or, to keep the designation simple, an adverbial phrase.

A prepositional phrase contains a preposition, the *object of the preposition* (usually a noun), and all the modifiers of the object. Those modifiers may themselves be prepositional phrases; thus one often encounters sentences such as this:

The rooms in the old building with the sagging roof were dark and damp.

The first prepositional phrase is *in the old building with the sagging roof*. The preposition is *in;* its object is *building. Building,* too, has a modifying prepositional phrase: *with the sagging roof. With* is the preposition; *roof* is the object of the preposition.

Remember that objects of prepositions are in the objective case. Fortunately, English does not have a separate form (or case) for nominative and objective uses of nouns. Pronouns do have separate cases, however; therefore, you must remember to use the objective case of the pronoun where the pronoun is the object of the preposition. Notice the following:

No one could distinguish *between **him** and **me**.*
Route your report *through **Mildred** and **her**.*

Occasionally, prepositional phrases can be used in somewhat unusual ways—for example, as subjects of sentences. The construction of the prepositional phrase remains the same:

Over the fence is a home run.
In shallow water is the place to find minnows.

After each of the following sentences, you'll find listed the prepositional phrases within that sentence, the preposition within each prepositional phrase, and the object of each prepositional phrase. If the sentence contains prepositional phrases within prepositional phrases, they will be so noted.

The tree in the meadow is an old oak.

> **Prepositional phrase:** in the meadow
> **Preposition:** in
> **Object of preposition:** meadow

I do not trust the bridge across the big river in Tennessee.

> **Prepositional phrase:** across the big river in Tennessee
> **Preposition:** across
> **Object of preposition:** river
> **Prepositional phrase:** in Tennessee
> **Preposition:** in
> **Object of preposition:** Tennessee

Cows with calves by their sides often remain in one area.

> **Prepositional phrase:** with calves by their sides
> **Preposition:** with
> **Object of preposition:** calves
> **Prepositional phrase:** by their sides
> **Preposition:** by
> **Object of preposition:** sides
> **Prepositional phrase:** in one area
> **Preposition:** in
> **Object of preposition:** area

Shagbark hickories are identified by their hard, peeling bark.

> **Prepositional phrase:** by their hard, peeling bark
> **Preposition:** by
> **Object of preposition:** bark

T-shirts with funny sayings on them are popular with the young set.

> **Prepositional phrase:** with funny sayings on them
> **Preposition:** with

Object of preposition: sayings
Prepositional phrase: on them
Preposition: on
Object of preposition: them
Prepositional phrase: with the young set
Preposition: with
Object of preposition: set

Into the hole ran the mouse, with the cat after it.

Prepositional phrase: into the hole
Preposition: into
Object of preposition: hole
Prepositional phrase: with the cat after it
Preposition: with
Object of preposition: cat
Prepositional phrase: after it
Preposition: after
Object of preposition: it

Except for dogs with fleas, I like most animals.

Prepositional phrase: except for dogs with fleas
Preposition: except
Object of preposition: dogs
Prepositional phrase: with fleas
Preposition: with
Object of preposition: fleas

The best place for a vacation is in the mountains.

Prepositional phrase: for a vacation
Preposition: for
Object of preposition: vacation
Prepositional phrase: in the mountains
Preposition: in
Object of preposition: mountains

During the night, the south wind brought rain and snow.

Prepositional phrase: during the night
Preposition: during
Object of preposition: night

We hiked through the woods and over the hills until late afternoon.

> **Prepositional phrase:** through the woods
> **Preposition:** through
> **Object of preposition:** woods
> **Prepositional phrase:** over the hills
> **Preposition:** over
> **Object of preposition:** hills
> **Prepositional phrase:** until late afternoon
> **Preposition:** until
> **Object of preposition:** afternoon

VERBALS

The three types of phrases discussed in this section—infinitives, gerunds, and participles—are known as *verbals* because they incorporate verb forms in their basic constructions. Verbals are employed as grammatical units within sentences, usually as nouns or modifiers. They are often classified as *nonfinite verbs* because they are not inflected (do not change form) to indicate person, number, or tense.

Infinitive Phrases

Infinitive phrases, like prepositional phrases, can be used in a number of ways. Fortunately, an infinitive phrase is fairly easy to recognize. First of all, it has as one of its constituents the infinitive from which the phrase gets its name. An infinitive is the word *to* followed by the base form of a verb, such as *run, jump, play, work, buy, see,* and so on. Infinitives, then, look like this: *to run, to jump, to play, to work, to buy, to see.*

An infinitive phrase contains an infinitive and words that pattern with it—modifiers, objects, and subjects. Like verbs that are used as predicators in sentences, an infinitive can have objects—in this case called *objects of the infinitive* rather than *direct objects*.

Note the infinitive phrases and the objects of the infinitives in the following sentences. The phrases are in italics, and the objects of the infinitives are in bold:

> My father tried *to find his missing **wallet.***
> *To buy a **house** in the country* was his life-long dream.
> She wanted *to play her **violin*** at a concert in New York.

Like verbs used as predicators, infinitives may have indirect objects, as the boldfaced words in the following sentences demonstrate:

The professor threatened *to give **us** a test*.
Matilda left *to get **Marty** an ice cream cone*.

Pronouns used as either objects or indirect objects of the infinitive must be in the objective case, unless the infinitive is constructed with the verb *to be*. Such a construction requires special consideration; however, the rules governing it are few and really quite simple:

- If the infinitive *to be* has no subject, the complement of the infinitive is in the *nominative* case:

    The girl with the red shorts was thought to be *she*.
    The winner turned out to be *he* whom we selected.

- If the infinitive *to be* has a subject, its subject (in bold) and complement (in italics) are in the objective case:

    They all thought **him** to be *me*.
    The principal believed the **leader** to be *him*.

Insofar as an infinitive has many of the characteristics of a verb, it can pattern in much the same way as a verb—with objects and indirect objects and with subjects and modifiers. Examine the following sentences and note the subjects, objects, and modifiers of the infinitives. The modifiers have been boldfaced for ease of identification; the infinitive phrases are in italics:

We all tried *to finish our work **quickly.***
The club wanted *Bill to construct a shelf **in the hall.***
*To write **well*** was his greatest ambition.
All the students wanted *him to cover **adequately** the material that would be on the test.*

Bill in the second sentence and *him* in the fourth sentence above are subjects of the infinitives in those sentences. Subjects of infinitives are in the objective case, as noted earlier in the discussion of the infinitive with the verb *to be*.

On Split Infinitives

Some grammar texts assert that one must never "split" an infinitive. That rule is a holdover from early studies of English based on observations about Latin. In Latin, infinitives cannot be split, because they are single words, not two words, as they are in English.

Because splitting the infinitive is still often frowned upon, you probably should avoid doing so as often as possible. At times, however, awkward constructions may result from trying to avoid splitting infinitives, and you must decide whether splitting the infinitive or sounding awkward— or even inane—is the greater error.

The infinitives are split in the sentences that follow. How would you avoid splitting infinitives in these sentences?

- *To* better *reflect* nutritional knowledge, the USDA revamped the food pyramid.
- We plan *to* completely *remove* partially weakened beams to satisfy the inspector from OSHA.

One could argue, of course, that a different type of construction could be used in place of the infinitive. For instance, one could use a participle and create this sentence:

- Revamping the food pyramid was an attempt by the USDA to better reflect nutritional knowledge.
- Our plan incorporating total removal of partially weakened beams is designed to satisfy the inspector from OSHA.

Such a position is valid; but in order to create sentences with a variety of constructions, you must understand all the options available to a writer and the fine points of using those options. Recognizing these options is in large part dependent upon knowing sentence parts, including infinitives.

The infinitive phrase is a versatile construction, capable of being used in a number of ways within a sentence: as the subject of various constructions, as the object of verbs and verbals, and as a modifier. In the sentences that follow, the infinitive phrases are in italics, and the use of the infinitive phrase in each sentence is indicated in parentheses:

The team wanted *to win the final game of the season*. (direct object)

To win the final game was the team's greatest goal. (subject)

The team knew that the game *to win* was the final game. (adjective, telling which game)

The puppy ran *to get the bone*. (adverb, telling why the puppy ran)

My goal is *to get an A in biology*. (subject complement)

His objective, *to climb K2*, is unrealistic. (appositive with subject)

We discovered his secret ambition, *to write a novel*. (appositive with direct object)

We laughed as we tried *to walk across the ice rink*. (direct object)

The colors *to wear in the summertime* are light colors. (adjective, telling which colors)

The students wanted *to solve as many problems as they could*. (direct object)

You must wear sunglasses *to protect your eyes from the sun's rays*. (adverb, telling why you must wear sunglasses)

Carl's job is *to eliminate needless paperwork*. (subject complement)

To eat much less at mealtime was his latest goal. (subject)

My role, *to play the fool,* was not very enjoyable. (appositive with subject)

The officer knew his task—*to apprehend the criminal.* (appositive with direct object)

You should try *to discover answers for yourself.* (direct object)

Students should take a variety of courses *to get a well-rounded education.* (adverb, telling why students should take a variety of courses)

After the following sentences, the infinitive phrases are listed. Also listed are any subjects and objects of the infinitives, if applicable:

Everyone wanted Elizabeth to win the contest.

> **Infinitive phrase:** Elizabeth to win the contest
> **Subject of the infinitive:** Elizabeth
> **Object of the infinitive:** contest

His goal was to bowl a perfect game.

> **Infinitive phrase:** to bowl a perfect game
> **Object of the infinitive:** game

The wrench to use to loosen the bolt is missing.

> **Infinitive phrase:** to use (used as an adjective modifying *wrench*)
> **Infinitive phrase:** to loosen the bolt (used as an adverb modifying *to use,* telling when or under what conditions)
> **Object of the infinitive:** bolt

The cowboy tried to lasso the wild mustang.

> **Infinitive phrase:** to lasso the wild mustang
> **Object of the infinitive:** mustang

We found Richard to be someone whom we could trust.

> **Infinitive phrase:** Richard to be someone whom we could trust
> **Subject of the infinitive:** Richard

The officer threatened to issue the driver a traffic citation.

> **Infinitive phrase:** to issue the driver a traffic citation
> **Object of the infinitive:** citation (*driver* is the indirect object of the infinitive)

In the closet he found the perfect costume to wear to the party.

> **Infinitive phrase:** to wear to the party

To move quietly through the brush takes the skill of a woodsman.

> **Infinitive phrase:** to move quietly through the brush

Strive to show yourself worthy of any praise you receive.

> **Infinitive phrase:** to show yourself worthy of any praise you receive
> **Object of the infinitive:** yourself

The hunters found orange to be visible during cloudy days.

> **Infinitive phrase:** orange to be visible during cloudy days
> **Subject of the infinitive:** orange

We all wanted to be in bed before midnight.

> **Infinitive phrase:** to be in bed before midnight

To do a good job, one must strive to follow instructions.

> **Infinitive phrase:** to do a good job
> **Object of the infinitive:** job
> **Infinitive phrase:** to follow instructions
> **Object of the infinitive:** instructions

The clothes to wear to a ball game are sports clothes.

> **Infinitive phrase:** clothes to wear to a ball game
> **Subject of the infinitive:** clothes

Try to keep calm during emergencies.

> **Infinitive phrase:** to keep calm during emergencies
> **Object of the infinitive:** calm

To achieve success does not always mean to win.

> **Infinitive phrase:** to achieve success
> **Object of the infinitive:** success
> **Infinitive phrase:** to win

Gerund Phrases

A *gerund phrase* is a type of verbal. Gerund phrases are recognized by two means: description and function. First, a gerund phrase is recognized by its characteristic verb form with an *ing* ending (although this is not always a sure-fire means of spotting a gerund). In addition to the *ing* ending, the gerund functions in a sentence in a manner similar to a noun. For purposes of this book, then, a gerund may be identified as a verb form ending in *ing* and used as a noun. And, of course, because this discussion concerns phrases, other words must be included with the gerund to form the phrase.

Notice the gerunds and gerund phrases in the sentences below. The gerunds are bold, and each entire gerund phrase is in italics:

> ***Painting** houses* can be very rewarding.
> We all enjoyed ***seeing** the pictures*.
> The team won the game by ***passing** the ball*.

In the first sentence, the gerund phrase functions as the subject of the verb *can be*. In the second sentence, the gerund phrase is the direct object of the verb, and in the third sentence, the gerund phrase is used as the object of the preposition *by*. Basically, the use of the gerund duplicates the use of the noun.

In the examples that follow, note the use of the gerund phrase as an indirect object in the first sentence, and as object of the infinitive in the second sentence:

> The boy gave ***flying** his kite* his undivided attention.
> The tourists found ***hiking** in the park* somewhat boring.

Gerund phrases may also be used as subject complements (as in the first sentence that follows) and as appositives (as in the second and third sentences that follow):

> His favorite pastime is ***building** model airplanes*.
> Her hobby, ***painting** miniatures*, requires great patience.
> The class finished the assignment, ***finding** gerund phrases*.

To complicate matters a bit, gerunds, like verbs and infinitives, may pattern with their own complements, such as objects and modifiers. The sentences in the group that follows demonstrate various patterns. The gerunds are underlined, and the various associated word groups are in bold. The entire gerund phrase is in italics:

> The artist enjoyed *<u>painting</u> **pictures of the sea.***
>> (*Pictures of the sea* is the object of the gerund.)

> *<u>Working</u> **in the hot sun*** was an unpleasant experience.
>> (The gerund phrase is used as the subject of the verb *was*, while *in the hot sun* is an adverbial prepositional phrase telling "where.")

> *<u>Crying</u> **hysterically*** is quite distracting.
>> (*Hysterically* is a single word adverb telling "how.")

> We learned the technique by *<u>watching</u> **the experts.***
>> (*Watching the experts* is the object of the preposition *by; the experts* is the object of the gerund.)

The swimmer enjoys *practicing diving* **into the new pool.**
> (The gerund phrase is the object of the verb *enjoys,* while the gerund *diving* is the object of the gerund *practicing*.)

Your greatest mistake was *giving* **your roommate your notes.**
> (*Notes* is the object of the gerund *giving,* while *your roommate* is the indirect object of the gerund. The gerund phrase is a subject complement.)

As you can see, if you understand the special relationships that exist between the verb and other parts of the sentence, along with the various uses of nouns, you should have very little difficulty understanding the gerund and its uses in the sentence. Two cautions must be exercised, however:

- You must be careful not to mistake a participle for a gerund. Participles may have the *ing* ending that is also characteristic of gerunds, but participles are used as modifiers, not as noun substitutes. (Participles are discussed in the next section.)
- A gerund without an auxiliary always consists of the *ing* form of the verb; if it has an auxiliary when a past-participial form is used, it will be preceded by an auxiliary ending in an *ing* form:

> Having **worked** for an attorney was a valuable experience.

The gerund *worked* has the past-participle form, thus it contains no *ing* ending; however, the auxiliary preceding it, *having,* does have the characteristic *ing* ending. In the following sentence, two auxiliaries are employed in the gerund phrase:

> *Having been* **found** *guilty* caused his consternation.

In both sentences above, the gerund phrases are subjects of the verb.

Showing Relationships among Gerunds and Actors

To show a relationship between an actor (noun) and a following gerund, always use a possessive pronoun (if a pronoun is required). If a noun is used, always use the possessive form. Notice the following:

> **His** *working late* always bothered his wife.
> No one seemed to mind **our** *mowing the lawn on Sunday.*
> **My** *singing so loud* was unappreciated by music lovers.
> **Roger's** *coming late* disturbed the class.

But, again, you must be able to distinguish between a gerund with a possessive pronoun and a participial phrase, as in the following sentences:

We did not appreciate ***his*** *walking through our garden*. (gerund phrase)
We saw ***him*** *walking through our garden*. (participial phrase)

In the first sentence above, the italicized element is a gerund phrase used as a direct object. Thus *his* is the properly employed pronoun form. In the second sentence, however, the pronoun *him* is the object of the verb *saw*. *Walking through our garden* is a participial phrase modifying *him*. The sentence can be read this way:

We saw him. He was walking through our garden.

Here's another example:

We saw the workers leaning against the building.

Leaning against the building describes the workers, thus it is a participial phrase, not a gerund phrase.

Recognizing Gerund Phrases

Following are sentences demonstrating the use of gerund phrases. After each sentence, the gerund and object of the gerund (if any) are listed.

Playing billiards was his favorite pastime.

> **Gerund phrase:** playing billiards (subject)
> **Gerund:** playing
> **Object of the gerund:** billiards

The scouts enjoyed swimming in the clear, cold water.

> **Gerund phrase:** swimming in the clear, cold water (direct object)
> **Gerund:** swimming

You will receive recognition for maintaining an *A* average.

> **Gerund phrase:** maintaining an *A* average (object of the preposition)
> **Gerund:** maintaining
> **Object of the gerund:** *A* average

Mowing grass on a hot afternoon is not very enjoyable.

> **Gerund phrase:** mowing grass on a hot afternoon (subject)
> **Gerund:** mowing
> **Object of the gerund:** grass

Trying to study is not the same as studying.

> **Gerund phrase:** trying to study (subject)
> **Gerund:** trying

Object of the gerund: to study
Gerund phrase: studying (object of preposition)
Gerund: studying

The old artist gave painting landscapes his undivided attention.

Gerund phrase: painting landscapes (indirect object)
Gerund: painting
Object of the gerund: landscapes

No one understood his rejecting such an attractive offer.

Gerund phrase: his rejecting such an attractive offer (direct object)
Gerund: rejecting
Object of the gerund: offer

We were recognized for keeping our streets free of trash.

Gerund phrase: keeping our streets free of trash (object of the preposition)
Gerund: keeping
Object of the gerund: streets

Searching for Civil War relics can be an exciting hobby.

Gerund phrase: searching for Civil War relics (subject)
Gerund: searching

Some people cannot endure coping with loud roommates.

Gerund phrase: coping with loud roommates (direct object)
Gerund: coping

The mechanic tried washing his hands in hot running water.

Gerund phrase: washing his hands in hot running water (direct object)
Gerund: washing
Object of the gerund: hands

By scaling the wall, the prisoners were able to escape captivity.

Gerund phrase: scaling the wall (object of the preposition)
Gerund: scaling
Object of the gerund: wall

Seeing is *not* believing.

> **Gerund phrase:** seeing (subject)
> **Gerund:** seeing
> **Gerund phrase:** believing (subject complement)
> **Gerund:** believing

Driving recklessly is against the law.

> **Gerund phrase:** driving recklessly (subject)
> **Gerund:** driving

Janet talked of seeing an interesting play while in Paris.

> **Gerund phrase:** seeing an interesting play while in Paris (object of the preposition)
> **Gerund:** seeing
> **Object of the gerund:** play

His hobby was building model airplanes.

> **Gerund phrase:** building model airplanes (subject complement)
> **Gerund:** building
> **Object of the gerund:** airplanes

We were all accustomed to seeing some students given special consideration.

> **Gerund phrase:** seeing some students given special consideration (object of the preposition)
> **Gerund:** seeing
> **Object of the gerund:** students

Vacationing in Hawaii is expensive.

> **Gerund phrase:** vacationing in Hawaii (subject)
> **Gerund:** vacationing

She tried losing weight by not eating.

> **Gerund phrase:** losing weight by not eating (direct object)
> **Gerund:** losing
> **Object of the gerund:** weight
> **Gerund phrase:** eating (object of the preposition)

He was given a citation for not yielding the right-of-way.

> **Gerund phrase:** yielding the right-of-way (object of the preposition)
> **Gerund:** yielding
> **Object of the gerund:** right-of-way

Participial Phrases

The participle of a verb has two basic forms—the *present participle* and the *past participle:*

- The present participle is always the base form of the verb with *ing* added to it—for example, *play + ing, work + ing, go + ing.*
- The past-participle form of regular verbs ends in *ed* and patterns with auxiliaries such as *have* and *had*—for example, *worked, tried, moved, cleaned.*
- Various forms, of course, represent the irregular verbs: *swept, seen, caught, run, rung,* and so on.

A participial phrase, then, is one that contains a participle. Such phrases can function in various ways:

- They can follow noun phrases:

  The plane *landing presently at Gate C11* is three hours late.

- They can function as dependent clauses to indicate time, result, reason, and so on:

  While skiing off-piste, Klaus discovered an old mining shack. (time)
  Obscured by the hedge, Grover was not detected by the police officer. (reason)
  Bert tripped, *dropping the jug of milk.* (result)

- They can follow an object and a verb of the senses (*see, feel, hear, smell, taste,* and so on):

  I could hear Heidi *playing in her crib.*

In all the preceding examples, the participial phrases act as adjectives; in fact, participial phrases pattern and function exactly as do adjectives. The difference between the two sets of words (adjectives and participles) is in form only (and, of course, the action indicated by the participles), with participles having the characteristic verb form plus the *ing* ending. Following are several sentences with participles, which appear in italics:

Lazily, the *yawning* miners returned to work.
We watched the *setting* sun with feelings of sadness and delight.
We felt the *rising* wind against our *perspiring* bodies.
The *fainting* shopper fell against the *moving* escalator.
The *smitten* student knew his heart was breaking. (*Smitten* is the past participle of *smite.*)
Huffing and *chuffing,* the little train left the *bustling* station behind.
The *sleeping* children rest in the shade of the *sheltering* oak tree.
Jogging is *exhilarating* exercise for some ambitious souls.

Discerning the Difference between Gerunds and Participles

As noted, participles and gerunds often have the same form: the base form of the verb plus the *ing* ending. The difference between a gerund and a participle is in their respective functions, with gerunds functioning as nouns and participles functioning as adjectives. Notice the similarities between regular adjectives and participles in this sentence:

The lazy, *sleeping* cat did not see the quiet, *creeping* mouse.

In contrast, a gerund typically acts as a noun, as in the following sentence, of which *snowboarding* is the subject:

Snowboarding is Ethan's favorite activity.

Participial Modifiers and Objects

Because a participle—like a gerund and an infinitive—is, in reality, a form of a verb, it can have modifiers and objects. In other words, a participle can be incorporated into its own grammatical unit: the *participial phrase*. Notice the modifiers and objects of the participles in the sentences that follow. The participial phrases are in italics and the participles are in bold:

The children, **sitting** *quietly*, waited for the teacher.
Finding *a dollar*, the boys headed to the candy store.
Working *in the hot sun*, the laborers soon grew weary.
Not **worrying** *about the others*, the guides soon left the stragglers behind.
Jane, *having* **studied** *the most*, received the highest score.

The adjectival function of the participles and participial phrases is apparent in the preceding sentences. Also, the various elements of the participial phrases are generally apparent. In the first sentence, the participle *sitting* has a single modifying adverb, *quietly*. In the second sentence, the participle *finding* has an object, called, logically enough, the *object of the participle*. What was found? A dollar. Thus, *dollar* is the object of the participle. In the third sentence, the participle *working* has a modifying prepositional (adverbial) phrase, *in the hot sun*. The fourth sentence contains a participial phrase preceded by a negative, *not*. The fifth sentence contains a participial phrase with the participle in the past-participle form. (Although *having* does have the participial *ing* ending, in this sentence it is used as an auxiliary, not as the head word of the participial phrase.)

Recognizing Participial Phrases

Following are several sentences containing participial phrases. Listed with each sentence are the phrase, the participle, and the object of the participle (if any):

My brother, repairing his car at the last minute, was able to enter the race.

> **Participial phrase:** repairing his car at the last minute
> **Participle:** repairing
> **Object of the participle:** car

We enjoyed watching the ducks swimming peacefully on the small pond.

> **Participial phrase:** swimming peacefully on the small pond
> **Participle:** swimming

Repairing the roof with new shingles, the roofer prevented further leaks.

> **Participial phrase:** repairing the roof with new shingles
> **Participle:** repairing
> **Object of the participle:** roof

The members of the class, anxiously awaiting the professor, talked among themselves.

> **Participial phrase:** anxiously awaiting the professor
> **Participle:** awaiting
> **Object of the participle:** professor

Trying to unfasten the window, the burglar awakened the family's dog.

> **Participial phrase:** trying to unfasten the window
> **Participle:** trying
> **Object of the participle:** to unfasten the window

Directing traffic with confidence, the rookie officer impressed his sergeant.

> **Participial phrase:** directing traffic with confidence
> **Participle:** directing
> **Object of the participle:** traffic

The fire truck, leading the holiday parade, was involved in a mishap.

> **Participial phrase:** leading the holiday parade
> **Participle:** leading
> **Object of the participle:** parade

The photographer watched the lion tracking its prey.
> **Participial phrase:** tracking its prey
> **Participle:** tracking
> **Object of the participle:** prey

We watched the cat climbing up the curtains.
> **Participial phrase:** climbing up the curtains
> **Participle:** climbing

The old gardener was angry at the squirrels eating his vegetables.
> **Participial phrase:** eating his vegetables
> **Participle:** eating
> **Object of the participle:** vegetables

Working with old lumber, the craftsman manufactured beautiful furniture.
> **Participial phrase:** working with old lumber
> **Participle:** working

Leaving the office early, the workers went to the ball game.
> **Participial phrase:** leaving the office early
> **Participle:** leaving
> **Object of the participle:** office

Knowing he was being watched, the spy left a fake message.
> **Participial phrase:** knowing he was being watched
> **Participle:** knowing
> **Object of the participle:** he was being watched

Sitting in the shade, the workers ate their lunches.
> **Participial phrase:** sitting in the shade
> **Participle:** sitting

We all knew the woman singing the song so beautifully.
> **Participial phrase:** singing the song so beautifully
> **Participle:** singing
> **Object of the participle:** song

The victim, pretending injury, sat in the street crying.
> **Participial phrase:** pretending injury
> **Participle:** pretending
> **Object of the participle:** injury
> **Participial phrase:** crying

Trapped by the tide, the swimmers drifted off course.
> **Participial phrase:** trapped by the tide (past-participle form)
> **Participle:** trapped

The person lying in the sun trying to sleep is my brother.
> **Participial phrase:** lying in the sun
> **Participle:** lying
> **Participial phrase:** trying to sleep
> **Participle:** trying
> **Object of the participle:** to sleep

Dangling Participles

Writers have long been warned about dangling participles—that is, a participial phrase located in the wrong place in the sentence (not next to the word it modifies). Although the results are often humorous, such a lapse in style indicates carelessness on the part of the writer that one can ill afford to convey to a reader.

The sentences that follow contain dangling participial phrases in italics. Laugh if you wish, but be able to explain what needs to be done to make the sentences say what they were probably meant to say:

Spurting gas all the way, the little old lady slowly drove her car into town.
Changing her diapers, the baby-sitter made the young child warm and comfortable.
After *paying my fine,* the judge told me I was free to leave.
Walking on two wooden legs, the little puppy tripped the unsteady man.
Holding his spear in front of him, the old lion charged the native.
Chased by the hound, the rock pile offered shelter for the frightened rabbit.

Nominative Absolute Phrases

Nominative absolute phrases are not, strictly speaking, participial phrases. In fact, they function differently from participial phrases in an English sentence. They do, however, contain participles, and they do function as modifiers. Therefore, students of grammar and usage should be aware of these types of phrases.

In order to understand nominative absolute phrases, you may need a crash course in nominals. A *nominal* names one or more people, places, objects, or events. If you think that the definition of a nominal is rather similar to that of a noun, you're absolutely correct. In fact, nouns and pronouns are the most common types of nominals, which are the following:

- Nouns

    Heidi
    flower
    laundromat

  letter opener
  boy
  Wimbledon

- Pronouns

  he
  her
  who
  it

- Noun phrases

  the man in the airplane

- Noun clauses

  whether she is absent

- Gerunds and gerund phrases

  seeming composed

- Infinitives and infinitive phrases

  to seem composed

A nominative absolute phrase, then, is a phrase without a finite verb that modifies the whole sentence:

 The game being over, the crowd left the stadium.

In the two sentences that follow, the first contains a participial phrase, and the second contains a nominative absolute phrase. Note the differences in structure and relationship to the main clause of each:

 Being the leader, I was responsible for the group.
 The leader being absent, I was responsible for the group.

The first sentence could be reconstructed in this manner:

 I was the leader. I was responsible for the group.

In the second sentence, no such relationship can be established. Two separate ideas are presented:

 The leader was absent. I was responsible for the group.

Here are some basic differences between the two constructions:

- The participial phrase in the first sentence relates specifically to the following noun or pronoun—in this case to *I,* which is not a part of the participial phrase itself.
- The participle in the second sentence is tied to a nominal, *leader,* within the confines of the phrase.
- The absolute phrase in the second sentence does not appear to modify any single word within the following clause. In fact, if anything, it seems to modify the entire main clause.
- The subject of the main clause cannot be related to the object of the participle in the second sentence, as it can be in the first sentence.

Nominative absolute phrases are capable of mobility within a sentence, because they are not directly tied to any single sentence element. Participial phrases do not enjoy such mobility. Notice the placement of the absolute phrase in each of the following sentences:

> *The ship having sailed earlier than expected,* we were forced to take a plane to Europe.
> We were forced to take a plane to Europe, *the ship having sailed earlier than expected.*

Following are some sample sentences, some with participial phrases (in italics), others with nominative absolute phrases (in bold):

> We found the boys *smoking cigarettes behind the school building.*
> **The tree having fallen across the drive,** we were forced to walk to the store for groceries.
> The students were studying for the examination, **the finals having been scheduled for the next day.**
> *Choked by the weeds,* the daisies simply would not grow as tall as the climbing roses.
> **The dog having been found by its master,** the reward of $100 was canceled.
> The trucker spotted the hitchhiker *sitting under the overpass.*
> The scouts, *needing shelter from the storm,* entered the old house.
> **The jury having found the defendant guilty,** the judge, *having a luncheon engagement,* adjourned the court.
> We thought we had spotted a UFO *flying overhead.*
> *Seeing their English professor coming up the walk,* the class began studying, **the bell having already rung.**

Identifying Verbals

To better help you identify the various types of verbals, the following sentences contain infinitive phrases, gerund phrases, participial phrases, and/or nominative absolute phrases:

The bell having rung, the students ceased their talking to friends.
    Nominative absolute phrase: the bell having rung
    Participial phrase: having rung
    Gerund phrase: talking to friends

We wanted to find our friends, so we began shouting to attract them.
    Infinitive phrase: to find our friends
    Gerund phrase: shouting to attract them
    Infinitive phrase: to attract them

By pinpointing the North Star, the scouts were able to locate the trail leading out of the woods.
    Gerund phrase: pinpointing the North Star
    Infinitive phrase: to locate the trail leading out of the woods
    Participial phrase: leading out of the woods

Realizing the professor was late, the class decided to leave early.
    Participial phrase: realizing the professor was late
    Infinitive phrase: to leave early

When we returned, the bus, having loaded early, was already departing.
    Participial phrase: having loaded early

The sun having set, we decided to set up camp.
    Nominative absolute phrase: the sun having set
    Participial phrase: having set
    Infinitive phrase: to set up camp

We refused to waste time by studying astrology.
    Infinitive phrase: to waste time by studying astrology
    Gerund phrase: studying astrology

Relying on Lynne's instructions, we tried eating wisely in an effort to lose weight.
    Participial phrase: relying on Lynne's instructions
    Gerund phrase: eating wisely
    Infinitive phrase: to lose weight

The thing to do in an emergency is to yell "Fire," hoping to attract attention.
    Infinitive phrase: to do in an emergency
    Infinitive phrase: to yell "Fire"
    Participial phrase: hoping to attract attention (modifying an understood "you")
    Infinitive phrase: to attract attention

Clauses

A *clause* is a group of words having both subject and predicate and incorporated as a part of the sentence. The two main types of clauses are the following:

* Independent clauses
* Dependent (or *subordinate*) clauses

INDEPENDENT CLAUSES

An *independent clause* conveys complete meaning and can stand alone. It could be a sentence in its own right; but because it patterns with other elements within the framework of a sentence, an independent clause is a part of a sentence. In the following examples, the independent clauses are in italics:

> Because I was ill, *I was not able to attend class.*
> *We were all stranded,* because the car wouldn't start.
> *Jake and I were friends,* but *we weren't roommates.*

Coordinate Clauses

A clause connected to one or more other clauses of equal status is called a *coordinate clause;* such clauses are joined through the use of coordinating conjunctions such as *for, and, nor, but, or,* and *yet.* (Note that the coordinating conjunction is not considered part of the independent clauses it joins; however, subordinating conjunctions, such as *because* and *since,* are considered a part of dependent clauses.)

A coordinating conjunction joining coordinate clauses is preceded by a comma—unless a comma is already used in one of the coordinate clauses. If such is the case, a semicolon is used. The first sentence below shows the use of a comma; the second shows the use of a semicolon:

> The puppy was playful, *but* the cat was not.
> As expected, the bus was late; *but* we didn't mind waiting.

Coordinate clauses may pattern *without* the coordinating conjunction joining them. In such cases, a semicolon is employed to separate them:

> We refused to cross the river; the current was too swift.

Very short coordinate clauses in a series may be written without coordinating conjunctions and separated by commas:

> I ran, I fell, I broke my leg.

Dependent (Subordinate) Clauses

Subordinate clauses are called *dependent clauses* because they cannot stand alone—that is, they cannot function independently as sentences. Instead, they are employed as parts of speech (adjectives, adverbs, and nouns); as such, they may be used as the specific parts of speech are used. Dependent clauses usually begin with a relative pronoun (such as *who, which,* or *that*) or with a subordinating conjunction (*if, as, since, although, until, because, where, when,* or *although*).

Adjective Clauses

An *adjective clause*, as does a single-word adjective, modifies a noun or pronoun. It is introduced by a relative pronoun (*who, whose, whom, which,* or *that*) or by a subordinating conjunction (*where, when,* or *why*):

> The boy **who** *is speaking* is my cousin.
> Give the money to him **who** *needs it most*.
> The racket **that** *I bought* has nylon strings.
> This is the spot **where** *we had a flat tire*.
> Sue, **who** *is a fine skier* and *who arrived today,* will teach us how to improve our form.
> The reason **why** *he left* is a mystery to everyone.
> The girl **who** *caught the fish* <u>*that are displayed here*</u> is ten years old.

The underlined clause in the preceding sentence is an additional adjective clause.

The relative pronoun is an important part of the adjective clause. It may be a subject, a direct object, an object of a preposition, or a possessive modifier. *Where, when,* or *why* in an adjective clause modifies the verb within that clause.

Often, the relative pronoun or subordinating conjunction that usually introduces an adjective clause is omitted or understood. In formal English, these joining words probably ought to be employed. In any case, you should be able to recognize adjective clauses without the relative pronouns and subordinating conjunctions and not confuse such clauses with independent clauses. Note these examples in which the missing relative pronoun or conjunction is shown in brackets, with the empty brackets showing where the relative pronoun or conjunction would normally occur. The adjective clauses are in italics:

> The bike ( ) *you wanted* has been sold. (that)
> He knew the reason ( ) *my car wouldn't start*. (why)
> The man ( ) *you met* is my uncle. (whom)

Restrictive versus Nonrestrictive Clauses

Adjective clauses that are not essential to sentence meaning are called *nonrestrictive clauses* or *nonessential clauses*. They can be omitted from a sentence without a loss of the basic meaning of the sentence. Nonrestrictive clauses should be set off by commas.

Adjective clauses beginning with *that* are always restrictive clauses. They are necessary to restrict the meaning of the sentence; in other words, they indicate the essential meaning of the sentence):

> The dog *that you saw* came back again. (restrictive)
> Mr. Smith, *whom you met at the lecture,* is from Texas. (nonrestrictive)

In the first sentence above, the adjective clause *that you saw* is essential to the sentence to identify the exact dog that came back. In the second sentence, the nonrestrictive adjective clause *whom you met at the lecture* is merely an aside adding more information than is required to garner full meaning from the sentence.

That versus Which

Although many people use *that* and *which* interchangeably, they should not be so used. *That* should be used only to introduce a restrictive clause; *which* should be used only to introduce a nonrestrictive clause:

Correct: The puppy that I trained tore up my Birkenstocks.

(This sentence implies that there is more than one puppy; the speaker is referring specifically to the one she trained. This is a restrictive clause.)

Correct: The puppy, which I trained, tore up my Birkenstocks.

(In this sentence, the clause "which I trained" simply provides more information about the puppy in question; if the clause were removed, the sentence's essential meaning would still be conveyed. This is a nonrestrictive clause.)

Note that generally speaking, *which* should be preceded by a comma, while *that* should not be.

Adverb Clauses

An *adverb clause*, as does a single-word adverb, modifies a verb (including the verb form in a *verbal*—that is, a *gerund,* an *infinitive,* or a *participle*), an adjective, or an adverb. Adverb clauses are introduced by subordinating conjunctions such as the following:

even if
as though
when
although
because
as long as
as
until
before
than
wherever
while
whenever
though
after
whether
since
whereas
so that
provided that
where
as if
in order that
as soon as

Here are some examples of dependent (subordinate) clauses used as adverbs to modify the verb, adjective, adverb, infinitive, and a participle:

When the bell rang, everyone hurried into the building.
    (Modifies the verb *hurried*.)

Today is much warmer *than yesterday was*.
    (Modifies the adjective *warmer*.)

The boys come here more often *than they came before*.
    (Modifies the adverb *often*.)

He wishes to leave *before the rain begins*.
    (Modifies the infinitive *to leave*.)

Grumbling *because he was tired,* Don retraced his steps.
    (Modifies the participle *grumbling*.)

Adverbial clauses can express nine relationships:

- Time

    The man fainted *when he saw the blood.*
    Since the sun rose, I have been watching the ducks.

- Place

    I found my wallet *where I had left it.*
    Wherever we go, we find interesting people.

- Manner

    The colt runs *as if he were lame.*
    Copy the message *just as you received it.*

- Condition

    The boat will sink *if the hull isn't repaired.*
    Even if I lose the race, I'll feel proud for having done my best.

- Cause

    Jerry's scooter wouldn't start *because it was out of fuel.*
    Because the buses weren't running, we walked to the store.

- Purpose

    Our neighbors landscaped their lawn *so that they would win the prize.*
    In order to remember to call, I wrote the number on my hand.

- Result

    The trees fell so that *the road was completely blocked.*
    The wind blew so hard *that the fire went out.*

- Comparison

    A dog is faster *than a cat (is).*
    No one talks *as much as my roommate (talks).*

- Concession

    She delivered the lecture *although she felt unsteady.*
    Even though I have a ticket, I can't find a seat.

In the following examples, the adverb clauses modify the verb *runs*. Each illustrates one of the typical adverbial functions of telling *how, when, where, why, to what extent,* and *under what conditions:*

He runs *as though he has been frightened*. (how he runs)
He runs *whenever he can*. (when he runs)
He runs *wherever he goes*. (where he runs)
He runs *because he likes to run*. (why he runs)
He runs *as far as he can*. (to what extent he runs)
He runs *if he feels like running*. (under what condition he runs)

Discerning the Difference between Adverb Clauses and Adjective Clauses

The following sentences contain adjective and/or adverb clauses. Following each sentence are the type of clause, each clause, and the word(s) it modifies:

The coin that I found on the sidewalk had been there since the sun rose this morning.

> **Adjective clause:** that I found on the sidewalk (coin)
> **Adverb clause:** since the sun rose this morning (had been [there])

If you see the person who used this book, have him or her report to me.

> **Adverb clause:** if you see the person who used this book (have)
> **Adjective clause:** who used this book (person)

We had never seen a squirrel that could dial a telephone.

> **Adjective clause:** that could dial a telephone (squirrel)

This is the place where we were stuck in the mud yesterday.

> **Adjective clause:** where we were stuck in the mud yesterday (place)

Try to be quiet when you come home late at night.

> **Adverb clause:** when you come home late at night (try)

If you are observant, you will be able to see the owl that built its nest in the old oak tree.

> **Adverb clause:** if you are observant (will be able)
> **Adjective clause:** that built its nest in the old oak tree (owl)

I liked the report that you presented to our group when you were here.

> **Adjective clause:** that you presented to our group (report)
> **Adverb clause:** when you were here (presented)

I talked with a boy who wants to be a race car driver when he grows up.

> **Adjective clause:** who wants to be a race car driver (boy)
> **Adverb clause:** when he grows up (wants)

We watched the volcano that erupted unexpectedly.

> **Adjective clause:** that erupted unexpectedly (volcano)

We became acquainted with the people who moved into the house that was rebuilt after the fire.

> **Adjective clause:** who moved into the house (people)
> **Adjective clause:** that was rebuilt after the fire (house)

When I returned home from school, I got a job for the summer.

> **Adverb clause:** when I returned from school (got)

Even though she is always very polite, she seems to annoy people.

> **Adverb clause:** even though she is always very polite (seems)

We'll surely win the game if we play well.

> **Adverb clause:** if we play well (win)

I plan to travel to Europe, where I'll trace my family's roots.

> **Adjective clause:** where I'll trace my family's roots (Europe)

The boy who was lost ate ice cream at the police station.

> **Adjective clause:** who was lost (boy)
> **Adverb clause:** at the police station

We sang songs until we were too tired to sing any longer.

> **Adverb clause:** until we were too tired to sing any longer (sang)

Whoever told you that story is not a person that I would trust.

> **Adjective clause:** that I would trust (person)

The witness identified the man who held up the bank.

> **Adjective clause:** who held up the bank (man)

Oscar wrote one of the most interesting stories I have ever read.

> **Adjective clause:** (that) I have ever read (stories)

The members of the road crew worked hard in the morning so that they could take the afternoon off.

> **Adverb clause:** so that they could take the afternoon off (worked)

I enjoy classical music, which is not popular with Sue.

> **Adjective clause:** which is not popular with Sue (music)

The skit, which was performed by professional actors, lasted until the next act was ready.

> **Adjective clause:** which was performed by professional actors (skit)
> **Adverb clause:** until the next act was ready (lasted)

Whenever you are ready, we'll meet the people who are waiting for us.

> **Adverb clause:** whenever you are ready (meet)
> **Adjective clause:** who are waiting for us (people)

We knew where we were when we saw the sign that pointed the way to Nashville.

> **Adverb clause:** when we saw the sign that pointed the way to Nashville (knew)
> **Adjective clause:** that pointed the way to Nashville (sign)

When I was a college student, I made a decision that changed my entire life—I decided to become a singer.

> **Adverb clause:** when I was a college student (made)
> **Adjective clause:** that changed my entire life (decision)

You should wear a hat with a large brim if you want to avoid sun damage on your face.

> **Adverb clause:** if you want to avoid sun damage on your face (wear)

Noun Clauses

Noun clauses function in sentences just as nouns function. If you understand the use of nouns as subjects, direct objects, objects of prepositions, indirect objects, appositives, subject complements, and objects of verbals, you should have little trouble understanding the use of noun clauses in a sentence. Following are examples of noun clauses used as various parts of the sentence:

> *What the professor said* was very confusing to the students. (subject of the verb *was*)
> I found *what I was looking for*. (direct object of *found*)
> Give the tools to *whomever needs them*. (object of the preposition *to*)

Tell *whomever you see* the story of the missing pens. (indirect object of *tell*)
We all knew the reason *that Sarah won the award.* (object complement of the noun *reason*)
The winner is *whoever crosses the line first.* (subject complement)
You think *whomever smiles at you* to be your friend. (subject of the infinitive *to be*)

A noun clause is usually introduced by *that, who, what, where, when, why, how, which,* or *whether.* Remember that some of these words also introduce other kinds of clauses, so take care not to attempt to identify clauses solely by the words that introduce them. The particular use of a clause within the framework of a sentence determines what type of clause it is:

I knew him *when he was a baby.*
> (The clause is an adverb clause telling *when* the speaker knew him.)

I knew *when she hurt himself.*
> (The clause is a noun clause used as the direct object of *knew.* What was known? When she hurt himself. Therefore, the clause is the direct object.)

He ran off the road *where it crosses the creek.*
> (The clause tells *where;* therefore, it is an adverb clause.)

At the last moment, we realized *where we were.*
> (The clause tells *what* we realized; therefore, it is a direct object and a noun clause.)

As with adjective clauses, a noun clause may sometimes occur without the relative pronoun *that.* In fact, *that* is often unnecessary in a sentence and serves only to introduce a following clause. (Some texts, however, treat *that* as a major part of a sentence—the direct object—and the following clause as a complement of *that.*) In the following sentence, the parentheses indicate where *that* would sometimes occur:

The minister believed ( ) his sermon was inspiring.

The following sentences contain noun clauses and indicate how those clauses are being used (as subjects, direct objects, object complements, objects of prepositions, subject complements, appositives, or indirect objects):

We told whoever would listen to us our sad story.

> **Noun clause:** whoever would listen to us
> **Usage:** indirect object

He told her he would help her move her belongings.

> **Noun clause:** he would help her move her belongings
> **Usage:** direct object

Our futures depend upon how we discipline ourselves.

> **Noun clause:** how we discipline ourselves
> **Usage:** object of the preposition

Whatever you prepare for dinner will be fine with me.

> **Noun clause:** whatever you prepare for dinner
> **Usage:** subject

The final decision will be whatever you choose.

> **Noun clause:** whatever you choose
> **Usage:** subject complement

The doctor knew what it was to suffer extreme pain.

> **Noun clause:** what it was to suffer extreme pain
> **Usage:** direct object

Who wins the race is secondary to how he or she wins it.

> **Noun clause:** who wins the race
> **Usage:** subject
> **Noun clause:** how he or she wins it
> **Usage:** object of the preposition

No one paid any attention to what the speaker told us about safety.

> **Noun clause:** what the speaker told us about safety
> **Usage:** object of the preposition

He knew his horse was becoming tired.

> **Noun clause:** his horse was becoming tired
> **Usage:** direct object

We were disappointed by what they told us.

> **Noun clause:** what they told us
> **Usage:** object of the preposition

Most people are not impressed by how fast others drive.

> **Noun clause:** how fast others drive
> **Usage:** object of the preposition

The message that the singer had canceled the engagement disappointed her fans.

> **Noun clause:** that the singer had canceled the engagement
> **Usage:** appositive (actually, this is a complement to the noun *message*)

Jack found his wallet just a short distance from where he thought he had lost it.

> **Noun clause:** where he thought he had lost it
> **Usage:** object of the preposition

Everyone should know the earth cannot support an indefinite number of people.

> **Noun clause:** (that) the earth cannot support an indefinite number of people
> **Usage:** direct object

The family reached the decision that it would vacation at the seashore.

> **Noun clause:** that it would vacation at the seashore
> **Usage:** object complement (this clause complements the direct object *decision*)

The president informed us that she was ready to start the meeting.

> **Noun clause:** that she was ready to start the meeting
> **Usage:** direct object

I hope the rain stops, because we want to go camping.

> **Noun clause**: the rain stops
> **Usage:** direct object

The old mariner told whomever would listen his tale.

> **Noun clause:** whomever would listen
> **Usage:** indirect object

Whoever travels there will find that things are different in California.

> **Noun clause:** whoever travels there
> **Usage:** subject
> **Noun clause:** that things are different in California
> **Usage:** direct object

General Observations about Sentence Parts

- A sentence can be composed of many parts. Some of these parts, such as the following, are required:
  - Subjects and predicates
  - Punctuation
- Other parts are not required but frequently appear in sentences nonetheless:
  - Direct objects
  - Indirect objects
  - Complements
  - Appositives
  - Sentence modifiers
  - Phrases
  - Clauses
- An English sentence comprises two parts: a subject and a predicate.
- With some sentences, answering a simple "who" or "what" question identifies the simple subject of the sentence.
- The *predicate* of a sentence is all the words that do not pattern with the subject, as long as the entire sentence (or clause) fits into one of the patterns discussed in Chapter 7.
- A major sentence element contained in many predicates is the *direct object*, which occurs in sentences that have transitive verbs. A *transitive verb* is a verb that requires a direct object to give the sentence a sense of completeness. To identify direct objects, you may again ask the "what" question in conjunction with the verb.
- *Indirect objects* are those parts of the predicate that occur in sentences containing direct objects and that are closely related to the direct objects by identifying the person/thing to whom or for whom something is done or given, or of whom a question is asked. Indirect objects are usually nouns or pronouns.
- A *complement,* which can be a noun, an adjective, a pronoun, or a phrase, is added to a verb to complete the predicate of a sentence. The complement provides information about a clause's subject or object. There are four main types of complements:
  - Object complement
  - Subject complement
  - Adverbial complement
  - Adjectival complement

- An *appositive* is a word, a phrase, or a clause usually located after a nominal (a noun, a noun phrase, or a noun substitute) to identify, explain, or describe the nominal. Although adjectives can be used in apposition, appositives are usually nouns and pronouns.
- Certain types of adverbials can be employed as *sentence modifiers*. Usually set off by a comma, a sentence modifier relates to an entire sentence, not to any single element within the sentence.
- The traditional definition of a *phrase* is somewhat as follows: "A phrase is a group of words not containing a subject and predicate and used as a single part of speech." The various types of phrases include the following:
  - Noun phrases
  - Prepositional phrases
  - Verbals

- A *clause* is a group of words having both subject and predicate and incorporated as a part of the sentence. The two main types of clauses are the following:
  - Independent clauses
  - Dependent (or subordinate) clauses

PART III

HANDLING CAPITALIZATION AND SPELLING

Two elements of grammar are unusual in that they apply only to writers, not to speakers: capitalization and spelling. Although English does put forth some rules with regard to both these grammatical elements, the sad truth is that the language breaks those rules quite often. In this part, you learn the rules—and exceptions—for capitalization and spelling.

Chapter 10

Capitalization

The use of capital, or uppercase, letters is a mechanical aid to clarify meaning in written communication. When you write, you use capital letters to distinguish certain elements from other elements of the sentence. This section presents those elements that, according to custom, should be capitalized. It also emphasizes certain elements that should *not* be capitalized.

Although there are a few principles for the use of capital letters that do not readily submit to reason, you can easily learn the customs to follow by analyzing the general principles and the detailed examples presented in this section. If you follow these principles, you will be correct in all situations, with the possible exception of some journalistic writing, which tends to use less capitalization.

Just as other conventions of language—and language itself—are changing, so too is capitalization. Therefore, if you discover a practice that differs from this guide, you should pursue the matter to see how widespread the practice is. Bear in mind, also, that different publications use different style guides, and what may be acceptable style for one publication may need modifications for another.

Conventions for Capitalization

The following should be capitalized:

- The first word of any sentence
- The pronoun *I* and the vocative *O*

    O say, can you see, by the dawn's early light, what so proudly we hailed at the twilight's last gleaming?

- The first word of a formal statement following a colon

    Mrs. Smith released this statement to the press: "The fact that Mr. Smedley chose to resign is regrettable."

- The first word of a direct quotation for which the beginning has been included

    Miss Lovelace replied, "Today we shall study book reports."

Do not, however, capitalize the first word of a quoted fragment (unless the first word of the quotation is also the first word of a sentence)

> Was it Franklin who said that "fools will learn in no other"?
> I agree with Dr. Cole that Peter is his "own worst enemy."

- The first word of each outline topic and subtopic
- The first word of a statement or a question inserted into a sentence without quotation marks

> Our question is, How can we finish the work if our tools have been misplaced?

- The first word of a complete line of poetry
- The first word and any noun in the salutation of a letter

> Dear Friends and Neighbors,

- The first word of a complimentary close

> Very truly yours,

In addition, you should capitalize initials; titles (or abbreviations of titles) preceding proper names; the abbreviations Jr., Sr., and Esq. following names; and the abbreviations of academic degrees:

> Martin Luther King, Jr.
> J. R. Ewing
> Sir Anthony Hopkins
> Mrs. Robinson
> Superintendent Jones
> Chief Maddox
> Dr. James Herriott
> Murgatroyd Peterson, Ph.D.

On the subject of academic degrees, the formal names of academic degrees should be capitalized:

> Master of Arts degree
> Doctor of Philosophy degree
> Bachelor of Science

Do not, however, capitalize types of degrees unless the formal name is intended:

> She received her master's degree last summer.
> The university awarded more than 1,000 bachelor's degrees this year.

Capitalize a title only if it precedes a person's name or is used to directly address a person:

the president of the United States
President Barack Obama

Dr. Jones, superintendent of schools
Superintendent Jones

I was elected senator from my state.
No, Senator, I don't agree.

In addition, you must capitalize proper nouns and proper adjectives. These include the following:

- Words of family relationship when those words can be replaced by proper nouns or when they are used as part of the name

  Are you Jolene's uncle?
  We hope Uncle Ed will sing for us.
  I know, Uncle, that you are very tired.

- The names of persons

  Before writing a name beginning with Mc or Mac, determine whether it should include two capital letters. The custom is not constant: McDonald, MacKay, Macdonald, Macmillan, Macduff.

- Names beginning with O'

- Geographical names, including the names of the following:
  - Cities, townships, parishes, counties, states, provinces, countries, and continents
  - Recognized sections of the country or world
  - Islands, peninsulas, straits, beaches, and deserts
  - Bodies of water
  - Mountains
  - Forests, parks, canyons, and dams
  - Planets, stars, satellites, and constellations, except in the case of *sun, earth,* and *moon*

    Note: It is considered correct to capitalize *earth* in scientific texts and when it is used in a sentence with another capitalized astrological body.

  Do not capitalize *east, west, north,* and *south* when these words indicate direction. However, when they are part of a geographical location's proper name, they should be capitalized. Following are some examples:

  Incorrect: Jerry lives on the North side of town.
  Correct: Terre Haute is west of Indianapolis.

Incorrect: I think the Pacific northwest is one of the most intriguing regions in America.
Correct: There are many interesting books about the history of the South.

Incorrect: The Crawfords moved to the East Coast.
Correct: The Crawfords moved to the east coast of Bermuda.

- The names of pets
- The names of firms
- The names of institutions

    Benton-Marshall County Hospital
    Notre Dame University

- The names of organizations

    Boy Scouts of America
    National Organization for Women
    Amvets

- The names of buildings and other human-made structures

    the Taj Mahal
    the Great Pyramids at Giza

- Brand names (note that the common noun that follows the name of the product should not be capitalized, except in advertising displays)

    Levi's jeans
    Wilson racket

- The names of ships, planes, trains, railways, and airlines

    the Andrea Doria
    Air Force One
    Santa Fe Railroad
    Southwest Airlines

- The names of historical events and periods

    the Civil War
    the Renaissance

- The names of historical documents

    the Magna Carta
    the Declaration of Independence

- The names of holidays, including the words *day* and *eve*

    New Year's Day
    Christmas Eve

- The names of government bodies

    the U.S. Senate
    the House of Lords

- The names of races, religions, denominations, and nationalities

    Methodist
    Buddhism
    Asian
    Haitian

- The names of all languages
- The names of the months of the year and days of the week
- School subjects that are languages or that are followed by a numeral or a letter

    History 110
    history
    Chemistry B
    chemistry
    Biology 101
    biology
    French

- The names of political parties (but not the word *party*)

    Republican party
    States Rights party

- All things that are personified when they are addressed directly

    O Wind, if winter comes, can spring be far behind?

- An epithet or a nickname

    James "Big Dog" Boomhauser

- Words referring to a specific deity, to Christ, and to Mary, and the names applied to the Bible and its parts and to other sacred books

    O Lord
    the Virgin
    Genesis
    Old Testament
    Koran
    Talmud
    Mishnah

- A noun or an abbreviation of a noun that is followed by a numeral or a letter, except the word *page*

Stalag 14
Laboratory C
Deck A
ER 6
page 303

- The names of streets, boulevards, and other such road designations

    Maple Street
    Parklane Drive
    Glendale Road

- Abbreviations of proper nouns

    WW II
    Ph.D.
    MBA
    AA
    AFL-CIO
    CIA
    GSA
    FFA
    4-H
    FBI

- Proper nouns used as parts of names

    Queen Anne's lace
    Alaskan husky
    Persian rug
    Lou Gehrig's disease
    Chinese checkers
    Russian roulette

- Copyrighted names of games, but not common names used to identify games

    Concentration
    Clue
    Stratego
    bingo
    checkers
    golf
    chess

- The abbreviations A.M., P.M., B.C., B.C.E., and A.D., C.E., as well as the abbreviations for any expression that would be capitalized were it spelled out in full

Acceptable variations of A.M. and P.M. are a.m. and p.m, as well as A.M. and P.M.

- Do not capitalize the name of a season unless the season is personified.

   > I know that winter will soon arrive.
   > I know you, Winter—an old, cold, grandfather.

- Do not capitalize a generic term used in plural.

   > Chestnut and Walnut streets
   > the Atlantic and Pacific oceans
   > the Lutheran and Episcopal churches

In titles of publications, documents, musical compositions, radio and television programs, motion pictures, and works of art, you should capitalize the first word, the last word, and all other words except *a, and, the,* and prepositions and conjunctions that are one syllable or that contain fewer than five letters:

> *Gone with the Wind*
> *I Am Legend*
> "Texas Tech Second Behind Alabama"
> Titian's *Portrait of a Man in a Red Cap*
> "General Observations About Capitalization"

Examples of Correctly Capitalized Sentences

The following sentences demonstrate correct capitalization:

> Heather said, "Do you suppose this winter will be harsh?"
> Our family traveled to eastern Kentucky to visit Natural Bridge State Park.
> Sarah presented this idea to the group: "We should all save our soft-drink cans to use in an art project."
> The national anthem begins, "O say, can you see . . . ."
> The McGurtys have lived in the South for six generations.
> The travelers drove north until they crossed the Mackinac Bridge into Michigan's Upper Peninsula.
> Last Christmas Eve, we watched the aurora borealis for over an hour.
> Some members of the Presbyterian Church of America met in Louisville before the national convention.
> I talked with Senator Eric Haas about the national health care situation.

He loved to quote Paul Goodman's "and may my buddy-seat carry friendly freight."

The West is suffering from a drought.

She lived in Crittenden County until she became a U.S. senator.

The Panama Canal was built to aid intercontinental shipping.

I don't believe the *Spruce Goose* will ever fly again.

A brave man, Uncle Ted served in World War II until he was wounded.

Patricia is an engineer at IBM Corporation.

Next semester, I will have to take French, History 111, Chemistry II, and linguistics.

We played with Skippy, my dog, for several hours.

Did the professor say, "Tomorrow this class will have a test"?

Have you met Aunt Sophie yet?

This is my brother, Anthony.

One of his favorite television shows is *Cheers*.

Northwest Airlines has just completed a new financial arrangement with Delta Airlines.

The socialite wore Jimmy Choo shoes to the gala.

Have you ever watched geese fly south for the winter?

General Observations about Capitalization

- The use of capital letters is a mechanical aid to clarify meaning in written communication. When you write, you use capital letters to distinguish certain elements from other elements of a sentence.
- The rules regarding capitalization are rather complex and, seemingly, illogical. That said, you absolutely must capitalize the first word of any sentence, as well as proper nouns and proper adjectives.
- In titles of publications, documents, musical compositions, radio and television programs, motion pictures, and works of art, you should capitalize the first word, the last word, and all other words except *a, and,* and *the* and one-syllable prepositions and conjunctions containing fewer than five letters.

Chapter 11

Spelling

No matter how well you construct your sentences, a misspelled word in your text can result in the immediate loss of your credibility as a writer. Unfair though it may be, picky readers will, without doubt, hold misspellings against you, no matter how brilliant your prose may otherwise be.

Sadly, learning to spell correctly can be difficult due to the hodgepodge nature of the English language. Today's English has its roots in the language spoken by the Germanic tribes that colonized Britain in the middle of the fifth century and in French, spoken by the Normans who conquered Britain in 1066. During the Renaissance, the English language borrowed numerous words from other languages, particularly from Greek, Latin, and French. In addition, German, Yiddish, Italian, Spanish, and even Persian have contributed to the complexity of modern English.

That said, when it comes to learning how to spell correctly, you have a few strategies at your disposal:

- When you are unsure of the spelling of a word, try sounding it out.
- You can use your dictionary to look up the correct spelling of the word.
- You can employ mnemonic devices to remember the correct spellings of words that consistently baffle you.

Sounding Out Words

One way to handle those situations in which you are unsure of a word's correct spelling is to "sound out" the word piece by piece.

Although sounding out a word can be helpful in many instances, it is not the most reliable way of ensuring correct spelling. This is because a large number of words in the English language are not, in fact, spelled phonetically. (Ironically, an example of a word that is not spelled phonetically is *phonetically*, which, if it was spelled phonetically, would start with the letter *f*.) In proving this point, many grammarians refer to a story in which a girl, when asked to spell the word "fish," writes "ghoti" on the chalkboard. Her reasoning? The letters *gh* generate an *f* sound, as in the words *laugh, trough,* and *cough; o* can be used to sound like *i*, as in the word *women;* and the letters *ti* can indicate an *sh* sound, as in the words *function, nation, intervention,* and so on.

WATCHING FOR HOMOPHONES

Homophones—words that sound alike but that have different meanings and different spellings—complicate spelling. Following are several examples of homophones; notice how many instances there are of multiple homophones for a single word.

Definitions in the following entries have been culled from *Webster's New World College Dictionary, Fourth Edition*. (Only the first definition of each word is provided here.)

air: The elastic, invisible mixture of gases (chiefly nitrogen and oxygen, as well as hydrogen, carbon dioxide, argon, neon, helium, etc.) that surrounds the earth; atmosphere
err: To be wrong or mistaken; fall into error
heir: A person who inherits or is legally entitled to inherit, through the natural action of the law, another's property or title upon the other's death

aisle: A part of a church alongside the nave, choir, or transept, set off by a row of columns or piers
isle: An island, esp. a small island: poetic except as part of a place name

altar: A place, esp. a raised platform, where sacrifices or offerings are made to a god, an ancestor, etc.
alter: To make different in details but not in substance; modify

ate: Past participle of the verb *to eat*
eight: The cardinal number between seven and nine; 8; VIII

carat: A unit of weight for precious stones and pearls, equal to 3.0864 grains (200 milligrams): abbrev. *C*
caret: A mark (^) used in writing or in correcting proof, to show where something is to be inserted
carrot: A biennial plant (*Daucus carota*) of the umbel family, with fernlike leaves and compound umbels of white flowers, usually with one red flower in the center: only the cultivated variety is edible
karat: One 24th part (of pure gold)

cease: To bring or come to an end; stop; discontinue
seize: To take forcible legal possession of; confiscate

cede: To give up one's rights in; surrender formally
seed: The part of a flowering plant that typically contains the embryo with its protective coat and stored food and that can develop into a new plant under the proper conditions; fertilized and mature ovule

ceiling: The inside top part or covering of a room, opposite the floor
sealing: Present participle of the verb *to seal*

cel: Films: from use of celluloid, esp. formerly, for photographic films
cell: A small convent or monastery attached to a larger one
sell: To give up, deliver, or exchange (property, goods, services, etc.) for money or its equivalent

cent: A monetary unit of the U.S., equal to 1/100 of a dollar; penny
scent: To smell; perceive of the olfactory sense
sent: Past participle of the verb *to send*

cereal: Any grain used for food, as wheat, oats, or rice
serial: Of, arranged in, or forming a series

chute: A waterfall; rapids in a river
shoot: To move swiftly over, by, across, etc.

cite: To summon to appear before a court of law
sight: Something seen; view
site: A piece of land considered from the standpoint of its use for some specified purpose

colonel: A military officer ranking above a lieutenant colonel and below a brigadier general, and corresponding to a captain in the navy
kernel: A grain or seed, as of corn, wheat, etc.

cue: A bit of dialogue, action, or music that is a signal for an actor's entrance or speech, or for the working of curtains, lights, sound effects, etc.
queue: A line or file of persons, vehicles, etc., waiting as to be served

ewe: A female sheep
you: The person or persons to whom one is speaking or writing

flew: Past participle of the verb *to fly*
flue: A tube, pipe, or shaft for the passage of smoke, hot air, exhaust fumes, etc., esp. in a chimney
flu: Short for *influenza*

for: In place of; instead of
fore: At, in, or toward the bow of a ship
four: The cardinal number between three and five; 4; IV

gibe: To jeer or taunt; scoff (at)
jibe: To shift from one side of a ship to the other when the stern passes across a following or quartering wind

holey: Having a hole or holes
holy: Dedicated to religious use; belonging to or coming from God; consecrated; sacred
wholly: To the whole amount or extent; totally; entirely

key: An instrument, usually of metal, for moving the bolt of a lock and thus locking or unlocking something
quay: A wharf, usually of concrete or stone, for use in loading and unloading ships

knew: Past participle of the verb *to know*
new: Never existing before; appearing, thought of, developed, made, produced, etc., for the first time

know: To have a clear perception or understanding of; be sure of or well informed about
no: Not

meat: Food; esp. solid food, as distinguished from drink
meet: To come upon or encounter; esp. to come face to face with or up to (a person or thing moving from a different direction)
mete: To allot; distribute; apportion: usually with the word *out*

medal: A small, flat piece of metal with a design or inscription stamped or inscribed on it, made to commemorate some event, or awarded for some distinguished action, merit, etc.
meddle: To concern oneself with or take part in other people's affairs without being asked or needed; interfere (in or with)
metal: Any of a class of chemical elements, as iron, gold, or aluminum, generally characterized by ductility, malleability, luster, and conductivity of heat and electricity
mettle: Quality of character or temperament; esp. high quality of character; spirit; courage; ardor

one: Being a single thing or unit; not two or more
won: Past participle of the verb *to win*

pair: Two similar or corresponding things joined, associated, or used together

pare: To cut or trim away (the rind, skin, covering, rough surface, etc.) of (anything); peel
pear: A tree (*Pyrus communis*) of the rose family, with glossy leaves and greenish, brown, or reddish fruit

peak: To become sickly; waste away; droop
peek: To glance or look quickly and furtively, esp. through an opening or from behind something
pique: Resentment at being slighted or disdained; ruffled pride

poor: Lacking material possessions; having little or no means to support oneself; needy; impoverished
pore: To read or study carefully
pour: To cause to flow in a continuous stream

rain: Water falling to earth in drops larger than 0.5 mm (0.02 in) that have been condensed from the moisture in the atmosphere
reign: Royal power, authority, or rule; sovereignty
rein: A narrow strap of leather attached to each end of the bit in the mouth of a horse, and held by the rider or driver to control the animal

right: Formed by, or with reference to, a straight line or plane perpendicular to a base
rite: A ceremonial or formal, solemn act, observance, or procedure in accordance with prescribed rule or custom, as in religious use
wright: A person who makes, constructs, or repairs: used chiefly in compounds
write: To form or inscribe (words, letters, symbols, etc.) on a surface, as by cutting, carving, embossing, or, esp., marking with a pen or pencil

rote: A fixed, mechanical way of doing something; routine
wrote: Past participial of the verb *to write*

rye: A hardy cereal grass (*Secale cereale*) widely grown for its grain and straw
wry: Turned or bent to one side; twisted

sew: To join or fasten with stitches made with needle and thread
so: In the way or manner shown, expressed, indicated, understood, etc.; as stated or described; in such a manner
sow: To scatter or plant (seed) for growing

their: Of, belonging to, made by, or done by them
there: At or in that place
they're: A contraction from the words *they are*

to: In the direction of; toward
too: In addition; as well; besides; also
two: The cardinal number between one and three; 2; II

vain: Having no real value or significance; worthless, empty, idle, hollow, etc.
vane: A flat piece of metal, strip of cloth, etc., set up high to swing with the wind and show which way it is blowing; weather vane
vein: Any blood vessel that carries blood from some part of the body back toward the heart

If you use a word-processing program on a computer to write, be wary of relying too heavily on its spell-checker. Although spell-checkers can help you locate and correct many misspelled words, most cannot determine whether you have misused a homophone—that is, if you correctly spelled the word *mettle,* it cannot detect whether you have used it incorrectly in place of the word *meddle, medal,* or *metal.*

SELECTING THE CORRECT HOMOPHONE

Following are numerous sample sentences that demonstrate the selection of the correct homophone:

The swimmer gasped for (*air, err, heir*) upon reaching the surface.
air

Luisa's father walked her down the (*aisle, isle*).
aisle

(*Ate, Eight*) of us went to the movie.
Eight

Jeff presented Lisa with a two-(*carat, caret, carrot, karat*) diamond ring when he proposed to her.
carat

(*Cease, Seize*) this nonsense at once!
Cease

Billy agreed to (*cede, seed*) possession of his Power Ranger figurine in exchange for Joey's Luke Skywalker toy.
cede

Ed painted the (*ceiling, sealing*) using a long-handled paintbrush.
ceiling

You can purchase an original animation (*cel, cell, sell*) at this auction.
cel

Much to Max's chagrin, Jillian refused to pay back one (*cent, scent, sent*) of the money she owed him.
cent

Fruity Pebbles is my favorite type of (*cereal, serial*).
cereal

Phoebe's sweatshirt clogged the laundry (*chute, shoot*).
chute

When you write a research paper, you must (*cite, sight, site*) your sources.
cite

I think it was (*Colonel, Kernel*) Mustard in the hall with a candlestick.
Colonel

Franklin ruined the show when he missed his cue to enter stage right (*cue, queue*).
cue

The (*ewe, you*) nuzzled her newborn kid.
ewe

A bird just (*flew, flue, flu*) into the window!
flew

I bought these flowers (*for, fore, four*) my mother.
for

I typically (*gibe, jibe*) the ballplayers from the opposing team.
gibe

Even though Renata's favorite jeans are (*holey, holy, wholly*), she wears them almost every day.
holey

Brigitta lost her house (*key, quay*) and was stuck outside in the snow.
key

Alas, poor Yorick, I (*knew, new*) him well . . . .
knew

I (*know, no*) the answer, but I've forgotten it.
know

Vegetarians don't eat (*meat, meet, mete*).
meat

Becky's father won a silver (*medal, meddle, metal, mettle*) in the 1976 Olympic Games.
medal

(*One, Won*) of us will have to sleep on the sofa.
One

It seems like every time I (*pare, pair, pear*) down the items in my closet, my closet fills right back up!
pare

Solange climbed the (*peak, peek, pique*) while carrying a 40-pound backpack.
peak

I urge you to (*pore, poor, pour*) over these materials before the exam.
pore

After the heavy (*rain, reign, rein*), it seemed as though the garden sprouted weeds overnight.
rain

Returning the wallet to its owner was the (*right, rite, wright, write*) thing to do.
right

Freddy learned his multiplication tables by (*rote, wrote*).
rote

I'll have a tuna sandwich on (*rye, wry*), please.
rye

Because I didn't have enough money to buy a dress, I decided to (*sew, so, sow*) one instead.
sew

My parents gave us (*their, there, they're*) old patio furniture.
their

Give the candle (*to, too, two*) me.
> **to**

Some people think it's (*vain, vane, vein*) to dye one's hair.
> **vain**

To (*air, err, heir*) is human.
> **err**

My grandmother was born on the (*Aisle, Isle*) of Wight.
> **Isle**

After the show, we (*ate, eight*) pizza.
> **ate**

To indicate where in the manuscript a comma should be placed, first draw a (*carat, caret, carrot, karat*).
> **caret**

(*Cease, Seize*) the day!
> **Seize**

Jessica buried a (*cede, seed*) in the dirt to see if it would grow.
> **seed**

Tiffany used a (*ceiling, sealing*) agent to caulk the window.
> **sealing**

Time passes slowly in a prison (*cel, cell, sell*).
> **cell**

What is that bewitching (*cent, scent, sent*) you're wearing?
> **scent**

Ted Bundy was a (*cereal, serial*) killer.
> **serial**

I saw him (*chute, shoot*) across the yard before tripping over the shrub.
> **shoot**

(*Cite, Sight, Site*) is one of the five senses.
> **Sight**

A popcorn (*colonel, kernel*) is stuck in my teeth.
   kernel

If you are waiting to speak to the postmaster, please stand in this (*cue, queue*).
   queue

I'll share the car with (*ewe, you*) if you'll help pay for the gas.
   you

Please open the (*flew, flue, flu*) before lighting the fire.
   flue

Please bring your papers to the (*for, fore, four*).
   fore

At this point in the course, the captain of the yacht must (*gibe, jibe*).
   jibe

Christmas is a (*holey, holy, wholly*) day for Christians.
   holy

The men who work on the (*key, quay*) reek of fish.
   quay

The (*knew, new*) kid in school lives behind me.
   new

Mom said that under (*know, no*) circumstances was I allowed to go to the party.
   no

I plan to (*meat, meet, mete*) Sam after work.
   meet

Leave it to Aunt Susan to (*medal, meddle, metal, mettle*) in our affairs!
   meddle

I can't believe Randy's brother (*one, won*) the lottery!
   won

Would you hand me that (*pare, pair, pear*) of socks?
   pair

No, you cannot (*peak, peek, pique*) at your presents; your birthday isn't until tomorrow!
   peek

Tax breaks could really benefit the working (*pore, poor, pour*).
   poor

The (*rain, reign, rein*) of Queen Elizabeth I lasted from 1558 to 1602.
   reign

Getting one's driver's license has become a (*right, rite, wright, write*) of passage in this country.
   rite

Evelyn practically (*rote, wrote*) the book on horseback riding.
   wrote

Kevin has a (*rye, wry*) sense of humor.
   wry

Before you paint the wall, you cover it with primer like (*sew, so, sow*).
   so

Could you please set those plates down (*their, there, they're*)?
   there

I want to go, (*to, too, two*)!
   too

Edgar installed a new (*vain, vane, vein*) on the roof.
   vane

Prince William is (*air, err, heir*) to the throne.
   heir

Use shredded (*carat, caret, carrot, karat*) to add color to your salad.
   carrot

Ian decided to (*cel, cell, sell*) his motorcycle.
   sell

Lizzie says she (*cent, scent, sent*) the parcel yesterday.
sent

This plot of land is the building (*cite, sight, site*) for the new mall.
site

Jake caught a nasty strain of the (*flew, flue, flu*).
flu

I've made enough food for (*for, fore, four*) people.
four

Linda has proved herself to be (*holey, holy, wholly*) competent.
wholly

Because of the rationing, the baker was forced to (*meat, meet, mete*) out the bread.
mete

Many products that used to be made of (*medal, meddle, metal, mettle*) are now made of plastic.
metal

(*Pare, Pair, Pear*) is my favorite type of fruit.
Pear

Ned knew his decision would (*peak, peek, pique*) his father.
pique

Could you please (*pore, poor, pour*) me a glass of milk?
pour

Victor was so excited, we practically had to (*rain, reign, rein*) him in.
rein

You reap what you (*sew, so, sow*).
sow

(*Their, There, They're*) the ones who wanted to visit Monticello in the first place!
They're

After Jackson took a slice, only (*to, too, two*) were left.
two

Before the nurse could take a sample of my blood, she had to locate a (*vain, vane, vein*).
vein

This necklace is made of 24-(*carat, caret, carrot, karat*) gold.
karat

The hurricane really tested our (*medal, meddle, metal, mettle*).
mettle

Don't forget to (*right, rite, wright, write*) to your grandmother!
write

Looking Up Words in a Dictionary

Looking up a word in your dictionary is the best way of ensuring that you are spelling the word correctly. A simple pocket dictionary should suffice in most instances; that said, it would serve you well to invest in a more comprehensive dictionary for obscure words. In addition, spelling dictionaries are available; these dictionaries contain the correct spellings, but not definitions of, thousands of English words. Because these dictionaries lack the definitions of words, they are less cumbersome than full-sized regular dictionaries.

If you're in the market for a new dictionary, consider *Webster's New World College Dictionary, Fourth Edition*.

There may be times, however, when you can't even determine a word's first letter. For example, if you were trying to determine the correct spelling of the word *mnemonic*, it might not cross your mind to look under the *M*s in your dictionary. In times such as these, a phonetic dictionary may be helpful. Phonetic dictionaries enable you to look up words phonetically rather than alphabetically.

If you have access to the Internet, you'll find several online dictionaries at your disposal. To access several dictionaries, as well as other useful tools, visit www.refdesk.com.

It's best to look up words during the revision phase of writing rather than as you compose your prose. Otherwise, you risk losing your train of thought. As you write, simply highlight any words about whose spelling you are unsure.

Using Mnemonics

A *mnemonic* is a memory device that you can use to remember something, such as how to spell a word. For example, a mnemonic device to help you remember whether the word for "a person who has controlling authority or is in a leading position" is *principle* or *principal* might be "*A* stands for *authority;* therefore, the correct ending is *al* and not *le*."

Spelling Rules

Aside from the strategies listed earlier in this chapter, there are several rules you can learn to aid in the improvement of your spelling. The following are, of course, general rules. It should be noted that there are exceptions, even beyond those ones listed in the entries that follow.

You should be particularly careful to spell proper nouns—especially the names of people—correctly. Misspelling a person's name can be construed to indicate a lack of interest on your part about the person whose name you've misspelled.

I BEFORE *E* EXCEPT AFTER *C*

Nearly every person who attended grammar school in the United States remembers this rhyme: "*i* before *e* except after *c*." Here are some examples of words that follow that rule:

shield
hygiene
sobriety
niece
wield
friend
deceit
perceive
ceiling

There are, however, many exceptions to this rule. They include the following words:

weird
seize
either
neither

caffeine
foreign
forfeit
leisure

This rule is further complicated by this exception: When the vowel combination is intended to sound like an *a,* the *i* should follow, not precede, the *e*:

neighbor
weigh
eight
sleigh
vein
beige

HANDLING THE ADDITION OF PREFIXES AND SUFFIXES

The addition of a prefix to a word does not affect the spelling of the root word:

un + easy	uneasy
un + necessary	unnecessary
il + literate	illiterate
mis + spell	misspell
dis + content	discontent

Much spelling confusion arises, however, when a suffix is added to a root word. Should the silent *e* at the end of a root word be dropped before the suffix is added? If the root word ends in a consonant, should that consonant be doubled before the suffix is added? Following are some guidelines for answering these and other suffix-related questions.

Adding Suffixes to Words That End in a Silent *E*

When adding a suffix to a root word that ends in a silent *e,* drop the *e* if the suffix begins with a vowel:

ridicule + ous	ridiculous
hate + ing	hating
write + ing	writing

An exception to the preceding rule is this: If the root word ends in *ge* or *ce,* the final *e* is not dropped unless the suffix begins with the letter *i,* in which case the *e* is dropped:

outrage + ous	outrageous
trace + able	traceable
age + ing	aging

Don't be surprised to discover exceptions to the exceptions. For example, some words ending in *ge* or *ce* do drop the final *e* when a suffix is added—for example, *mortgage + or* becomes *mortgagor*, and *pledge + or* becomes *pledgor*.

In addition, if eliminating the silent *e* will create confusion or mispronunciation, it should remain:

acre + age	acreage
mile + age	mileage

When adding a suffix to a root word that ends in a silent *e*, keep the *e* if the suffix begins with a consonant:

love + ly	lovely
commence + ment	commencement

Likewise, if the suffix begins with the letter *y*, the silent *e* at the end of the root word is typically dropped:

ice + y	icy
ease + y	easy
rose + y	rosy

Exceptions to this rule include such words as *cagey*, *dicey*, and *pricey*.

If another vowel precedes the silent *e*, you should drop the *e*, regardless of whether the suffix begins with a consonant or with a vowel:

glue + ed	glued
true + ly	truly

If you are adding the suffix *ing* to a word that ends in *ie*, the *ie* is usually changed to *y* before the *ing* is added:

vie + ing	vying
die + ing	dying
lie + ing	lying

Adding Suffixes to Words That End in Y

When adding a suffix—whether it begins with a vowel or a consonant—to a word that ends in *y*, change the *y* to *i* when the *y* is preceded by a consonant:

happy + ness	happiness
hearty + ly	heartily

An exception to this rule is this: If you are adding the suffix *ing*, the *y* should remain as is:

ply + ing	plying
dry + ing	drying

Likewise, the *y* remains intact when a suffix is added if the *y* is preceded by a vowel:

play + ing	playing
stray + ed	straycd

Doubling the Final Consonant

When adding a suffix to a word that ends in a single consonant (except *w, x,* or *y*) preceded by a vowel (as in *hug, quip, strap, equip,* and so on), you should double the consonant at the end of the root word if the root word is monosyllabic or if the last syllable of the root word is accented:

hug	hugging
quip	quipped
strap	strapping
infer	inferred

If, in the case of a multisyllabic root word, the accent changes from the final syllable to the preceding one when a suffix is added, you should not double the final consonant::

defer + ence	deference
confer + ence	conference

In addition, the final consonant of a multisyllabic root word should not be doubled if the root word ends in a single consonant preceded by a single vowel, and the accent is not on the last syllable:

prophet + ic	prophetic
credit + ing	crediting

Likewise, if the root word, whether it be monosyllabic or multisyllabic, ends in a single consonant preceded by multiple vowels, the final consonant should not be doubled:

hear + ing	hearing
treat + ment	treatment
lean + ed	leaned
view + ing	viewing
cheat + er	cheater

If the root word, be it monosyllabic or multisyllabic, ends with more than one consonant, the final consonant is not doubled before the suffix is added:

sand + y	sandy
health + y	healthy
skirt + ing	skirting
mass + ive	massive
warm + ly	warmly

-Able versus *-Ible*

Many words in the English language end in *-able* or *-ible*. Alas, there are no hard-and-fast rules about which suffix is correct in which situation. When in doubt, consult your dictionary.

Adding Suffixes to Words That End in *C*

If you are adding a suffix to a word that ends in the letter *c* with a hard sound, you must usually add the letter *k* to the end of the root word before adding the suffix to preserve the hard sound of the *c*:

picnic + ing	picnicking
traffic + ed	trafficked

SPELLING COMPOUND WORDS

Many writers have difficulty when it comes to spelling compound words. Should the words remain separate, should they be hyphenated, or should they be joined into a single word? For example, which is correct: *horse play, horse-play,* or *horseplay?*

The best way of determining which spelling is correct for any given compound word is to consult a dictionary. If the compound you seek does not appear, it's probably wise to assume that the words should remain separate. Whether the words should be hyphenated depends on the role they play in the sentence. (For more information, refer to Chapter 8, "Punctuation," under the heading "The Hyphen (-).")

Commonly Misspelled Words

Following is a list of commonly misspelled words:

absence	absorption	abundance	acceptable
accessible	accidentally	acclaim	accommodate
accumulate	achieve	achievement	acquaintance
acquire	acquit	acquitted	address
advantageous	advice	advise	affect
affiliated	aggression	aggressive	alignment
allege	all right	a lot	aluminum
amateur	ambience	among	analysis
analyze	annual	apartment	apparatus
apparent	appearance	appropriate	arctic
arguing	argument	arithmetic	ascend
asphalt	assistant	asterisk	atheist
athlete	athletic	attendance	auditor
auxiliary	balance	balloon	bankruptcy
barbecue	bargain	basically	battalion
beggar	beginning	belief	believable
believe	bellwether	beneficial	benefit
benefited	besiege	biscuit	boundaries
brilliant	Britain	bulletin	bureau
bureaucracy	burglar	business	calendar
camouflage	campaign	candidate	Caribbean
category	ceiling	cemetery	challenge
changeable	changing	chaotic	chief
choose	chose	clientele	collateral
collectible	colonel	column	coming
commission	committee	committed	comparative
compelled	competitor	concede	conceivable

(continued)

conceive	condemn	condescend	conferred
congratulations	connoisseur	conscience	conscientious
conscious	consensus	control	controversial
controversy	convenient	convertible	correlate
correspondence	corroborate	councilor	counselor
counterfeit	courteous	courtesy	criticism
criticize	daiquiri	deceive	defendant
deferred	definite	definitely	definition
dependent	descend	describe	description
desirable	despair	desperate	despise
develop	dictionary	dilemma	dining
disappear	disappearance	disappoint	disastrous
disbursement	discipline	discrepancy	dispensable
dissatisfied	dissipate	dormitory	drunkenness
dumbbell	duel	dyeing (to dye)	dying (to die)
ecstasy	effect	efficiency	eighth
either	eligible	eliminate	emanate
embarrass	embarrassing	embarrassment	eminent
emperor	encouragement	encouraging	endorsement
environment	environmental	equipment	equipped
equivalent	especially	exaggerate	exceed
excellence	exhaust	exhilarate	existence
existent	experience	experiment	exorbitant
explanation	extraordinary	exuberance	facsimile
fallacious	fallacy	familiar	fascinate
fascinating	February	fictitious	fiery
finally	financially	flexible	fluctuation
fluorescent	forcibly	foreign	foresee
forfeit	formerly	forty	fourth
frantically	fuelling	fulfill	fundamentally
gauge	generally	genius	gesture

gorilla	government	governor	grammar
grandeur	grateful	grievance	grievous
gruesome	guarantee	guerilla	guidance
handkerchief	haphazard	harass	harassment
height	heinous	hemorrhage	heroes
hesitancy	hierarchy	hindrance	hoarse
holiday	hoping	humorous	hypocrisy
hypocrite	ideally	idiosyncrasy	ignorance
illegible	imaginary	immediate	immediately
immigrant	implement	incidentally	incredible
indelible	independence	independent	indicted
indispensable	inevitable	infinitely	inoculate
insistent	intellectual	intelligence	interesting
interference	intermediary	interrupt	introduce
irrelevant	irreplaceable	irresistible	island
jealousy	jeopardy	jewelry	judgment
judicial	kernel	knowledge	laboratory
laid	later	latter	labeling
led	legitimate	leisure	length
liaison	library	license	lieutenant
lightning	likelihood	litigation	loneliness
lose	losing	luxury	magazine
maintenance	manageable	maneuver	manufacture
marriage	mathematics	maybe	medicine
medieval	mediocre	memento	mere
millennium	miniature	minimum	miniscule
minutes	miscellaneous	mischief	mischievous
missile	misspell	mortgage	mosquito
mosquitoes	murmur	muscle	mysterious
naïve	narrative	naturally	necessary

(continued)

necessity	negligence	negotiable	neighbor
neutron	newsstand	ninety	ninth
noticeable	nowadays	nuisance	obedience
obstacle	occasion	occasionally	occurred
occurrence	official	omission	omitted
opinion	opponent	opportunity	oppression
optimist	optimistic	orchestra	ordinarily
origin	outrageous	overrun	paid
pamphlet	parallel	paralysis	paralyze
particular	pastime	pavilion	peaceable
peculiar	perceive	performance	permanent
permissible	perseverance	persistent	personal
personnel	perspiration	persuade	phony
physical	picnicking	pitiful	playwright
pleasant	pleasurable	portray	possess
possesses	possession	possibility	possible
potato	potatoes	practically	prairie
precede	precedence	preceding	predictable
preference	preferred	prejudice	preparation
prescription	prevalent	primitive	principal
principle	privilege	probably	procedure
proceed	profession	professor	prominent
pronunciation	propaganda	psychology	publicly
pursue	quantity	quarantine	questionnaire
quizzes	realistically	realize	recede
receive	receiving	receipt	receive
recognize	recommend	reference	referring
relevant	relieve	religious	remembrance
reminiscence	repetition	representative	rescind
resemblance	reservoir	resistance	restaurant

rheumatism	rhyme	rhythm	rhythmical
ridiculous	roommate	sacrifice	sacrilegious
salable	salary	satellite	scary
scenery	schedule	secede	secretary
seize	sense	separate	separation
sergeant	several	severely	shepherd
sheriff	shining	siege	similar
simile	simply	simultaneous	sincerely
skiing	sophomore	souvenir	sovereign
specifically	specimen	sponsor	spontaneous
statue	strenuous	stubbornness	studying
subtle	subtlety	subtly	succeed
succession	succumb	sufficient	suddenness
superintendent	supersede	suppress	surprise
susceptible	suspicious	syllable	symmetrical
synonymous	tangible	tariff	technical
technique	temperamental	temperature	tenant
tendency	than	their	then
theory	there	therefore	they're
thorough	threshold	tomato	tomatoes
too	tournament	toward	tragedy
tranquility	transferred	transferring	tries
truly	twelfth	tyranny	unanimous
unconscious	undoubtedly	unforgettable	unique
unmistakable	unnecessary	until	unwieldy
usable	usage	usually	utilization
vacillate	vacuum	valuable	vengeance
vicious	vigilant	vigilante	village
villain	violence	visible	vision
virtue	warrant	warrior	weather

(continued)

Wednesday	weird	whether	wholly
wield	withdrawal	withhold	woeful
woman	women	yacht	yield
young			

Many words have alternate spellings. Sometimes, the alternate spelling is the less common, and therefore the less acceptable, variant; other times, both variants of the same word are equally acceptable. Typically, if the two spellings are of equal acceptability, the dictionary will precede the second spelling with the word *or*. If one spelling is preferred, it will be listed first, with the second spelling preceded by the word *also*.

Unless you are writing in the most informal of circumstances, avoid shortening or altering common words, as in the following:

> lite (light)
> nite (night)
> thru (through)

U.S. Spelling versus British and Canadian Spellings

If you enjoy reading and have read books published in other English-speaking nations, you may have noticed inconsistencies in the spellings of certain words. Following are examples of words whose spellings differ depending on whether the writer is a U.S. writer, a British writer, or a Canadian writer:

In some cases, multiple variants of a word may be acceptable in a given country, as indicated by an asterisk (*). Here, however, only the most common usages appear.

U.S.	*British*	*Canadian*
acknowledgment	acknowledgement	acknowledgement
aging	ageing	aging
airplane	aeroplane	airplane
aluminum	aluminium	aluminum
amortize	amortise	amortize
amoxicillin	amoxycillin	amoxicillin

amphitheater	amphitheatre	amphitheatre
analog	analogue	analogue
anemia	anaemia	anemia
anemic	anaemic	anemic
anesthesia	anaesthesia	anaesthesia
anesthetic	anaesthetic	anaesthetic
analyze	analyse	analyze
apnea	apnoea	apnea
apologize	apologise	apologize
appall	appal	appall
appetizer	appetiser	appetizer
arbor	arbour	arbour
archeology	archaeology	archaeology
ardor	ardour	ardour
armor	armour	armour
armory	armoury	armoury
artifact	artefact	artifact
authorize	authorise	authorize
ax	axe	axe
bandanna	bandanna	bandana
baptize	baptise	baptize
barreled	barrelled	barrelled
barreling	barrelling	barrelling
behavior	behaviour	behaviour
behoove	behove	behoove
belabor	belabour	belabour
Breathalyzer	Breathalyser	Breathalyzer
burned	burnt	burned
bused	bussed	bused

(continued)

busing	bussing	busing
caldron	cauldron	cauldron
caliber	calibre	calibre
canceled	cancelled	cancelled
canceling	cancelling	cancelling
candor	candour	candour
capitalize	capitalise	capitalize
caramelize	caramelise	caramelize
carburetor	carburettor	carburetor
catalog	catalogue	catalogue
catalyze	catalyse	catalyze
categorize	categorise	categorize
cauterize	cauterise	cauterize
center	centre	centre
centering	centring	centring
centimeter	centimetre	centimetre
centralize	centralise	centralize
Cesarean	Caesarean	Caesarian
characterize	characterise	characterize
check (noun: money draft)	cheque	cheque
checkered	chequered	checkered
chili	chilli	chili
civilization	civilisation	civilization
civilize	civilise	civilize
clamor	clamour	clamour
collectible	collectable	collectible
colonize	colonise	colonize
color	colour	colour
commercialize	commercialise	commercialize
computerize	computerise	computerize

convener	convenor	convenor
costumer	costumier	costumer
councilor	councillor	councillor
counselor	counsellor	counsellor
counseled	counselled	counselled
counseling	counselling	counselling
cozy	cosy	cozy
criticize	criticise	criticize
crystallization	crystallisation	crystallization
crystallize	crystallise	crystallize
curb (noun: raised edge of sidewalk)	kerb	curb
customize	customise	customize
defense	defence	defence
demeanor	demeanour	demeanour
dependent (noun)	dependant	dependant
diarrhea	diarrhoea	diarrhea
dietician	dietician	dietitian
digitize	digitise	digitize
disheveled	dishevelled	dishevelled
dolor	dolour	dolour
donut	doughnut	doughnut
draft (noun: current of air)	draught	draft
dreamed	dreamt	dreamt
dueled	duelled	dueled
dueling	duelling	duelling
edema	oedema	edema
empathize	empathise	empathize
emphasize	emphasise	emphasize

(continued)

enamor	enamour	enamour
endeavor	endeavour	endeavour
enroll	enrol	enrol
enrollment	enrolment	enrolment
enthrall	enthral	enthrall
enthrallment	enthralment	enthrallment
eon	aeon	eon
epicenter	epicentre	epicentre
equalization	equalisation	equalization
equalize	equalise	equalize
equaled	equalled	equalled
equaling	equalling	equalling
esophagus	œsophagus	esophagus
estrogen	oestrogen	estrogen
familiarize	familiarise	familiarize
favor	favour	favour
favorite	favourite	favourite
fervor	fervour	fervour
fetid	foetid	fetid
fetus	foetus	fetus
fiber	fibre	fibre
flavor	flavour	flavour
flutist	flautist	flutist
fontanel	fontanelle	fontanelle
fueled	fuelled	fuelled
fueling	fuelling	fuelling
fulfill	fulfil	fulfil
funneled	funnelled	funnelled
funneling	funnelling	funnelling
furor	furore	furor

galvanize	galvanise	galvanize
generalize	generalise	generalize
glycerin	glycerine	glycerin
goiter	goitre	goitre
gonorrhea	gonorrhoea	gonorrhea
gray	grey	grey
grueling	gruelling	gruelling
gynecology	gynaecology	gynecology
harbor	harbour	harbour
harmonize	harmonise	harmonize
hauler	haulier	hauler
hematology	haematology	hematology
hematoma	haematoma	hematoma
hemoglobin	haemoglobin	hemoglobin
hemophilia	haemophilia	hemophilia
hemorrhage	haemorrhage	hemorrhage
honor	honour	honour
honorable	honourable	honourable
honored	honoured	honoured
honoring	honouring	honouring
hospitalize	hospitalise	hospitalize
humor	humour	humour
hyperglycemia	hyperglycaemia	hyperglycemia
hypnotize	hypnotise	hypnotize
hypoglycemia	hypoglycaemia	hypoglycemia
hypothesize	hypothesise	hypothesize
idolize	idolise	idolize
immortalize	immortalise	immortalize
immunization	immunisation	immunization

(continued)

immunize	immunise	immunize
industrialization	industrialisation	industrialization
industrialize	industrialise	industrialize
initialize	initialise	initialize
inquiry	enquiry	inquiry
installment	instalment	instalment*, installment
institutionalize	institutionalise	institutionalize
ionize	ionise	ionize
jail	gaol	jail
jeweled	jewelled	jewelled
jeweler	jeweller	jeweller
jewelry	jewellery	jewellery*, jewelry
judgment	judgement	judgement
labeled	labelled	labelled
labeling	labelling	labelling
labor	labour	labour
laborer	labourer	labourer
lasagna	lasagne	lasagna
leaned	leant	leaned
learned	learnt	learned
legalize	legalise	legalize
leukemia	leukaemia	leukemia
leveled	levelled	levelled
leveling	levelling	levelling
libeled	libelled	libelled
libeler	libeller	libeller
libelous	libellous	libellous
license (noun)	licence	licence
licorice	liquorice	licorice
liter	litre	litre

louver	louvre	louvre
louvered	louvred	louvred
luster	lustre	lustre
maneuver	manoeuvre	manoeuvre
marveled	marvelled	marvelled
marveling	marvelling	marvelling
marvelous	marvellous	marvellous
math	maths	math
matte (i.e., not glossy)	matt	matte
maximize	maximise	maximize
meager	meagre	meagre
memorialize	memorialise	memorialize
memorize	memorise	memorize
mesmerize	mesmerise	mesmerize
meter (i.e., unit of length)	metre	metre
militarize	militarise	militarize
miniaturization	miniaturisation	miniaturization
miniaturize	miniaturise	miniaturize
minimize	minimise	minimize
misdemeanor	misdemeanour	misdemeanour
miter	mitre	mitre
mobilize	mobilise	mobilize
modeled	modelled	modelled
modeling	modelling	modelling
mold	mould	mould
molder	moulder	moulder
mollusk	mollusc	mollusc
molt	moult	moult
mustache	moustache	moustache

(continued)

naïveté	naivety	naïveté
neighbor	neighbour	neighbour
neighborhood	neighbourhood	neighbourhood
neutralize	neutralise	neutralize
ocher	ochre	ochre
odor	odour	odour
offense	offence	offence
omelet	omelette	omelette
optimization	optimisation	optimization
optimize	optimise	optimize
organization	organisation	organization
organize	organise	organize
orient	orientate	orient
oriented	orientated	oriented
orthopedic	orthopaedic	orthopaedic
oxidize	oxidise	oxidize
pajamas	pyjamas	pyjamas
Paleocene	Palaeocene	Paleocene
paneled	panelled	panelled
paralyze	paralyse	paralyze*, paralyse
parlor	parlour	parlour
paralleled	parallelled	paralleled
paralleling	parallelling	paralleling
pasteurize	pasteurise	pasteurize
pediatrics	paediatrics	pediatrics
pedophile	paedophile	pedophile
penalization	penalisation	penalization
penalize	penalise	penalize
personalize	personalise	personalize
philosophize	philosophise	philosophize

plagiarize	plagiarise	plagiarize
plow	plough	plow
polarize	polarise	polarize
practice (verb)	practise	practise
pretense	pretence	pretense
prioritize	prioritise	prioritize
privatize	privatise	privatize
program (noun: television show)	programme	program
pulverize	pulverise	pulverize
pummeled	pummelled	pummelled
pummeling	pummelling	pummelling
rancor	rancour	rancour
realize	realise	realize
recognize	recognise	recognize
repellent	repellant	repellent
reveled	revelled	revelled
reveler	reveller	reveller
reveling	revelling	revelling
rigor	rigour	rigour
rumor	rumour	rumour
saber	sabre	sabre
sanitization	sanitisation	sanitization
sanitize	sanitise	sanitize
sapor	sapour	sapour
savior	saviour	saviour
savor	savour	savour
savory	savoury	savoury
scepter	sceptre	sceptre
scrutinize	scrutinise	scrutinize

(continued)

sensationalize	sensationalise	sensationalize
shriveled	shrivelled	shrivelled
shriveling	shrivelling	shrivelling
signaled	signalled	signalled
signaler	signaller	signaller
signaling	signalling	signalling
skeptic	sceptic	sceptic
skeptical	sceptical	sceptical
skillful	skilful	skilful
smelled	smelt	smelled
smolder	smoulder	smoulder
snorkeled	snorkelled	snorkelled
snorkeling	snorkelling	snorkelling
somber	sombre	sombre
specialize	specialise	specialize
specialty	speciality	specialty
specter	spectre	spectre
spiralcd	spiralled	spiralled
spiraling	spiralling	spiralling
splendor	splendour	splendour
stabilize	stabilise	stabilize
standardization	standardisation	standardization
standardize	standardise	standardize
sterilize	sterilise	sterilize
story (i.e., building floor)	storey	storey
stylize	stylise	stylize
succor	succour	succour
sulfur	sulphur	sulphur
summarize	summarise	summarize
symbolize	symbolise	symbolize

synthesize	synthesise	synthesize
systemize	systemise	systemize
theater	theatre	theatre
tidbit	titbit	tidbit
tire (noun)	tyre	tire
ton	tonne	tonne
totaled	totalled	totalled
totaling	totalling	totalling
toward	towards	toward
tranquility	tranquillity	tranquillity
tranquilize	tranquillise	tranquillize
tranquilized	tranquillised	tranquillized
tranquilizer	tranquilliser	tranquillizer
tranquilizing	tranquillising	tranquillizing
traveled	travelled	travelled
traveler	traveller	traveller
traveling	travelling	travelling
triple	treble	triple
tumor	tumour	tumour
tunneled	tunnelled	tunnelled
tunneler	tunneller	tunneller
tunneling	tunnelling	tunnelling
unionize	unionise	unionize
utilize	utilise	utilize
valor	valour	valour
vapor	vapour	vapour
vaporization	vaporisation	vaporization
vaporize	vaporise	vaporize
vaporizer	vaporiser	vaporizer
vaporer	vapourer	vapourer

(continued)

vise (noun: clamping device)	vice	vice
vigor	vigour	vigour
visualize	visualise	visualize
willful	wilful	wilful
willfully	wilfully	wilfully
willfulness	wilfulness	wilfulness
woolen	woollen	woollen
yodeled	yodelled	yodelled
yodeling	yodelling	yodelling
yogurt	yogurt	yogourt

Foreign Words

You may find yourself employing foreign words as you write. If so, you'll likely wonder whether you are presenting them correctly. For example, should a particular foreign word appear in italics? How can you ensure that a foreign word has been spelled correctly? What is the correct use of diacritical marks?

ITALICIZING FOREIGN WORDS

If a foreign word you are employing is familiar within the English language, as is the case with such words and phrases as the following, the word or phrase is not italicized:

barrio
soup du jour
haute couture
protégé
bona fide
en route
non sequitur
Mardi Gras
sang-froid
subpoena
gesundheit
al fresco

If, however, the foreign word is not a familiar one, it should be italicized. The rub, then, is determining which foreign words are considered familiar. Here's a litmus test: If the word in question appears in an English-speaking dictionary, it can be considered familiar and thus need not be italicized.

Ensuring That Foreign Words Have Been Correctly Spelled

To ensure that a foreign word has been correctly spelled, you should—you guessed it—consult your trusty dictionary. If the word does not appear in your English dictionary, you should then resort to using a dictionary for the language of the word in question.

If you have access to the Internet, visit the Language Automation Web site at www. lai.com/lai/glossaries.html for links to dictionaries for languages from Afrikaans to Yiddish, and everything in between. This site even provides links to dictionaries for artificial languages, such as Esperanto and Klingon.

Using Diacritical Marks

Unlike words in English, many foreign words employ *diacritical marks*—accents, diacritics, or special alphabetic characters for native words. The diacritical marks most commonly used in European and Asian languages written in the Latin alphabet are listed in the following table:

Mark	Name	Purpose
´	Acute accent	Placed over a vowel to indicate length or high pitch, or to indicate primary stress of a syllable
`	Grave accent	Placed over a vowel to indicate length or low pitch, or to indicate secondary stress of a syllable
¨	Dieresis	Placed over a vowel to indicate that it is pronounced in a separate syllable
¨	Umlaut	Placed over the vowel to indicate a more central or front articulation
^	Circumflex	Originally used in Greek over long vowels to indicate a rising-falling tone; used in other languages to mark length, contraction, or a particular vowel quality
~	Tilde	Placed over the letter n to denote the sound ny or over vowels to indicate nasality
¸	Cedilla	Placed under a letter to indicate an alteration or modification of its usual phonetic value

Again, you should consult a dictionary for the language in question to determine whether a word in that language uses diacritical marks.

Numerals

The difficult part of using numerals in text is determining when those numerals should be spelled out and when they should be represented by numerical symbols. There are few consistent rules on this issue; in fact, different publications espouse the use of different styles. Some grammar texts urge writers to spell out whole numbers from one to ninety-nine, while representing all others with numerical symbols; others suggest that writers spell out whole numbers from one to twenty. Still others insist that only numerals one through nine be spelled out.

No matter which style you choose, however, a few rules do apply:

- Use the style you choose consistently within a single sentence or paragraph. For example, if a single sentence contains numbers that should typically be spelled out in addition to numbers that would normally be represented by numerical symbols, you should use numerical symbols for all the numbers in the sentence:

    Correct: Among the 482 graduates, 111 majored in Spanish, 71 majored in German, 34 majored in French, and 4 majored in Swahili.
    Incorrect: Among the 482 graduates, 111 majored in Spanish, seventy-one majored in German, thirty-four majored in French, and four majored in Swahili.

  If the sentence or paragraph contains numbers in varying categories, it is acceptable to spell out some while representing others with numerals. Here's an example:

    In the past five years, I've read 43 books, watched 391 movies, and listened to 1,412 records.

  Notice that *five* is spelled out, but the other numerals are not. This is because the other numerals are all members of the same category—that is, they are entertainment experiences. In contrast, *five* refers to years.

- If your sentence or paragraph contains several numbers that would normally be spelled out, it's better to represent them with numerals to avoid creating cumbersome-looking text:

    Correct: I have several children; their ages are 1, 4, 7, 9, 10, and 14.
    Incorrect: I have several children; their ages are one, four, seven, nine, ten, and fourteen.

- Numbers that are approximations are typically spelled out.
- If a number is at the beginning of the sentence, it is always spelled out, even if it normally would not be:

> **Correct:** Three hundred twenty members of Congress abstained from voting on the issue.
> **Incorrect:** 320 members of Congress abstained from voting on the issue.

There may be times when spelling out a number that appears at the beginning of a sentence is cumbersome. In such cases, it's best to recast the sentence so that the number no longer appears at the beginning:

> **Incorrect:** Nineteen hundred forty six is the year my father was born.
> **Correct:** My father was born in 1946.

There are instances, however, in which numbers that would normally be spelled out should not be (unless appearing at the beginning of a sentence), including the following:

- Percentages and decimals
- Physical quantities (distances, masses, and so on)
- Sums of money
- Dates

Although dates are not spelled out, the numerical designation of centuries are (twenty-first century, eighteenth century, and so on):

> **Correct:** Colleen renovated a house that was built in the eighteenth century.
> **Incorrect:** Vermeer is a famous 17th-century Dutch painter.

Word Division

If possible, you should avoid dividing a word at the end of a line using a hyphen. There are situations, however, in which avoiding word division is impossible. If you find yourself in such a situation, attempt to divide the word according to pronunciation. That is, avoid dividing the word in the middle of a syllable; make the break at the end of a syllable:

> **Correct:** pronun-ciation
> **Incorrect:** pronu-nciation
> **Correct:** etymo-logical
> **Incorrect:** etymol-ogical

Beyond that, consider the following:

- Compounds should be divided in such a way that the words comprising the compound remain intact:

    Correct: dis-association
    Incorrect: disassoc-iation
    Correct: butter-fly
    Incorrect: but-terfly

- When two consonants separate a pair of vowels, it's best to divide the word between the two consonants:

    Correct: war-rant
    Incorrect: warr-ant
    Correct: mean-der
    Incorrect: mea-nder

- Avoid dividing words (or phrases) that already contain hyphens anywhere other than at the existing hyphen:

    Correct: compound-complex sentence
    Incorrect: com-pound-complex sentence
    Correct: red-letter day
    Incorrect: red-let-ter day

- Avoid dividing proper nouns (especially names of people), and avoid separating a person's initials from the name:

    Correct: Marilyn Monroe
    Incorrect: Marilyn Mon-roe
    Correct: J. D. Salinger
    Incorrect: J. D. Salin-ger

- Avoid leaving a row of hyphens at the edge of your page; do not break the last word in more than two lines in a row.

General Observations about Spelling

- No matter how well you construct your sentences, a misspelled word in your text can result in the immediate loss of your credibility as a writer.
- Learning to spell correctly can be difficult due to the hodgepodge nature of the English language.

- When you are unsure of the spelling of a word, try sounding it out.
- You can use your dictionary to look up the correct spelling of the word.
- You can employ mnemonic devices to remember the correct spellings of words that consistently baffle you.
- *Homophones* are words that sound alike but that have different meanings and different spellings.
- Several rules can be learned to aid in the improvement of one's spelling. These are, of course, general rules. It should be noted that there are exceptions.
- Unless you are writing in the most informal of circumstances, avoid shortening or altering common words.
- The spellings of many words differ depending on whether the writer is a U.S. writer, a Canadian writer, or a British writer.
- If a foreign word or phrase you are employing in your text is familiar within the English language, the word or phrase is not italicized.
- The difficult part of using numerals in text is determining when those numerals should be spelled out and when they should be represented by numerical symbols. There are few consistent rules on this issue.

Appendix A

On Writing

No doubt you'll use your newfound grammar expertise when you speak, but it's when you write that it really comes into play. After all, in order to speak correctly, you need not have a grasp of the correct use of the colon or the semicolon, or even of the accepted spelling of the words you're saying. In fact, grammar and writing are so intertwined that the word *grammar* stems from the Greek *graphein*, meaning *to write*.

When writing, however, you must be concerned with more than the simple mechanics of grammar. It's not enough to ensure that every word has been spelled correctly, that every sentence has been correctly punctuated, that every verb agrees with every subject. Additional issues, such as structure and style, arise. And, as with speech, writers must consider their audience; it doesn't do to write as though your piece will be read by a Girl Scout troop when, in fact, your company's board of directors is your audience.

Although there is no precise process for writing—whether it be a short story, a novel, a play, a poem, an article, a school paper, a screenplay, a case study, or a research grant—most writing involves four basic steps:

- Prewriting
- Writing
- Revising
- Proofreading

The amount of time you spend on each step will vary widely depending on the type of piece you are writing and on you yourself. For example, a person writing a research paper might spend more time in the prewriting phase than a person writing a short story for the simple reason that the research paper probably involves more, well, *research*. That said, some fiction writers research copiously and may remain in the prewriting stage for some time before moving on.

Prewriting

E. L. Doctorow once said, "Planning to write is not writing. Outlining . . . researching . . . talking to people about what you're doing, none of that is writing. Writing is writing." And of course, he's right. Only writing is writing. That said, the prewriting phase of a writing project can be an important one. In this phase, the writer might do any of the following:

- Generate ideas
- Research
- Organize the piece

GENERATING IDEAS

Generating ideas can occur in any number of ways. While perusing the newspaper, for example, you might read a story that plants an idea in your brain. Or you might see a person on the street who captures your interest and begin imagining his or her life. You might even generate ideas through your own experiences—for example, if you're buying a house, you may be inspired to write an article about it. Then again, your writing may be the result of a school assignment, in which case you may be limited in your choice of topic. Even so, you'll need ideas about how you want to present your information or what aspect of the topic you want to cover.

Regardless of what you are writing, the idea-generating phase is critical. Following are some ways in which you can get your creative juices flowing:

- **Live.** In her memoir *An American Childhood,* Annie Dillard writes, "Admire the world for never ending on you—as you would admire an opponent, without taking your eyes from him or walking away." The world is a fascinating place; participating in life, and observing the people and things around you, can inspire incredible stories, articles, plays, and more.
  Always carry a notebook with you. When you see or hear something that sparks an idea, write it down immediately so that you don't forget it.
- **Talk to people.** Every person on this planet has at least one incredible story to tell. If you listen, you'll be amazed at the material you can gather.
- **Reflect.** Reflecting on your own experiences can lend incredible insight that can be very helpful in the realm of writing.
- **Write in a journal or blog.** Recording the events in your own life, as well as your general observations about life itself and the world around you, can help you hone your writing in general, as well as help you decide what topics are worth pursuing.
- **Read.** Read anything you can get your hands on, be it *The Wall Street Journal, Hamlet,* or the back of a Cheerios box. Reading brings the world to you, and with it, ideas for your own stories. As a bonus, by reading you will develop a strong sense of language and, as a result, improve your writing skills.
- **Brainstorm.** Give yourself time to think; open your mind, and let the ideas pour forth. This process can be especially effective in a group setting.

When brainstorming, don't discard any ideas, no matter how farfetched they seem. Write down everything that crosses your mind and evaluate your ideas later.

RESEARCHING

After you've generated ideas, you're probably eager to get started writing. Before you do, however, you'll likely need to engage in some form of research. Indeed, if you are writing an academic paper, the research phase might be quite prolonged.

If you intend to write a novel, short story, or similar piece, you might believe yourself exempt from the research portion of the prewriting phase—and you may well be if you wish to write a story that is rooted entirely in your own experience. After all, you conducted your "research" when you lived through the experiences about which you are writing. If, however, your story is about people who are different from you— perhaps they live in a different town, or hold different jobs, or experience things you can only imagine—you'll need to do some research before moving on.

When it comes to research, more is better. Learn as much as you can about the topic at hand. As Ernest Hemingway once said, "If a writer . . . knows enough about what he is writing about, he may omit things that he knows . . . The dignity of movement of an iceberg is due to only one ninth of it being above water."

Your research may involve any of the following:

- Reading books, magazines, newspapers, pamphlets, or other materials
- Watching films, videos, or other broadcasts
- Listening to audio recordings
- Interviewing people
- Searching the Internet

The Internet has revolutionized the way people research. No longer must you trek to the library to access information about a topic, no matter how obscure. That said, you must take care when using the Internet as a research tool; because the Internet is so wide open, information found on it can sometimes be of questionable value. For this reason, you should consider the following when conducting research online:

- Make sure your sources are valid. Gather information only from those sites you trust (taking care, of course, to avoid plagiarism, and to cite the Web site from whence the information came).
- Make sure any Web site you're quoting is up to date.
- Avoid using the Internet to the exclusion of all other research methods.

As you're researching, be sure to gather the information you find into a file so that you can refer to it as you write. Such a file might include photocopied passages from books you've used in your research, printouts of articles you've found online, newspaper clippings, brochures, and so on. Paper trails such as these are also useful in the event your finished piece is published; editors or other staff can use them to fact-check your story.

ORGANIZING THE PIECE

There are some types of writing, such as journal entries and love letters, for which organization, or structure, is insignificant. Such pieces are, in essence, outpourings of the feelings or views of the writer, and the order in which those feelings and views are presented is unimportant. Other types of writing, such as academic papers, case studies, and certain types of poems, have strict rules on structure. Sonnets, for example, must contain exactly fourteen lines in iambic-pentameter lines. Most types of writing, however, fall somewhere in the middle, requiring you to pay at least some attention to organization and structure before putting pen to paper.

Suppose, for example, that you are writing a suspenseful novel. Most likely, you would want to withhold certain details until the end of the story rather than reveal them at the beginning. That said, if your story ends with a twist, you must lay the foundation for that twist earlier in the book to make it believable. As another example, suppose your story jumps back and forth in time. You may begin with a relatively short section set in the present, flash back to a short section set in the past, and then slowly increase the lengths of subsequent sections as the story moves forward. All these issues relate to the organization of your piece.

USING AN OUTLINE

Although some people can park themselves in front of a computer and crank out the great American novel, organizing it in their head as they go, many writers need to construct outlines before progressing to the writing stage. Whether you're writing a *War and Peace*–type saga or a 500-word article for your school paper, an outline can help you focus your ideas and organize your piece. Outlines can range from the very broad to the very detailed; some writers create outlines that are hundreds of pages long. Of course, the more detailed your outline, the easier it is to write your piece.

As you build your outline, pay particular attention to the way the parts of your outline relate to the whole. In other words, in addition to looking at the big picture, be sure to look at the individual pieces and find a logical way to connect them. For example, in writing this chapter, we first discussed writing as a whole, then broke down the various components of writing, and finally attempted to illustrate how those components relate to the whole as well as to each other.

If you are creating an outline for your own use—that is, no one but you will look at it—you can list the key points in your piece any way you want. If, however, your outline will be viewed by others, such as a professor or an editor, it's best to use a more formal outline structure.

Writing

You've come up with an idea. You've researched. You've organized your piece and (we hope) generated an outline. Finally, you're ready to begin writing. At this stage, your goal is to simply get your ideas on paper in a relatively cohesive form (you'll revise your work later), using your outline as a template. This first pass is called the *rough draft*.

When creating a rough draft, you should first examine your outline, making sure your research has addressed all the points contained in it. Then, formulate sentences that express the points in your outline, filling in the missing pieces as you go. You don't necessarily have to start at the beginning of your outline. If you prefer, begin in the middle and catch up as you go. When you finish, you should have a cohesive piece that conveys your idea.

Of course, these instructions for writing are rather simplified; unfortunately, the scope of this book does not permit an exhaustive examination of the writing process. There are, however, numerous titles on this topic available to the curious reader. A good one to try is *Webster's New World Student Writing Handbook, Second Edition*.

As you write, don't fret if your sentences contain grammatical errors or misspellings or if they don't seem to flow. You'll fix these problems when you revise your piece. Do, however, concern yourself with the following:

- Style
- Showing versus telling

STYLE

The word *style* typically means "a way of doing things." In terms of writing, style can refer to two things:

- The form of a piece of writing (for example, whether a letter has an inside address, a salutation, and a complimentary close)
- The use of words and sentence patterns

It is the second sense with which this section is concerned. The two primary ways to describe a style are by its preference for words of a certain kind (for example, familiar or unfamiliar, monosyllabic or polysyllabic, ornate or spare, and so on) and by its preference for certain sentence patterns or structures. As you write, notice whether your style is spare or ornate, simple or complex. Understand that there is no universally preferable style; find the one that suits you (and your piece) and go with it.

SHOWING VERSUS TELLING

Compare the following two paragraphs:

> When he heard the news, David was sad.

> When David learned that his mother was ill with cancer, his face crumpled, and his shoulders slumped. He swayed momentarily before folding his unsteady frame into his threadbare recliner and covering his face with his hands.

Notice that the second paragraph conveys David's sadness without explicitly stating that he was sad. This occurs through the use of specific details. You learn what "the news" is, and you "see" David's reaction. This is, in the world of writing, known as "showing versus telling." By showing the reader what is happening and enabling him to draw his own conclusions about what David is feeling, you engage him in a way that simply telling him how David felt won't allow. In essence, by showing rather than telling, you are proving to the reader that what you say is true.

The use of details can also help readers understand what kind of person or event is being portrayed in your writing. For example, noting that your subject (fictional or real) drinks decaffeinated lattes with skim milk and two packets of raw sugar is more revealing than simply noting that she drinks coffee. Likewise, noting that your subject drives a mint-condition cherry-red 1968 Mustang convertible is more revealing than noting that he drives a car. Of course, the most effective details are the ones that are the least expected—a hard-nosed cop's hidden love of haiku, for example, or a kindergarten teacher's heavy-metal CD collection.

Revising

After you finish your rough draft, it's time to hone your manuscript. This process is called *revision*—literally, "re-seeing." During this process, you "re-see" your piece, looking at it anew to determine what stays and what goes. During revision, you separate the wheat from the chaff of your piece, ensuring, as Rust Hills puts it in *Writing in General and the Short Story in Particular,* that "everything enhances everything, interrelates with everything else, is inseparable from everything else, and all this is done with a necessary and perfect economy."

During the revision phase of your writing, examine the following:

- Word choice
- Variety in sentence structure
- Flow

WORD CHOICE

To paraphrase the venerable William Strunk, Jr., coauthor of the classic grammar book *The Elements of Style,* just as a machine has no extra parts and a drawing has no extra lines, your writing should have no extra words. You must make every word in your piece count. If you can strip words from paragraphs or sentences while still retaining your intended meaning, do so. If you can use a single word to convey the meaning of several words (while maintaining the intended tone), do so. If you can use expressive language rather than passive language, do so.

Stripping Words

Eliminating unnecessary words, also called *tightening,* can help you focus your prose. Here's an example of a paragraph that, in addition to containing a sentence fragment, needs to be tightened:

> Since the beginning of time, technology has always been a business issue. From the growing copper-working industry looking for more efficient transportation methods, constructing two-wheeled carts in Mesopotamia about 3500 B.C.E., to today's struggle with information technology. Industry has struggled with taking the phone, fax, steam, electricity, computer, etc., and implementing them within their business processes.

Here's the same paragraph after it's been tightened. Notice how much easier it is to read:

> Technology has always been a business issue. Even in 3500 B.C., Mesopotamia's growing copper-working industry constructed two-wheeled carts for more efficient transportation; more recently, businesses have struggled to implement steam, electricity, phones, faxes, and computers into their processes.

One way to tighten your prose is to join several short sentences into one long one. Examine the sentences below:

> I enjoy surfing. I also enjoy scuba diving. I would like to surf and scuba dive more often.

You could combine these sentences into a single sentence:

> I enjoy surfing and scuba diving, and I would like to do both more often.

Here are other examples of sentences that were combined:

> Virgil was a Roman poet. Virgil is featured in Dante's *Inferno*.
> Virgil, the Roman poet, is featured in Dante's *Inferno*.

> Loveland Pass is a mountain pass. It is in the Colorado Rockies.
> Loveland Pass, a mountain pass, is in the Colorado Rockies.

> My neighbor is a painter. He painted our house.
> My neighbor, who is a painter, painted our house.

In addition, when tightening your prose, be on the lookout for wordy phrases that can easily be replaced by one or a few words, as in the following:

Wordy Phrase	Suggested Replacement
a majority of	most
a sufficient amount of	enough
along the lines of	like
at such time as	when
at the present time	now
at this point in time	now
be in a position to	can, be able to
by means of	by
come to a conclusion	conclude
despite the fact that	although
due to the fact that	because
during the time that	while
for the purpose of	to, for
for the reason that	because
give consideration to	consider, examine
give indication of	show, indicate, suggest
in a number of	several, many
in all cases	always
in close proximity to	near
in many cases	often
in most cases	usually

Wordy Phrase	Suggested Replacement
in no case	never
in some cases	sometimes
in the event that	if
in the near future	soon
in the neighborhood of	near, about, nearly
in the vicinity of	near
in this case	here
in view of the fact that	because
is capable of	can
is found to be	is
is in a position to	can
it is our opinion that	we think
it is possible that	perhaps
manner in which	how
notwithstanding the fact that	although
on the basis of	from, because, by
prior to	before
provided that	if
put an end to	end
reach a conclusion	conclude
subsequent to	after
the question as to	whether
with reference to	about
with the exception that	except that

Similar to wordy phrases are phrases that contain redundancies, such as the following:

Redundant Phrase	Suggested Replacement
added bonus	bonus
adequate enough	adequate (or enough)
advance planning	planning
basic essentials	basics (or essentials)
brief overview	overview

(continued)

Redundant Phrase	Suggested Replacement
close proximity	proximity
definite decision	decision
first priority	priority
free gift	gift
general rule	rule
green colored	green
joint cooperation	cooperation
major breakthrough	breakthrough
most optimal	optimum
necessary requirement	requirement
outside periphery	periphery
rate of speed	speed
resemble in appearance	resemble
twelve in number	twelve
unexpected surprise	surprise
usual rule	rule
very unique	unique

CHOOSING THE RIGHT WORD

If you take the time to select exactly the right word to express your intended meaning, you can increase the impact of your writing. When determining whether a word is the right one, you should consider the following:

- **Is the word specific?** That is, is there a word or phrase that would more completely convey your intended meaning? Mentioning that your character is wearing a skirt is less specific, and thus less descriptive, than mentioning that she is wearing a black leather micro-mini.
- **Does the word have unwanted connotations?** Many car dealerships have begun advertising their vast selection of "pre-owned cars" because, in their view, the word "used" has a negative connotation. You can control the way readers respond to your writing by recognizing the emotional overtones of certain words.
- **Is the word ambiguous?** Some sentences contain words that can mean more than one thing. For example, "Eloise has a funny expression on her face" could indicate that her expression is funny as in "amusing" or funny as in "odd." A better sentence might be "Eloise stuck out her tongue and crossed her eyes."

On Clarity

Avoiding the use of ambiguous words is only one way to improve the clarity of your writing. Here are a few other tips:

- Be precise.
    Vague: You shouldn't watch too much television.
    Better: You shouldn't watch more than one hour of television per day.
- Eliminate misplaced modifiers.
    Incorrect: Jack gave Joe his toy.
    Correct: Jack gave his toy to Joe.
    Correct: Jack returned Joe's toy to him.
- Avoid squinting modifiers.
    Vague: Seeing the children eating quickly caused Mother to lose her temper.
    Better: Mother quickly lost her temper upon seeing the children eating.
    Better: Mother lost her temper upon seeing the children eating quickly.
- Avoid hedge words.
    Vague: Smith died of an apparent heart attack.
    Better: Apparently, Smith died of a heart attack.
    Better: Smith died, apparently of a heart attack.
- **Is the word overused?** Has the word grown trite? Has its novelty gone? Such words are called *clichés* and should be avoided. If you must use a cliché, however, be certain you don't muddle it. For example, many people use the phrase "I could care less" instead of the correct version, "I couldn't care less," even though these two phrases convey opposite meanings.
- **Is it appropriate for the context in which it is being used?** If you are writing a novel about NASA scientists, it is unlikely that they would speak using street jargon (and vice versa).

EMPLOYING EXPRESSIVE LANGUAGE

The use of expressive language can improve your writing immensely. As an example, compare the following two paragraphs:

Bruges was pretty but the weather was lousy and I was in a bad mood. But I walked around and finally found a nice bench to rest on and read. Later, I walked back to the station but just missed a train to Brussels—I ran all the way from one end of the station to the other and took the steps to the platform two at a time, but an unsmiling worker wouldn't let me board.

Bruges, all cobblestones and spires, appealed to me, but the cold drizzle wrecked my mood. After trudging around town all morning, I collapsed on a sheltered bench and read a few chapters of *Les Miserables*. When the rain abated, I ambled to the train station; as I straggled in, a voice on the intercom announced the imminent departure of the Brussels-bound train. I sprinted the length of the station and scrambled up the steps to the platform two at a time, but a domineering conductor blocked my way when I tried to squeeze through the closing doors of the train.

Notice how the text in the second paragraph seems more vibrant, more descriptive. The narrator doesn't just "walk around"; rather, she "trudges." The weather isn't "lousy"; it's a "cold drizzle." The narrator doesn't "rest on" a bench; she "collapses" on it. She doesn't "run from one end of the station to the other"; instead, she "sprints" and "scrambles." The use of powerful verbs and precise details makes the second paragraph come alive.

Following are some tips to help you employ expressive language in your writing:

- Use active voice rather than passive voice.

  Passive: The carpet was designed by Elias.
  Active: Elias designed the carpet.

- Substitute descriptive verbs for vague verbs.

  Vague: Katherine went to the park.
  Better: Katherine walked to the park.
  Even Better: Katherine sauntered to the park.

- Condense your sentences to avoid wordiness and redundancy.

  Wordy: An appointment will prevent me from attending the meeting. I am going to the dentist, so I won't be there.
  Better: A dentist appointment will prevent me from attending the meeting.

- Eliminate overkill.

  Overkill: A peninsula surrounded on three sides by ocean
  Better: A peninsula

- Delete pointless words.

  Wordy: There is a woman who lives nearby who works as a waitress.
  Better: A woman who lives nearby works as a waitress.

- Replace long words with short words when possible.

  Long Word: Rudy had a huge contusion on his calf.
  Better: Rudy had a huge bruise on his calf.

- Eliminate adverbs that repeat an idea already expressed in the verb.

  Wordy: Jillian sped quickly to the scene.
  Better: Jillian sped to the scene.

- Eliminate adjectives that repeat an idea already expressed in the noun.

> **Wordy:** The ugly hag scolded us for trespassing.
> **Better:** The hag scolded us for trespassing.

VARIETY IN SENTENCE STRUCTURE

In addition to paring your sentences to their leanest form, it's important that you use many different sentence patterns so that readers don't perceive your writing as monotonous. For more information about sentence patterns, refer to Chapter 7, "Sentence Patterns."

On Repetition

Although it's a good practice to avoid repetition—be it in sentence structure or in content—there are times when repetition can help you emphasize an important point or lend a lyrical quality to your prose. That said, repetition, even when it's intentional, should be used sparingly.

In addition to using various sentence patterns, you should use both loose sentences and periodic sentences. Before you learn about the difference between loose and periodic sentences, however, you must understand that every sentence, whether it's loose or periodic, contains a basic statement, which may stand alone or may be buried in a longer sentence. Following are examples of basic statements:

Dogs slobber.
Rain is wet.
Christmas is on Tuesday.

A *loose sentence*, then, is one that contains a basic statement, along with a string of details. Loose structures typically expand on the verb or object:

> **Basic Statement:** Carrie wore a dress.
> **Loose Sentence:** Carrie wore a dress, which was a green taffeta Dior.

A *periodic sentence,* on the other hand, is one in which additional details are placed before or within the basic statement. Periodic structures typically expand on the subject or verb:

> **Basic Statement:** Snow is cold.
> **Periodic Sentence:** Snow, although it is received each year with open arms by kids and grownups alike, is cold.
> **Periodic Sentence:** Snow is, and always has been, cold.

Some sentences are both loose and periodic:

Basic Statement: Games are fun.
Combination Sentence: Games, especially card games, are fun—so much so that I frequently lose all sense of time when I play.

FLOW

You've pared down your sentences, taken care to choose the right words, revised your text to employ more expressive language, and made sure your sentences vary in structure—but something is still wrong: Your piece seems choppy. What's missing are *transitional devices,* which can help you ease your prose from one point to the next. These devices help you link each paragraph—or even each sentence—to the ones before and after it.

Following is an example of a paragraph lacking flow:

Jennifer was prepared for the test. Joseph was not. He hadn't even read the book on which he was being tested. He was nervous about the exam. He was sweating.

Here is the same paragraph, incorporating transitional devices to improve the flow:

Jennifer was prepared for the test. Joseph, on the other hand, was not. Indeed, he hadn't even read the book on which he was being tested. For this reason, he was nervous about the exam. In fact, he was sweating.

The main type of transitional device is the *transitional expression,* of which there are several types:

- **Contrast and qualification.** Using this type of device, you heighten the contrast between the point you've just made and the point you're about to make. This type of transitional device includes such words and phrases as the following:

    on the contrary
    conversely
    alternatively
    however
    in contrast
    still
    yet
    nevertheless
    on the other hand

The following sentences provide examples of the contrast and qualification transitional device:

> In light of the present circumstances, quitting your job seems the thing to do. On the other hand, the economy is slow, which may make finding other work difficult.

> I realize David can be annoying. Nevertheless, he is a decent man, and he means well.

- **Continuity.** Using this type of device, you further the point you are attempting to make by providing a secondary argument. This type of transitional device includes such words and phrases as the following:

  > besides
  > furthermore
  > in addition
  > also
  > secondly
  > to continue
  > next
  > similarly
  > likewise
  > moreover
  > indeed
  > again
  > in other words

These sentences make good use of continuity transition:

> Bill is an asset to the company. Furthermore, he's an upstanding citizen. The food at Wellington's is much tastier than the food at Joe's Grill. Besides, Wellington's is less expensive.

- **Cause and effect.** Using this type of device, you illustrate how one point relates to the next. This type of transitional device includes such words and phrases as the following:

  > thus
  > therefore
  > as a result
  > consequently
  > hence
  > for this reason

The following sentences suggest cause and effect in their use of this type of transitional device:

Patrick is very tall and athletic. For this reason, he is an excellent candidate for the varsity basketball team.

Denzel is a horrible cook. Therefore, we will order out tonight.

- **Exemplification.** This type of device enables you to support a point you are attempting to make by providing specific details. This type of transitional device includes such words and phrases as the following:

> for instance
> for example
> in fact
> in particular
> specifically
> to illustrate

The following sentences provide examples of reinforcing a point with this type of transitional device:

> Several children in the class are excellent readers. In particular, Jose, Hiro, and Jamie have demonstrated great reading comprehension.

> Dogs are very loyal. In fact, our dog follows me wherever I go and protects me from strangers.

- **Summation.** Using this type of device, you sum up points you've already made. This type of transitional device includes such words and phrases as the following:

> finally
> in conclusion
> to sum up
> in brief
> as we have seen

These sentences demonstrate the summation transitional device:

> As we have seen, dinosaurs were fascinating creatures.
> To sum up, planning a wedding can be a daunting task.

Proofreading

No matter what type of writing you perform—be it an essay, a technical document, a novel, or a simple advertisement—proofreading is an important component of the writing process. It is the very last step of your journey, occurring after you have revised your piece—perhaps more than once—for clarity and accuracy (but, obviously, before you submit the final piece to your publisher, professor, or peers). Proofreading enables you to catch those small embarrassing mistakes that can make or break your writing.

In its strictest sense, the word *proofreading* refers to the inspection and marking of proofs during the printing process. As such, proofreaders are concerned not only with grammatical errors but also with such issues as spacing, leading, alignment, and the like. This section employs the word *proofreading* in a less strict sense—that is, as concerning the correction of grammatical errors.

WHAT TO LOOK FOR

Proofreading is, it would seem, a simple process: You read your piece and, drawing on what you've learned in earlier parts of this book, locate and correct errors. You'll want to check in particular for errors in punctuation, grammar, and usage. Chances are these errors will leap out at you as you carefully read your work; even so, here are some common problems for which you should be on the lookout:

- Misspelled words

    Incorrect: Our neighborhood nursery sells shurbs.
    Correct: Our neighborhood nursery sells shrubs.

- Improperly capitalized words

    Incorrect: Kevin and I visited Kevin's Mother.
    Correct: Kevin and I visited Kevin's mother.

- Subjects and verbs that disagree

    Incorrect: Gerry and I was exhausted after spending the day in the hot sun.
    Correct: Gerry and I were exhausted after spending the day in the hot sun.

- Pronouns and antecedents that disagree, either in number or in gender

    Incorrect: The smart painter cleans their brushes after finishing work.
    Correct: The smart painter cleans his or her brushes after finishing work.
    Correct: Smart painters clean their brushes after finishing work.

- Incorrect verb forms, particularly with irregular verbs

    Incorrect: We drug the garbage to the curb.
    Correct: We dragged the garbage to the curb.

- Inaccurate punctuation that dilutes the meaning of a sentence

  Incorrect: Franklin, and George, bought a puppy, at the pet store.
  Correct: Franklin and George bought a puppy at the pet store.

- Shifts in tense

  Incorrect: We walk into the bar, and the bartender served us each a beer.
  Correct: We walked into the bar, and the bartender served us each a beer.

- Shifts in person

  Incorrect: Janis is my favorite waitress. She'll never lets me down. She pours you a cup of coffee before you've even sat down.
  Correct: Janis is my favorite waitress. She never lets me down. She pours me a cup of coffee before I've even sat down.

- Misrelated modifiers

  Incorrect: Helen purchased a new jacket from the store that she liked.
  Correct: Helen purchased a new jacket that she liked from the store.
  Correct: Helen purchased from the store that she liked a new jacket.

- Run-ons and sentence fragments

  Incorrect: I saw Peter he was sleepy but he was going to work anyway.
  Correct: I saw Peter. He was sleepy, but he was going to work anyway.
  Incorrect: I was buzzing. Wired from the long flight.
  Correct: I was buzzing, wired from the long flight.

If you have written your piece using a word-processing program on your computer, you may be tempted to simply use that program's spell-checking feature instead of proofreading it with your own eyes. Relying on your word processor to find mistakes, however, is a risky endeavor. For example, although your spell-checker will bring to your attention any words that do not appear in its dictionary, it may not alert you to words that are incorrectly used—especially if you are working with an older word-processing program. Thus, common errors, such as the use of *there* instead of *their* or *it's* instead of *its* may well be overlooked.

PROOFREADER'S SIGNS AND SYMBOLS

If you are proofreading your own work, and you will be the person to draft the final, corrected version, you can mark up your pages any way you want. You may have developed your own personal shorthand over the years; feel free to use it.

If, however, someone else will be applying your corrections to the final version (a secretary or typist, for example), or if you are proofreading the work of another person, you'll likely need to use the standardized proofreader's marks employed by journalists, editors, printers, and the like.

The following table lists the proofreader's marks you'll most likely encounter or need to use. (Note that there are more marks at your disposal than are discussed here; most of the marks not included in this list relate to typesetting rather than style or grammar per se. For a complete list, refer to *The Chicago Manual of Style, 15th Edition*.)

Be aware that proofreader's marks may vary somewhat; the ones shown in the following table are currently in common, but not ubiquitous, usage.

Mark	Meaning
♪	Delete. Place this mark in the margin to indicate that something be removed from a line—be it a single letter, a word or words, or the entire line—without substitution. Then draw a diagonal line through the letter to be deleted or a straight line through the word or words to be deleted to indicate where the deletion should be made. If you are deleting several lines, draw a circle around the lines to be deleted and add the delete mark in the margin. Note: Do not use this mark if the the deleted matter should be substituted with another letter, word, or line; in that case, circle the letter, word, or words to be replaced, and write the correct text in the margin.
⌣	Close up. Use this mark to indicate too much space between letters.
⌒	Delete and close up. Use this mark when deleting a letter or letters within a word.
stet	Let stand. Use this notation to indicate that a previous notation should be disregarded. To clarify what text should remain unchanged, place dots under the incorrectly marked word or words in the body of the text.
#	Insert space. Draw this symbol in the margin to indicate that a space should be added; place a vertical line or caret in the body of the text where the space should be inserted.
¶	Begin new paragraph. Place this symbol in the margin to indicate that a paragraph should be broken in two. To indicate the first word in the new paragraph, place an L-shaped mark to the left and partly under the word in the body of the text.
run in	Run in. Write *run in* in the margin and draw a line from the end of the one paragraph to the beginning of the next to indicate that the two paragraphs should be combined.

(continued)

Mark	Meaning
∿	Transpose. If you discover that words or letters are out of order, draw the transpose symbol over and under the affected text and write *tr* in the margin. You can move a word or words to a different line by circling the text to be moved and drawing a line from the circle to the spot where the text should be inserted (avoid drawing the line through words or punctuation).
(sp)	Spell out. Circle any abbreviations or numerals that should be spelled out and place the spell-out sign in the margin.
ital	Set in italic type. Draw a single line under the word you want to italicize and write *ital* in the margin.
rom	Set in roman type. If text has been incorrectly italicized, circle it and write *rom* in the margin.
bf	Set in boldface type. Draw a wavy line under the word you want boldfaced and write *bf* in the margin.
lc	Set in lowercase. Draw a slash through any capital letters that should be changed to lowercase and write *lc* in the margin.
cap	Set in capital letters. Circle or draw three short lines under any lowercase letter that should be capitalized and write *cap* in the margin.

These marks should be made in the margin on the same line as the error. If a line requires more than one correction, the marks should appear in order, with a slash after each one. If a line requires many corrections, cross out the entire line and write the correct text in the margin. For longer corrections, cross out the entire passage, type the correct text on a separate sheet, attach the separate sheet to the marked-up page, and write *insert attached* in the marked-up page's margin.

MARKING CHANGES IN PUNCTUATION

As you proofread your work (or the work of others), you'll no doubt encounter instances of punctuation that you'd like to change either for accuracy or for effect.

The best way to change one punctuation mark to another is to circle or draw a line through the offending mark and then place the correct mark in the margin. To add a mark where none appears, draw a caret (^) at the spot where the mark belongs and then draw the correct mark in the margin. Certain marks, however, may seem indistinguishable from each other. For example, handwritten commas, apostrophes, and parentheses may appear identical. For this reason, you should draw these marks in the margin as follows:

- Place a caret over a comma.
- Place an inverted caret under an apostrophe or quotation marks.
- Draw your parentheses in such a way that they are large enough not to be confused with commas and apostrophes. Alternatively, you can draw two short, horizontal lines through each parenthesis to distinguish it from other marks.

Likewise, hyphens, en dashes, and em dashes are often indistinguishable when drawn by hand. Differentiate them by employing their appropriate symbols in the margin:

=	Insert hyphen
M̲	Insert em dash
N	Insert en dash

Here are a few more marks that can cause confusion:

- Periods can be so small as to seem invisible in the margin. For this reason, you should circle any periods you mark.
- A question mark in the margin might be mistaken for a query. If you mean to add a question mark to a point in the text, you should follow the mark in the margin with the word *set* and circle the word.
- A letter with a missing or incorrect accent or diacritical mark should be completely crossed out, and the letter and correct accent should be written in the margin.

Semicolons, colons, and exclamation points, if written clearly, need no further identifying marks.

The sample paragraph on page 308 has been proofread and marked using the symbols and techniques discussed in this chapter.

Try to find someone to look over your work for you. Sometimes, if you've been staring at the same piece of writing for several hours, it's impossible to catch the errors it contains. A fresh pair of eyes can be a lifesaver. Alternatively, if you have time, put the piece away for a few days and then come back to it. You'll likely find many more errors than you would have otherwise.

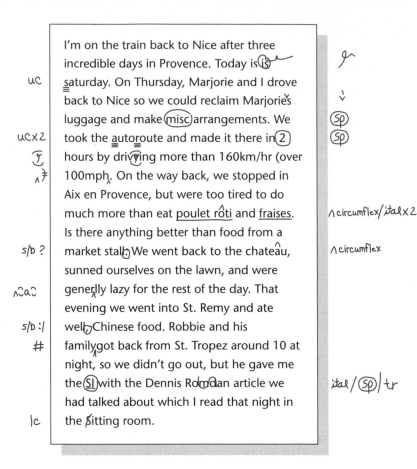

I'm on the train back to Nice after three incredible days in Provence. Today is saturday. On Thursday, Marjorie and I drove back to Nice so we could reclaim Marjorie's luggage and make misc arrangements. We took the autoroute and made it there in 2 hours by driving more than 160km/hr (over 100mph. On the way back, we stopped in Aix en Provence, but were too tired to do much more than eat poulet rôti and fraises. Is there anything better than food from a market stall We went back to the chateau, sunned ourselves on the lawn, and were generlly lazy for the rest of the day. That evening we went into St. Remy and ate well Chinese food. Robbie and his family got back from St. Tropez around 10 at night, so we didn't go out, but he gave me the SI with the Dennis Roman article we had talked about which I read that night in the sitting room.

Margin markings: uc · uc×2 · s/b ? · s/b :/ · # · lc · ∧circumflex/ital×2 · ∧circumflex · ital/sp/tr

General Observations about Writing

- In the prewriting phase, the writer might generate ideas, research, and organize the piece.
- When trying to generate ideas, try any or all of the following:
  - Draw on life experiences
  - Talk to people
  - Reflect
  - Write in a journal or blog
  - Read
  - Brainstorm
- Your research might involve any of the following:
  - Reading books, magazines, newspapers, pamphlets, or other materials

- ○ Watching films, videos, or other broadcasts
- ○ Listening to audio recordings
- ○ Interviewing people
- ○ Searching the Internet
- Most types of writing require one to pay at least some attention to organization and structure before putting pen to paper.
- Many writers need to construct outlines before progressing to the writing stage. The more detailed your outline, the easier it is to actually write your piece.
- In the writing stage, your goal is to simply get your ideas on paper in a relatively cohesive form, using your outline as a template. (You'll revise your work later to correct grammatical errors and misspellings and to improve flow.) This first pass is called the *rough draft*.
- As you write, concern yourself with the following:
  - ○ Style. The word *style* in this case refers to the use of words and sentence patterns.
  - ○ Showing versus telling. By showing the reader what is happening and enabling him to draw his own conclusions about what he is reading, you engage him in a way that simply telling him won't allow.
- During the revision process, you "re-see" your piece, looking at it anew to determine what stays and what goes.
- During the revision phase of your writing, examine the following:
  - ○ Word choice
  - ○ Variety in sentence structure
  - ○ Flow
- Eliminating unnecessary words, also called *tightening,* can help you focus your prose.
- If you take the time to select exactly the right word to express your intended meaning, you can increase the impact of your writing.
- The use of expressive language—for example, active voice rather than passive voice—can improve your writing immensely.
  - ○ It's important to use many different sentence patterns so that readers don't perceive your writing as monotonous.
  - ○ Try to employ both loose sentences and periodic sentences in your writing. A *loose sentence* is one that contains a basic statement, along with a string of details. A *periodic sentence* is one in which additional details are placed before or within the basic statement.
- Transitional devices can help you ease your prose from one point to the next. These devices help you link each paragraph—or even each sentence—to the ones before and after it.

- Proofreading enables you to catch those small embarrassing mistakes that can make or break your writing. It is the very last step of your journey, occurring after you have revised your piece but before you submit the final piece to your publisher, professor, or peers.
- When proofreading, be on the lookout for these common problems:
  - Misspelled words
  - Improperly capitalized words
  - Subjects and verbs that disagree
  - Pronouns and antecedents that disagree, either in number or in gender
  - Incorrect verb forms, particularly with irregular verbs
  - Inaccurate punctuation that dilutes the meaning of a sentence
  - Shifts in tense
  - Shifts in person
  - Misrelated modifiers
  - Run-ons and sentence fragments
- If someone else will be applying your corrections to the final version, or if you are proofreading the work of another person, you'll likely need to use the standardized proofreader's marks employed by journalists, editors, typesetters, printers, and the like.
- Proofreading marks should be made in the margin on the same line as the error. If a line requires more than one correction, the marks should appear in order, each separated by a slash.
- Try to find someone to look over your work for you; a fresh pair of eyes can be a lifesaver.

MISUSED WORDS AND EXPRESSIONS

Some problems of language command cannot be discussed according to principles of function. These problems consist of words and expressions that have been misused by many people over a long period of time or words that, while acceptable in slang form, are not appropriate in formal speaking and writing. The ensuing list illuminates such troublesome problems and provides practical applications in usage for many of the problem words or expressions.

Bear in mind that language is in a constant state of change. What was once unacceptable may be acceptable today. The words *awful* and *sick* are good examples. While *awful* once meant "inspiring awe" or "exalted," it now has taken on the meaning (in informal usage) of "very" or "unpleasant."

> My brother was awfully tired after the race.
> We all felt just awful after eating the pie.

When the word is used with its original meaning of "inspiring awe," it is sometimes given a special (though generally unrecognized) spelling of aweful. The word is best avoided.

Likewise, many of us were informed as young children that *sick* and *ill* had special meanings: *sick* meant "mentally imbalanced," and *ill* meant "physically ailing." Of course, this distinction is no longer recognized. Now, when *sick* is used, it may mean "affected with disease," "ill," "ailing in body or mind," or "suffering from an upset stomach." *Ill* means "not in good health" or "suffering from a physical disorder caused by poor health." In other words, the two terms are now generally used interchangeably—although a distinction does exist in formal usage.

Nevertheless, various words have been used in specific ways and with specific meanings for a long enough period of time to be accorded certain stature in English usage. To be certain that your language employs words with precise meanings and reflects creditably upon you—especially in formal situations—you would indeed be wise to learn distinctions between similar words that are in common use. As such, in addition to presenting frequently misused expressions and idioms and slang terms that are best avoided, the guide presented in this appendix is designed to help you learn such distinctions.

You will find a variety of definitions for most of the words presented in this section if you consult any standard dictionary. This guide cannot present all the many uses and definitions of any given word. Instead, it is intended to help you navigate some of the many trouble spots that exist and to serve as a quick reference. As always, when you're uncertain about the use or definition of a word, you should rely on a good dictionary to help clarify the situation.

A, AN: Use *a* before a word beginning with a consonant sound, including the "long U" sound (as in *uniform*). Use *an* before a word beginning with a vowel sound, even if the first letter of the word is a consonant (as in *an honest person*).

> **Correct:** Most of us waited for *an* hour.
> **Correct:** John works for *a* utility company.
> **Correct:** Sally is truly *a* fine and honest person.

A HALF, A HALF A, HALF A: Use *half a* or *a half,* but avoid the redundant *a half a.*

> **Correct:** I'd love *half a* piece of cake.

A LOT, A WHOLE LOT, LOTS, LOTS OF: Avoid using these expressions, which are often employed to mean "much, many, a great deal." See *alot.*

> **Incorrect:** Almost everyone would enjoy having *lots of* money.
> **Incorrect:** We need *a whole lot* of help during the tournament.
> **Correct:** The visitor certainly had *many* friends.

A WHILE, AWHILE: Be sure to distinguish between the adverb *awhile* and the article and noun *a while.* As an object of a preposition, *a while* is always written as two words.

> **Correct:** Wait *awhile* to see if we've been chosen to be delegates.
> **Correct:** We played volleyball on the beach for *a while.*

A WHOLE LOT, LOTS, LOTS OF, A LOT: See *a lot, a whole lot, lots, lots of.*

A.D., B.C.: A.D. (*anno Domini*) should always precede the date; B.C. (before Christ) should always follow the date (A.D. 1936, 356 B.C.). B.C. is frequently replaced by B.C.E., meaning "before common era."

A.M., P.M. (also a.m., p.m.): Use these expressions only with figures; do not use them to stand for the words *morning* and *afternoon.*

> **Incorrect:** We plan to be finished early in the *p.m.*
> **Correct:** The flight is scheduled to depart at 7:00 *A.M.*

ABILITY, CAPACITY: *Ability* is one's power (mental or physical) to do a thing, or one's talent; *capacity* is the power to receive or to contain or acquire an ability.

> **Correct:** You have the *ability* to master calculus.
> **Correct:** This much information is beyond his capacity to retain.

ABOVE: Avoid using *above* to refer to that which has already been written—except in legal documents, unless, perhaps, the reference is to something on the same page. Use *preceding* instead.

> **Incorrect:** Be sure that you follow the *above* instructions.
> **Correct:** The text in the *preceding* paragraph introduces the list that follows.

ACCEPT, EXCEPT: Do not confuse these two words as verbs. *Accept* means "to receive"; *except* means "to exclude."

> **Correct:** John has been *accepted* into club membership.
> **Correct:** The committee *excepted* his infraction of the rules and *accepted* his report.

AD: This shortening of the word *advertisement* is unacceptable in formal writing.

> **Incorrect:** The fraternity ran a long *ad* in the campus newspaper.

ADMISSION, ADMITTANCE: *Admission* is the power to enter after paying a price; *admittance* is the physical act of entering.

> **Correct:** Your *admission* to (your right to enter) the club depends upon your attitude and behavior.
> **Correct:** The demonstrators' *admittance* to the president's home was blocked by the police.
> **Correct:** Sally gained *admittance* to the theater after she paid the price of *admission*.
> **Correct:** With this pass, I am guaranteed *admittance*.

ADVICE, ADVISE: *Advice* is a suggestion of how to act; *advise* means "to suggest to another person a course of action or behavior."

> **Correct:** May I offer you a piece of *advice* on handling your mother-in-law?
> **Correct:** Please *advise* me on selecting a college.

AFFECT, EFFECT: *Affect* is a verb meaning "to influence" or "to have a bearing upon"; it is also a noun meaning "the observable manifestations of a subjectively experienced emotion." *Effect* is also both a verb and a noun. As a verb, it means "to bring to pass"; as a noun, it means "result."

Correct: How this weather will *affect* the crops is uncertain.
Correct: The *effect* (noun) of loud noise on hearing ability is well known.
Correct: We hope to *effect* (verb) a solution to the impasse.

AGGRAVATE, ANNOY, IRRITATE: *To aggravate* is to make worse an already bad condition; *to annoy* is to cause worry, trouble, or concern; *to irritate* is to cause to be inflamed or sore.

Correct: The tight shoe *irritated* his blister.
Correct: Elena *aggravated* her shoulder injury by attempting an overhead serve.
Correct: Children often *annoy* parents by their selection of music.

AIN'T: This is an illiterate contraction for *am not, are not, is not, has not,* and *have not.* Avoid using *ain't.*

ALIBI: Do not use this expression to mean "excuse." *Alibi* is proper only in its technical legal sense—proof that one could not have committed an act because one was not present at the time and place where the act was committed.

Correct: What *excuse* do you have for arriving two hours late?
Correct: The suspect had an *alibi* for the night of the crime.

ALL READY, ALREADY: *Already* (one word) means "prior to some specified time, either past, present, or future." *All ready* (two words) means "completely ready."

Correct: The day just startcd, and I am *already* running late!
Correct: Having completed almost all my training runs over the last several months, I feel *all ready* to run in the marathon.
Correct: Are we *all ready* to go to the theater?

ALL RIGHT, ALRIGHT: *Alright* is a corrupt spelling of *all right.* It is not generally accepted in formal writing.

Correct: Betty is *all right* as our representative.
Incorrect: It should be *alright* for you to finish the job tomorrow.

ALL THE: *All the farther, all the faster, all the higher,* and similar expressions should not be used for *as far as, as fast as,* or *as high as.*

ALL TOGETHER, ALTOGETHER: *Altogether* (one word) means "wholly, in all, thoroughly." *All together* (two words) means "in a group."

Correct: Ms. Brown said to the class, "Many of you have written thesis statements that are *altogether* too vague."
Correct: Please bring your papers to me so that they will be *all together.*

ALLOW, LEAVE, LET, PERMIT: To allow is to tolerate or to approve, to show for-bearance. *To let* is to demonstrate indifference. *To permit* is to approve from a position of authority, to grant permission. *To leave* is to depart, to go away. Do not use these terms interchangeably.

> **Correct:** Our neighbor *let* his roof leak all spring.
> **Correct:** James *permitted* his daughter to drive his new car.
> **Correct:** *Leave* me alone; I don't want any company right now!
> **Correct:** We cannot *allow* students to make noise all night long.

ALLUDE, REFER: *To allude* is to make indirect reference; *to refer* is to mention something specifically.

> **Correct:** The story in the newspaper *alluded* to the candidate's war record but did not discuss it in explicit terms.
> **Correct:** The speaker *referred* to Act V, Scene ii, of *Macbeth*.

ALLUSION, DELUSION, ILLUSION: An *allusion* is an indirect reference; an *illusion* is an unreal image or a false visual impression; a *delusion* is an error of the mind or a false belief.

> **Correct:** The lecturer made an *allusion* to Beethoven's hearing loss.
> **Correct:** The oasis was only an *illusion*.
> **Correct:** My aunt has *delusions* of extreme wealth.

ALMOST, MOST: Do not use *most* in place of *almost*. *Almost* means "nearly"; *most* means "greatest in quantity or number."

> **Correct:** *Most* of the ponies were pintos.
> **Correct:** *Almost* all the money had been wasted on sweets.

ALOT: Avoid this misspelling and generally ineffective expression. See *a lot, a whole lot, lots, lots of.*

ALREADY, ALL READY: See *all ready, already*.

ALRIGHT, ALL RIGHT: See *all right, alright*.

ALTAR, ALTER: An *altar* is a raised structure used in worship; *alter* means "to change or modify."

> **Correct:** Could you please *alter* these pants to make them shorter?
> **Correct:** The archaeologist found an *altar* near the ancient burial grounds.

ALTERNATE, ALTERNATIVE: *Alternative* means "available as another choice," "unconventional," or "one of two possibilities." It should not be confused with *alternate*, which means "every other."

> **Correct:** You could mow the lawn or, as an *alternative,* you could clean out the basement.
> **Correct:** Our pottery class meets on *alternate* Tuesdays.

ALTERNATIVE, CHOICE: Use *alternative* only to show an option between two things; for more than two, use *choice.*

> **Correct:** Naturally, he selected the most expensive of the many *choices.*
> **Incorrect:** The stern father gave his son four *alternatives.*

ALTHOUGH, THOUGH: Both terms are acceptable and may be used interchangeably. However, you should be consistent in your use of the terms throughout a composition.

ALTOGETHER, ALL TOGETHER: See *all together, altogether.*

ALUMNA, ALUMNUS: *Alumnus* is a male graduate; *alumni,* two or more male graduates. *Alumna* is a female graduate; *alumnae,* two or more female graduates. *Alumni* is used when both male and female graduates are grouped together.

> **Correct:** She and Bess are both *alumnae* of the same university.

AMATEUR, NOVICE: An *amateur* is one who does not accept payment for his efforts; a *novice* is an unskilled beginner in some endeavor.

> **Correct:** The Olympics were originally designed for *amateur* athletes, although many professional athletes are now allowed to participate.
> **Correct:** This knitting book is perfect for the *novice* knitter; it covers the basics of that craft.

AMONG, BETWEEN: *Among* always refers to more than two. *Between* refers to only two.

> **Correct:** The conquered territory was divided *between* the two victors.
> **Correct:** Can we keep a secret *among* the four of us?

AMORAL, IMMORAL: *Amoral* means "without moral standards, without preconceived notions of right or wrong." *Immoral* means "contrary to moral codes or acceptable social standards, evil."

> **Correct:** Mrs. Sylvester taught the history of the Aztecs from an *amoral* perspective.
> **Correct:** Ultimately it was decided—and rightfully so—that slavery is *immoral.*

AMOUNT, NUMBER: Use *amount* to refer to things in bulk or mass; use *number* to refer to objects that can be counted.

>**Correct:** The *amount* of smog in the air is disturbing.
>**Correct:** The *number* of people at the concert was surprising.

AN, A: See *a, an.*

AND ETC.: Never place *and* before *etc.* The *and* is redundant, because *etc.* is an abbreviation for *et* (*and*) and *cetera* (*other things*).

>**Incorrect:** Write the alphabet in reverse order—that is, z, y, *and etc.*

AND WHICH, BUT WHICH: Do not corrupt subordination by inserting *and* or *but* before a subordinate clause. However, *and* or *but* may be used before *which* to join two *which* clauses.

>**Correct:** The car, which I bought yesterday and *which* was represented as being new was, in fact, well used.
>**Incorrect:** Katie read the trilogy by Crabb, and which she enjoyed very much.

ANGLE: Do not use *angle* to mean "point of view, phase, or facet."

>**Incorrect:** Let's look at another *angle* of this problem.
>**Correct:** If you want another *point of view* on the matter, ask Sue.

ANNOY, IRRITATE, AGGRAVATE: See *aggravate, annoy, irritate.*

ANTE-, ANTI-: *Ante-* means "before," as in *antebellum. Anti-* means "against," as in *anti-Castro.* The hyphen is used after *anti-* before words beginning with capital letters and before words beginning with the letter *I,* as in *anti-imperialist.*

ANYONE, ANY ONE: *Anyone* (one word) means "any person." *Any one* (two words) means "any single person or thing."

>**Correct:** *Any one* of the three sisters will baby-sit for you.
>**Correct:** Can *anyone* help me lift this table?

ANYWAYS: Do not use *anyways* for *anyway.*

ANXIOUS, EAGER: *Anxious* means "concerned, worried"; *eager* means "excited."

>**Correct:** The students were *anxious* about the final examination.
>**Correct:** I'm certainly not *eager* to see my test score.

APPARENTLY, EVIDENTLY: *Apparently* means "seems to be but may not be"; *evidently* means "both seems to be and is."

Correct: *Apparently,* the mail carrier has not been here; we don't have any mail. (Perhaps we received no mail today.)

Correct: *Evidently,* the mail carrier has been here; I see his tracks in the snow. (The evidence confirms the observation.)

APT, LIABLE, LIKELY: Use *likely* to express probability, *liable* to suggest the idea of responsibility, and *apt* to express predisposition or dexterity.

Correct: Louise has demonstrated that she is *apt* in music.

Correct: You are not *likely* to win the lottery.

Correct: The motorist is *liable* to pay for the damage.

AROUND: Do not use *around* to mean "about" or "near."

Incorrect: We had *around* five dollars between us.

Correct: We had *about* 40 dollars in the bank.

AS . . . AS . . . , SO . . . AS . . . : Use *as . . . as . . .* for a positive comparison; use *so . . . as . . .* for a negative comparison.

Correct: My horse is *as* fast *as* your horse, but it is not *so* fast *as* LuAnn's.

Incorrect: This new plane is not nearly *as* large *as* the older model.

AS, AS IF, LIKE: *Like* is a preposition and must have an object. *As* and *as if* are conjunctions; therefore, they connect but do not show an absolute relationship.

Correct: Ellen acts *as if* she were ill.

Correct: Tom looks *like* his father.

AS TO: Do not use *as to* as a substitute for *about* or *regarding.*

Incorrect: He spoke *as to* the need for more effort.

Incorrect: Mr. Fritzvold talked with me *as to* his conducting the tour.

ASSERT, MAINTAIN: To *assert* is "to declare, to state"; to *maintain* is "to affirm, to claim to be true, to defend."

Correct: James *asserted* that he would, in fact, win the game.

Correct: I *maintain* that I could outrun Jerry, if he would only agree to a race.

ASSET: *Asset* is grossly overused to mean "resource, support, or source of strength." In fact, *asset* means "a thing or quality of value."

Correct: Rich soil is a great *asset* to a farmer.

Questionable: Her friends were a great *asset* to her.

Incorrect: Your being here is a real *asset* to our cause.

ASSURE, ENSURE, INSURE: *Assure* means "to guarantee, convince"; *ensure* means "to make certain"; *insure* means "to protect against financial loss by means of a legal contract."

> **Correct:** I *assure* you, I have no intention of leaving.
> **Correct:** To *ensure* our safety, the pilot demanded we wear seatbelts.
> **Correct:** You should *insure* that necklace; it is very valuable.

AT: The *at* is redundant in such expressions as these: *Where is the book at? Where did you sleep at?* Avoid such uses.

AT ABOUT: The *at* is unnecessary. Use *about* without *at*.

> **Incorrect:** We left the house *at about* nine o'clock.

AVAIL: *Of no avail* should be used only with some form of *be* or a linking verb.

> **Correct:** Our efforts seemed *of no avail* against the flood.

AVOCATION, VOCATION: An *avocation* is a hobby; a *vocation* is one's regular work or profession.

> **Correct:** Golf is his *avocation* above all others.
> **Correct:** I'm an attorney by *vocation*, but I sing for fun.

AWFUL: Use *awful* or *awfully* to mean "bad, fearsome." Do not use *awful* for such adverbs as "very," "really," and "extremely."

> **Incorrect:** The accident had *awfully* bad results.
> **Correct:** This soup tastes *awful*.

AWHILE, A WHILE: See *a while, awhile*.

B.C., A.D.: See *A.D., B.C.*

BACK OF: See *in back of*.

BAD: Do not use *bad* as an adverb; use *badly*. Use *bad* as an *adjective*.

> **Correct:** She feels *bad* about the loss of her pet.
>   (The verb *feels* in this sentence is a linking verb; *bad* is a predicate adjective.)
> **Correct:** Eric behaved *badly* at Nan's birthday party.
>   (*Badly* indicates how Eric behaved. It is an adverb.)

BADLY: Do not use *badly* to mean "very much" or with verbs to signify *want* or *need*. Use a word such as *truly, seriously, surely, really*.

Incorrect: We *badly* need a new car.
Correct: Because of his injury, he plays *badly*.
Incorrect: The team *badly* needs your support.

BALANCE, REST: *Balance* is an accountant's term meaning "the excess shown on either side"; *rest* means "that which is left over."

Incorrect: The *balance* of the students have left the campus already.

BANK ON, TAKE STOCK IN: Avoid these two expressions to mean "rely on" or "trust in."

Incorrect: It is not a good practice to *bank* entirely *on* luck.

BE BACK: In formal writing, avoid using this expression to mean "return."

Correct: I expect to *return* at noon.

BECAUSE: Do not use *because* to introduce a noun clause.

Incorrect: The reason he did not attend was *because* he was in Chicago that evening.
Incorrect: *Because* I'm angry is why I've resigned.

BECAUSE, SINCE: Do not use these words interchangeably. Because is used to indicate the cause or reason for an action; since is meant to indicate the beginning point of an action.

Incorrect: Lainey ate only half her lunch since she wasn't hungry.
Correct: Lainey ate only half her lunch because she wasn't hungry.
Correct: It's been only two hours since Lainey ate.

BEING AS, BEING THAT: Do not use these two expressions to mean "because."

Incorrect: *Being that* you are ready, why don't you go first?
Correct: *Because* I was ill, I missed the last lecture.

BELOW: Avoid using *below* to refer to text or illustrations to come unless, perhaps, the reference is to something on the same page. Use *following* instead.

Incorrect: Discussed *below* is the procedure for tuning a guitar.
Correct: As shown in the following illustration, the automobile is quite large.

BESIDE, BESIDES: Do not confuse these two words. *Beside* is a preposition meaning "by the side of." *Besides,* used chiefly as an adverb, means "in addition to."

Correct: Martha usually sits *beside* me in class.
Correct: Who *besides* Leslie knows the answer to that problem?

BETWEEN, AMONG: See *among, between*.

BLAME ON: Use *blame for*.

Correct: They *blamed* us *for* the loss of power.
Incorrect: The coach *blamed* the loss *on* the quarterback.
(This sentence should be recast to read "The coach blamed the quarterback for the loss.")

BORN, BORNE: *Born* means "brought into being or existence"; *borne* means "carried" or "endured."

Correct: Heidi was *born* on September 19, 2000.
Correct: *Borne* aloft by a hot-air balloon, Jake surveyed the land below.

BOUND, DETERMINED: Bound means "obligated"; determined means "resolved." (The cliché "bound and determined" is acceptable.)

Correct: The child seemed *determined* to have his way.
Correct: According to this document, you are *bound* to remain for another year in your present position.
Correct: The twins seemed *determined* to injure themselves.

BRING, TAKE: Use *bring* to mean "to convey something to the person speaking"; use *take* to mean "to convey something away from the person speaking." *Bring* is related to *come; take,* to go.

Correct: *Take* the papers to the principal's office when you go.
Correct: I shall *bring* the books to class next time I come.

BUNCH: Do not use *bunch* to mean "group of people." *Bunch* properly refers to things that grow together in clumps—bananas, grapes, and so on.

Incorrect: Did you see that *bunch* of people who boarded the plane?

BURSTED, BUST, BUSTED: These are corrupt forms of the verb *burst,* which has the same form for all its principal parts.

Incorrect: Stevie *busted* through the door in hot pursuit of Mike.

BUT WHAT: Do not use this expression as a substitute for *that*.

BUT WHICH, AND WHICH: See *and which, but which*.

CALCULATE: Do not use this word to mean "think, guess, plan."

CAN, MAY: *Can* denotes ability; *may* denotes possibility or permission.

> **Correct:** Mother said we *may* go to the circus.
> **Correct:** Even with an injured leg, that horse *can* still run fast.
> **Correct:** *May* I help you with that package?

CANNOT HELP BUT: This is considered a double negative. Use *cannot help* with a gerund.

> **Incorrect:** We *cannot help but* feel compassion for those unfortunate people.
> **Correct:** I *cannot help* thinking I made a favorable impression.

CAN'T HARDLY: This is a double negative. Use *can hardly*.

> **Incorrect:** Susan's legs are so short, she *can't hardly* reach the brake pedal when she's driving.

CAN'T SEEM: Use *doesn't seem* or *don't seem* (as appropriate, for correct number agreement).

> **Incorrect:** It *can't seem* good that Eric has lost his job.

CAPACITY, ABILITY: See *ability, capacity*.

CAPITAL, CAPITOL: *Capital* means "money invested" or "the location of the seat of government"; *capitol* means "state house" or "an edifice."

> **Correct:** Before we could launch our new business, we needed to raise some *capital*.
> **Correct:** Indianapolis is the *capital* of Indiana.
> **Correct:** The dome atop the *capitol* is breathtaking.

CENSURE, CRITICIZE: *Criticize* means "to examine" or "to judge as a critic"; *censure* means "to find fault with" or "to condemn as wrong."

> **Correct:** Allow me to *criticize* your paper and point out its strengths and weaknesses.
> **Correct:** My father *censured* us for our poor behavior during dinner.

CENTER AROUND: Omit *around;* use *focus on* or *upon* or *center on* or *upon*.

> **Incorrect:** The story was *centered around* the vagaries of war.

CHARACTER, REPUTATION: *Character* is what a person really is; *reputation* is what others think he is.

Correct: She is a person of outstanding *character*.
Correct: Her *reputation* is as unblemished as her *character*.
Correct: Although Sid has a *reputation* for being miserly, he is in fact quite generous.

CHOICE, ALTERNATIVE: See *alternative, choice*.

CITE, SITE: *Cite* means "to quote from"; *site* is a geographical location.

Correct: Edwina *cited* Shakespeare during the course of her commencement speech.
Correct: This is the future *site* of the new dormitory.

CLAIM: Do not use *claim* to mean "assert, state, contend, maintain"; *claim* means "to demand on the basis of right."

Incorrect: He *claimed* that he was misquoted by the press.
Correct: Clutching the winning ticket in his hand, Andy rushed to *claim* his prize.

CLOTH, CLOTHE: *Cloth* refers to fabric; *clothe* is a verb meaning "to cover" or "surround."

Correct: Rico was wearing a shirt made of fine *cloth*.
Correct: Mothers should *clothe* their young children in warm playsuits in the winter time.
Correct: The speaker seemed to *clothe* himself in an aura of self-righteousness.

COARSE, COURSE: *Coarse* means "base, crude, or rough"; *course* means "route, plan, academic pursuit."

Correct: The *coarse* material chafed my skin and caused a sore.
Correct: Patrice wanted to enroll in an advanced *course* in guitar.

COMMON, MUTUAL: *Common* means "belonging to more than one"; *mutual* means "being reciprocal" or "interchanged."

Correct: Jane and I have many friends in *common*.
Correct: Elizabeth and I have a *mutual* respect for each other.

COMPARE, CONTRAST: Use *compare* to indicate similarities or to examine two or more entities to ascertain similarities or differences; use *contrast* to point out differences only.

Correct: In *comparing* Jeff's resume with Jason's, we noticed many similarities.
Correct: Phoebe's eyes are blue; in *contrast,* Max's are brown.

COMPLECTED: This is a corrupt form of *complexioned*.

Incorrect: Allison is an unusually fair-*complected* girl.

COMPLEMENT, COMPLIMENT: *Complement* means "that which completes or accents, a full or total number"; *compliment* means "to flatter, a flattering remark."

Correct: My granddaughter has a full *complement* of Barbie dolls.
Correct: The new drapes certainly *complement* our furniture.
Correct: I wish to *compliment* you on your fine performance.

COMPLETE, FINISH: *Complete* is properly used to show that nothing is lacking; all parts are present. *Finish* is used to show that all that was required has been done.

Correct: Edgar has a *complete* set of *Star Wars* action figures.
Correct: We *finished* painting the dining room on Saturday.

COMPLIMENT, COMPLEMENT: See *complement, compliment*.

COMPOSE, COMPRISE: Do not use *comprise* interchangeably with *compose,* as in "to make up the constituent parts of a whole." Use *comprise* when the subject of the sentence includes the constituent parts and the predicate contains the whole; use *compose* when the subject of the sentence is the whole and the predicate contains the constituent parts. Note that *compose* often patterns with the preposition *of*.

Correct: The musical group The Beatles was *comprised of* John Lennon, Paul McCartney, Ringo Starr, and George Harrison.
Correct: The musical group The Beatles was *composed of* John Lennon, Paul McCartney, Ringo Starr, and George Harrison.
Correct: John Lennon, Paul McCartney, Ringo Starr, and George Harrison *comprised* The Beatles.

CONNECT TOGETHER: The *together* in *connect together* is redundant. Simply use *connect*.

Incorrect: It's best to *connect together* the puzzle pieces around the edge before *connecting together* the ones in the middle.

CONSCIENCE, CONSCIOUS: *Conscious* means "being awake, alert"; *conscience* refers to one's feelings of right or wrong; one's morality.

Correct: Although the quarterback remained *conscious,* he had almost certainly suffered a concussion.
Correct: My *conscience* would not allow me to peek at Carlita's file.

CONSEQUENCE, IMPORTANCE: A *consequence* is a result; *importance* is significance.

> **Correct:** The accident was surely a *consequence* of carelessness.
> **Correct:** His objection is really of little *importance*.

CONTEMPLATE: This verb should not be followed by a preposition.

> **Incorrect:** We'll *contemplate* on this matter later in the meeting.
> **Correct:** Oliver *contemplated* the question for some time before answering.

CONTINUAL, CONTINUOUS: *Continual* means "occurring in steady, rapid, but not unbroken succession." *Continuous* means "without cessation or interruption."

> **Correct:** We had hoped to relax by the pool, but *continual* interruptions by the children prevented us from doing so.
> **Correct:** There is a *continuous* flow of the river from here to New Orleans.

CONTRAST, COMPARE: See *compare, contrast*.

COULD OF: This is a corrupt form of *could have*.

> **Incorrect:** Is it likely that anyone else *could of* won the election?
> **Correct:** No one *could have* lifted that huge stone by himself.

COUNCIL, COUNSEL: *Council* is a group of elected officials. *Counsel* means "to advise someone" or "to receive advice."

> **Correct:** The student *council* approved the new dress code.
> **Correct:** My advisor *counseled* me to enroll in a chemistry class.

COUPLE ARE, COUPLE IS: When referring to two people as a pair, *couple* may be either singular or plural. The plural form the *couple are* is becoming increasingly common today. Regardless of which form you use, you should ensure that any other related words in the sentence agree: "The couple *are* planning *their* wedding," or "The couple *is* planning *its* wedding."

COURSE, COARSE: See *coarse, course*.

CREDIBLE, CREDITABLE, CREDULOUS: *Credible* means "capable of being believed"; *creditable*, "worthy of esteem or honor"; *credulous*, "inclined to believe or easily convinced."

> **Correct:** Given Stan's tendency to exaggerate, I'm not certain his account of the fiasco is *credible*.
> **Correct:** The skaters gave a very *creditable* performance last evening.
> **Correct:** My mother—a very *credulous* person—believed the wild tale that we told her.

CRITICIZE, CENSURE: See *censure, criticize.*

DATA, MEDIA, PHENOMENA, STRATA: These words are the plurals of *datum, medium, phenomenon,* and *stratum.* As plurals, they require plural demonstrative modifiers and plural verbs.

> **Correct:** Those *data* are quite reliable.

DECIDED, DECISIVE: *Decided* means "definite, unquestionable, emphatic"; *decisive* means "final, conclusive, beyond any doubt."

> **Correct:** The rebels claimed a *decisive* victory against tyranny.
> **Correct:** The chairman cast the *decisive* vote.
> **Correct:** He made a *decided* effort to locate the missing dinosaur bones.

Do not confuse these words with the various forms of the verb *to decide,* which means "to make a decision."

DEFINITELY: Avoid this word as an intensifier.

> **Incorrect:** The professor was *definitely* wrong in his answer. (Is there an indefinite wrong?)
> **Correct:** Sue was *surely* wrong in her assessment of Joe.

DELUSION, ILLUSION, ALLUSION: See *allusion, delusion, illusion.*

DEPENDING, DEPENDS: These words are always followed by *on* or *upon.*

> **Correct:** Whether we visit Nina *depends on* how quickly you finish your lunch.

DETERMINED, BOUND: See *bound, determined.*

DEVICE, DEVISE: A *device* is a gadget or tool; *devise* is a verb meaning "to formulate or invent."

> **Correct:** This handy *device* should enable us to open our broken lock.
> **Correct:** We should *devise* a plan to increase our profits.

DIDN'T OUGHT, HAD OUGHT, HADN'T OUGHT: Avoid these combinations. Use *ought* or *ought not.*

> **Correct:** You *ought* to be more careful.
> **Correct:** You *ought not* get involved in that situation.

DIFFER FROM, DIFFER WITH: Use *differ from* to indicate that two separate items are different. Use *differ with* to indicate disagreement.

> **Correct:** My report *differs from* yours.
> **Correct:** Even though you *differ with* me on this issue, I respect your point of view.

DIFFERENT FROM, DIFFERENT THAN: Use *from,* not *than,* after *different.*

> **Incorrect:** Running the 100-meter dash is a lot *different than* running a marathon.

DIFFICULT, HARD: *Difficult* means "not easy, demanding"; *hard* means "solid, firm."

> **Correct:** Ascending K2 is among the most *difficult* feats a climber can accomplish.
> **Correct:** Stone is a *harder* surface than wood.

Some dictionaries indicate that both these terms are interchangeable with "not easy."

DISCOVERY, INVENTION: A *discovery* is the bringing to light of something that already exists. An *invention* is that which is created by ingenuity.

> **Correct:** The *discovery* of uranium did much to advance knowledge.
> **Correct:** The *invention* of the automobile ultimately marked the demise of the horse-and-carriage industry.

DISCREET, DISCRETE: *Discreet* means "careful, showing wise restraint"; *discrete* means "independent or separate."

> **Correct:** Sally is very *discreet;* she almost never gossips.
> **Correct:** Because the newspaper division of the company is *discrete* from the book-publishing arm, they do not share resources.

DISINTERESTED, UNINTERESTED: *Disinterested* means "impartial"; *uninterested* means "having no concern or interest whatsoever."

> **Correct:** *Disinterested* persons make the most reliable witnesses.
> **Correct:** We were *uninterested* in the outcome of the trial, so we left early.

DISASSEMBLE, DISSEMBLE: *Dissemble* means "to feign, to disguise or conceal something." *Disassemble* means "to take apart."

> **Correct:** He *dissembled* his intense shyness by singing a humorous song.
> **Correct:** In order to fix the garage-door opener, Katie first had to *disassemble* it.

DONE: This is the past participle of *to do.* Do not use *done* as a past tense; use *did.*

> **Incorrect:** We knew that he *done* it on purpose.
> **Correct:** I knew immediately that he had *done* what he promised.

DON'T: This is a contraction for *do not,* but not for *does not (doesn't).*

> **Incorrect:** He *don't* know a thing about taxidermy.

DRAGGED, DRUG: The past tense of *drag* is *dragged,* not *drug.*

> **Incorrect:** Mother *drug* me with her to the beauty parlor.

DRUNK: *Drunk* is the correct past-participle form of the verb *to drink.* Do not use the past-tense form *drank* as the past participle.

> **Incorrect:** The kitten has drank all her milk.

DUMB, MUTE, STUPID: *Dumb* means "not having the power of speech"; *mute,* "having the power of speech but choosing not to speak"; *stupid,* "dull-witted, foolish." *Dumb,* even when used correctly, is falling out of favor.

> **Correct:** To avoid incriminating himself, the witness remained *mute.*
> **Correct:** Removal of the vocal cords renders one *dumb.*
> **Correct:** Louise may be a *stupid* dog, but she is loyal, and we love her.

EACH OTHER, ONE ANOTHER: Use *each other* to refer to only two; use *one another* to refer to more than two.

> **Correct:** Sarah, Sue, and Sally help *one another* regularly.
> **Correct:** The twins will surely hurt *each other.*

EAGER, ANXIOUS: See *anxious, eager.*

EFFECT, AFFECT: See *affect, effect.*

EITHER, NEITHER: Use these words to designate one of only two persons or things.

> **Incorrect:** The book belongs to *either* Megan, Bryan, or Sal.
> **Incorrect:** *Neither* Will nor Sam nor Rianne ate their lima beans.

EMIGRANT, IMMIGRANT: *Emigrant* means "one who has moved *out* of a country"; *immigrant* refers to one who has moved *into* a country.

> **Correct:** My neighbor, Olivier, is an *immigrant* from France.

EMIGRATE, IMMIGRATE: *Emigrate* means "to move out of a country"; *immigrate* means "to move into a country."

> **Correct:** My ancestors *emigrated* from Europe to Canada in the eighteenth century.

EMINENT, IMMINENT, PROMINENT: *Prominent* means "conspicuous"; *eminent* means "distinguished in character or rank"; *imminent* means "impending, about to occur."

Correct: Place this picture of Uncle Oscar in a very *prominent* place.
Correct: Dr. Rogers is an *eminent* nuclear physicist.
Correct: The *imminent* flood resulted in a food shortage.

ENORMITY, ENORMOUSNESS: *Enormity* means "wickedness"; *enormousness* means "vastness."

Correct: The *enormity* of his crimes is nearly beyond belief.
Correct: The *enormousness* of the frontier startled some settlers.

ENSURE, INSURE, ASSURE: See *assure, ensure, insure.*

ENTHUSE: This is an illiterate attempt to develop a verb form to mean "make enthusiastic" or "become enthusiastic." While many words have been formed by this process of "back formation," this word has not yet gained the status of total acceptance. It is best avoided.

Incorrect: The talent show's emcee attempted to *enthuse* the audience in preparation for the first act.
Correct: I sincerely hope you become *enthusiastic* about the opera.

EQUABLE, EQUITABLE: *Equable* means "uniform, steady, consistently even, serene"; *equitable* means "just, impartial."

Correct: Miss Wheat certainly has an *equable* disposition.
Correct: An *equitable* solution is to cut the pie in half.

EQUALLY AS GOOD: The *as* is redundant. Use *equally good* or *as good as.*

Incorrect: That ice cream is equally as good as the other.

EQUITABLE, EQUABLE: See *equable, equitable.*

ETC.: Use this abbreviation only when it is obvious what follows. Too often, the expression is used vaguely to try to impress the listener or reader that the user knows more than he or she really does know.

Correct: Prime numbers include 2, 3, 5, 7, 11, *etc.*

EVACUATE: Do not use this word, which means "to empty or remove the contents from," as a substitute for the verb *leave.*

Incorrect: Jane's class *evacuated* the building when her teacher heard the fire alarm.
Correct: When the mayor learned of the coming hurricane, he ordered that the town be *evacuated.*

EVERY BIT: Do not use this expression to mean "in every way" or "quite." It is generally superfluous.

> **Incorrect:** He was *every bit* as happy as I thought he would be.
> **Incorrect:** This man is *every bit* as guilty as you are.

EVERY ONE, EVERYONE: *Everyone* (one word) means "every person." *Every one* (two words) means "every single person or thing."

> **Correct:** *Everyone* gather around; I want to tell you a story.
> **Correct:** *Every one* of those dogs is a contender for Best in Show.

EVERYPLACE: This is a corrupt form of *everywhere*.

> **Incorrect:** Lois looked *everyplace* for the lost mitten.

EVIDENTLY, APPARENTLY: See *apparently, evidently*.

EXCEPT, ACCEPT: See *accept, except*.

EXCEPTIONABLE, EXCEPTIONAL: *Exceptional* means "rare or superior"; *exceptionable* means "objectionable."

> **Correct:** These are diamonds of *exceptional* quality.
> **Correct:** The senator excised the *exceptionable* content in the speech before delivering it to the audience.

EXCUSE, PARDON: *Excuse* is to grant leave; *pardon* is to forgive. In asking forgiveness, however, small indiscretions may be excused; greater faults are pardoned. In formal situations, adhere to the distinction listed first.

> **Correct:** *Pardon* me; I didn't mean to trip you.

EXPECT, SUSPECT: *Suspect* means "to have suspicions, to doubt or distrust"; *expect* means "to anticipate, to believe likely, or nearly certain."

> **Correct:** We all *suspected* Marie of feigning illness.
> **Correct:** At what time do you *expect* him to return?

EXPLICIT, IMPLICIT: *Explicit* means "stated clearly or directly"; *implicit* means "suggested, implied."

EXTRA: Do not use this word to mean "unusually."

> **Incorrect:** The weather has been *extra* nice this spring.

FAMOUS, INFAMOUS, NOTORIOUS: *Famous* means "well-known, renowned, celebrated"; *notorious* means "well-known for unsavory reasons, disapproved of, deplored"—in other words, *infamous*.

> **Correct:** Rubinoff, the *famous* violinist, gave a concert in the hall.
> **Correct:** Fred Pinkerton, the *notorious* white-collar criminal, has been caught.
> **Correct:** John Dillinger, the *infamous* gunslinger, had roots in Indiana.

FARTHER, FURTHER: Use *farther* to express distance; use *further* to express the meaning of "more, in addition, to a greater degree."

> **Correct:** We walked *farther* today than we did yesterday.
> **Correct:** We must discuss this matter *further* before reaching a decision.

FAVOR: Do not use this word to mean "resemble."

> **Incorrect:** Don't you think he *favors* his father in the face?
> **Correct:** Do you think Eric *resembles* his uncle Fritz?

FAZE, PHASE: Use *faze* to mean "worry, disconcert." *Phase,* on the other hand, describes a distinct period in a sequence.

> **Correct:** It didn't *faze* Allen a bit to find a wild boar on his patio.
> **Correct:** I'm thrilled to be entering this new *phase* in life.

FELLOW: Avoid *fellow* in the general sense of "man, sweetheart, person." *Fellow* connotes comradeship or association.

> **Incorrect:** Two *fellows* were riding in that red convertible.
> **Correct:** The environment ended his speech by exhorting his *fellow* citizens of the world to act now to avert climate change.

FETCH: This word means both "go" and "bring." Do not use it with *go*.

> **Incorrect:** Go *fetch*, Fido!
> **Incorrect:** Will you go and *fetch* these items from the market?

FEWER, LESS: *Fewer* refers to numbers; *less,* to value, degree, amount. Use *fewer* with count nouns; *less* with mass nouns.

> **Correct:** My grandfather's trees have *fewer* apples this year than last.
> **Correct:** I seem to have *less* money than you have.

FIGURATIVELY, LITERALLY: *Literally* means "strictly, truly, exactly"; *figuratively* means "in a similar way" or "in a manner of speaking, but not really true."

Correct: Her clothes were *literally* smoking from the heat of the flames.
Correct: His father was *figuratively* boiling when he saw the dent in his new car.

FIGURE: Do not use this word as a verb to mean "plan, judge, deduce." Save *figure* for problems in mathematics.

Incorrect: I *figure* she's right about the cause of the fire.
Incorrect: No one *figured* that he would succeed.

FINISH, COMPLETE: See *complete, finish.*

FLUNK: Use *fail.*

Incorrect: Even though Edgar studied for the test all night, he *flunked* it.

FORMALLY, FORMERLY: *Formally* means "high regard for correctness"; *formerly* means "in the past."

Correct: The delegation was received very *formally* by the queen.
Correct: Doreen, *formerly* a clerk, has been promoted to assistant manager.

FORMER: Use this expression to refer to the first of only two persons, things, or groups. See *later, latter.*

Correct: Of Sarah and Susan, only the *former* is blonde.

FORMERLY, FORMALLY: See *formally, formerly.*

FORWARD, FORWARDS: Avoid *forwards.*

Correct: No matter how tired you become while jogging, it's important to keep moving *forward.*

FRIGHTEN, STARTLE: *Frighten* means "to induce fear, to cause to be afraid"; *startle* means "to surprise, to cause a reaction because of something unexpected."

Correct: The howling wolves *frightened* the campers.
Correct: The noise of the door slamming shut behind me *startled* me.

FUNNY, STRANGE: Avoid *funny* to mean "odd"; in this sense, use *strange. Funny* means "amusing."

Correct: Isn't it *strange* that Antoine doesn't care for cake?
Correct: The children thought it *funny* when the clown swung from the rope.

FURTHER, FARTHER: See *farther, further.*

GENDER, SEX: *Sex* is used in reference to creatures of the animal world. *Gender* refers to words in the study of grammar or to the "behavioral, cultural, or psychological traits typically associated with one sex."

> **Correct:** In French, you can indicate *gender* by using the antecedent *le* or *la*.
> **Correct:** What *sex* is the baby elephant that was just born at the zoo?

GENTLEMAN, LADY: Use these two words when your purpose is to indicate persons of refinement and culture. Use the plural forms in addressing an audience: *Ladies and Gentlemen*. Otherwise, use *man* and *woman*.

> **Correct:** We counted four *men* who had lost their hats.
> **Correct:** In all matters, Isabella shows herself to be a genteel *lady*.

GET, GOT: The verb *to get* is one of the most useful words in the language. It is common in such idioms as *get along with* (*someone*), *get the better of* (*someone*), *get at* (*information*), *get up* (*from a nap*), *get on* (*a horse*), or *get over* (*an illness*). Always be certain that *get* or *got* is used in good idiom, not in slang. *Must* is often usable in its stead.

> **Incorrect:** I've *got* to leave soon.
> **Correct:** I *must* leave before the wind blows any harder.

GIBE, JIBE, JIVE: A *gibe* is a taunt; to *jibe* is to agree. *Jive* is a slang term referring to jazz or swing music or to a nonsensical way of speaking.

> **Correct:** One of my favorite parts of William Shakespeare's *Hamlet* is when Hamlet says, "Where be your *gibes* now, your gambols, your songs, your flashes of merriment that were wont to set the table on a roar?"
> **Correct:** Jenkins' views on evolution *jibe* with mine.

GOES: Do not use *goes* to mean "says, states, replies," and so on.

> **Incorrect:** "Then Cyrus *goes,* 'Where were you? I couldn't find you,' and I *went,* 'We were in front of you the whole time!'"

GOOD, WELL: *Good* is properly a noun or an adjective; do not use *good* as an adverb. *Well* may function as either an adjective or an adverb, depending upon the meaning of the sentence.

> **Correct:** She looks *good* in her new dress.
> > (*Good* follows the linking verb *looks* and modifies *she*.)
> **Correct:** The choir sings *well*.
> > (*Well* is an adverb, modifying *sings*.)

Correct: The senator looks *well,* even though she has been ill.
(*Well,* meaning "not ill," follows the linking verb *looks* and modifies *senator.*)
Incorrect: Tom's '63 Chevy runs *good.*

GOOD AND: Avoid *good and* in the meaning of "very" or "really."

Incorrect: Father was *good and* angry with us last night.
Incorrect: Be sure that the floor is *good and* clean tomorrow.

GOT, GET: See *get, got.*

GRAND: Avoid the vague usage of *grand* to mean "excellent." Select the exact word to fit the desired meaning.

Incorrect: We had a *grand* time on the cruise.

GREAT DEAL OF: Do not use this as a substitute for *many.*

Incorrect: Marjorie knew a *great deal of* the women at the tea.
Correct: He knew *many* of the answers.

GUESS: Avoid *guess* to mean "think, suppose, believe." *Guess* means "to estimate, to conjecture"; *think* means "to reason, visualize, suppose."

Incorrect: I *guess* I'll go to bed now.
Incorrect: No one *guessed* that he would do what he had promised.
Correct: Mr. Boisson didn't know how many marbles were in the jar, but he guessed correctly.
Correct: I *think* I'll go to the theater tonight.

GUY: Do not use *guy* to mean "man, boy, person, fellow."

Incorrect: Tell that *guy* to drive more slowly.

HAD BETTER, HAD RATHER, WOULD RATHER: These are good idioms used to express advisability (with *better*) or preference (with *rather*). Do not use *better* as a shortening of *had better.*

Incorrect: We *better* do that work before dark.
Correct: It's getting dark; I think we *had better* turn back.
Correct: I *would rather* go to dinner before the movie.

HAD HE HAVE GONE: This is a corrupt expression of *had he gone.*

Incorrect: *Had he have gone* to work with a cold, he almost certainly would have spread it around.

Correct: *Had she gone* to college, she'd almost certainly have more employment opportunities now.

HAD OF: This is a corrupt expression of *had*.

Incorrect: *Had* we *of* left on time, we'd be home by now.
Correct: *Had* we planned ahead, we would no doubt have foreseen this problem.

HAD OUGHT, HADN'T OUGHT, DIDN'T OUGHT: See *didn't ought, had ought, hadn't ought*.

HAD RATHER, WOULD RATHER, HAD BETTER: See *had better, had rather, would rather*.

HADN'T OUGHT, DIDN'T OUGHT, HAD OUGHT: See *didn't ought, had ought, hadn't ought*.

HALF A, A HALF, A HALF A: See *a half, a half a, half a*.

HANGED, HUNG: Use *hung* unless speaking of death by hanging, in which case *hanged* is correct.

Correct: After Stephanie *hung* the picture on the wall, the room looked complete.
Correct: The outlaw was *hanged* at dawn.

HARD, DIFFICULT: See *difficult, hard*.

HARDLY, SCARCELY: These words are negative in implication and should not be used with another negative.

Incorrect: We couldn't *hardly* breathe.
Correct: We could *scarcely* believe our luck.

HATE: Avoid this expression to mean "regret, dislike."

Incorrect: I *hate* that I cannot see you this evening.
Correct: My sister *dislikes* having to get out of bed in the morning.

HAVE GOT: Do not use *have got* in the sense of "must" or to show possession. Use *have*.

Incorrect: *Have* you *got* an extra pencil in your pocket?
Incorrect: I *have got* to get a haircut; I can barely see through these bangs!

HEALTHFUL, HEALTHY: *Healthful* means "capable of giving health"; *healthy* means "having health."

Correct: Apples are a *healthful* snack.
Correct: Fergus' cat gave birth to seven *healthy* kittens.

HELP BUT: See *cannot help but*.

HIMSELF, MYSELF, YOURSELF: Use these forms as intensives or reflexives only. These forms are not substitutes for the nominatives and objectives. Also, never insert the word *own* between the syllables of these words.

> **Correct:** You *yourself* are responsible for your predicament.
> **Incorrect:** You are responsible *your ownself* for your problems.
> **Incorrect:** Alec and *myself* would prefer to deal with your brother and *yourself*.

HISSELF: This is a corrupt form of *himself*.

> **Incorrect:** Ralph drove *hisself* to the hospital.

HONORABLE, REVEREND: *Reverend* is not a title. It is an adjective that modifies a title such as *Mr., Dr.,* or *Ms. Honorable* is used as an official form of address for political figures.

> **Correct:** The *Reverend* Mr. Jones will speak to us on Sunday.
> **Correct:** The *Honorable* Judge Alice Tinser is a family friend.
> **Incorrect:** I spoke with *Reverend* McDonald yesterday.

HOPEFULLY: *Hopefully* means "with hope." Avoid *hopefully* to mean "We hope that" or a similar phrase.

> **Incorrect:** *Hopefully,* the engine will not fail us.
> **Correct:** We *hope* (or *are hopeful*) that the engine will not fail us.
> **Correct:** The farmer listened *hopefully* for the sound of rain on the roof.

HOW COME?: Avoid this expression, which is a corrupt form of "How did that come to be?" or "How came that to be?" Use *why* or *why not*.

> **Incorrect:** *How come* you didn't answer your phone?
> **Correct:** *Why* didn't you answer your phone?

HUMAN, HUMANE: *Human* means "having the characteristics of *Homo sapiens*"; *humane* means "merciful, having kindness or sympathy."

> **Correct:** It would appear that these life forms are not *human*.
> **Correct:** It's imperative that we all work to ensure that animals are treated *humanely*.

HUNG, HANGED: See *hanged, hung*.

IDEA, IDEAL: Use *idea* to mean "thought, mental plan, or conception." Use *ideal* to mean "standard of excellence, perfection; a model."

Correct: Chad had some great *ideas* about earning money.
Correct: Angelina was certain the *ideal* man was out there; she just had to find him.

IF, WHETHER: Use *if* to introduce clauses of condition; use *whether* (with *or* expressed or understood) to introduce noun clauses that contain alternatives.

When *whether* fits, *if* is incorrect.

Correct: *If* the sun shines, we'll go fishing.
Correct: *Whether* you go or stay, you'll need some money.
Incorrect: *If* you win or lose, you'll gain wide recognition.

ILL, SICK: Use *ill* to mean "not well" and *sick* to mean "nauseated" or "mentally imbalanced."

Correct: Steve became *sick* after eating the omelet.
Correct: Because Bob was *ill*, he stayed home from school.

ILLUSION, ALLUSION, DELUSION: See *allusion, delusion, illusion*.

IMMIGRANT, EMIGRANT: See *emigrant, immigrant*.

IMMIGRATE, EMIGRATE: See *emigrate, immigrate*.

IMMINENT, PROMINENT, EMINENT: See *eminent, imminent, prominent*.

IMMORAL, AMORAL: See *amoral, immoral*.

IMPACT: In its noun form, *impact* refers to the striking of one body against another, the force generated by a collision, or the effect of one thing on another; in its verb form, *impact* means "to pack firmly together" or "to strike forcefully." Do not use as a verb to mean "to have an effect on."

Correct: When Arthur fell from the ladder, the *impact* caused him to break his arm.
Correct: The *impact* of early education on a child's overall development can be measured in a number of ways.
Correct: Jason *impacted* the snow into a ball before hurling it at Sonja.
Incorrect: The storm *impacted* our ability to travel by plane.

IMPLICIT, EXPLICIT: See *explicit, implicit*.

IMPLY, INFER: The writer or the speaker *implies* with his or her words; the reader or listener *infers* from what he or she hears.

Correct: Are you *implying* that I am responsible for the accident?
Correct: I *infer* from your comments that you are angry.

IMPORTANCE, CONSEQUENCE: See *consequence, importance*.

IN, INTO: *In* indicates *location within; into* indicates *motion or direction to a point within*.

> **Correct:** The children jumped *into* the water (from the shore).
> **Correct:** The children were jumping *in* the water. (They were already in the water when they began jumping.)

IN-, UN-: Both prefixes have the meaning of "not." Check a dictionary if any doubt exists concerning the proper form to use with a particular root word.

> **Correct:** My friend is an *incompetent* mechanic.
> **Correct:** That comment was *unnecessary*.

IN BACK OF: Avoid this expression. Use *behind*.

> **Incorrect:** Park your car *in back of* the house.

IN REGARDS TO: Avoid this expression. Use either *in regard to, as regards*.

> **Incorrect:** Jason's message was *in regards to* your plans for this evening.

INCREDIBLE, INCREDULOUS: *Incredible* means "too extraordinary to admit of belief." *Incredulous* means "inclined not to believe on slight evidence."

> **Correct:** I believe your story about seeing a ghost to be *incredible* (unbelievable).
> **Correct:** Frank cast me an *incredulous* glance as I discussed my experience.

INDIVIDUAL, PARTY, PERSON: *Individual* refers to a single person, animal, or thing. *Party* refers to a group, never to a single person (except in legal language). *Person* is the preferred word for general reference to a human being.

> **Correct:** Will the *person* who took my book please return it?

INFAMOUS, NOTORIOUS, FAMOUS: See *famous, infamous, notorious*.

INFER, IMPLY: See *imply, infer*.

INFERIOR THAN: Use *inferior to* or *worse than*.

> **Incorrect:** From a speed standpoint, this car is *inferior than* that one.

INGENIOUS, INGENUOUS: *Ingenious* means "clever, resourceful"; *ingenuous* means "open, frank, artless."

> **Correct:** Your invention is an *ingenious* device.
> **Correct:** He seemed to give *ingenuous* answers to my sincere questions.

INSIDE OF, OUTSIDE OF: The *of* is superfluous. Do not use *inside of* to mean "within." Do not use *outside of* to mean "besides."

> **Incorrect:** Look *inside of* the drawer to find more paper.
> **Incorrect:** He did nothing wrong *outside of* missing class ten times.
> **Correct:** The cat was *inside* the box.

INSURE, ASSURE, ENSURE: See *assure, ensure, insure.*

INTO, IN: See *in, into.*

INVENTION, DISCOVERY: See *discovery, invention.*

INVITE: Do not use *invite* as a noun. Use *invitation.*

> **Incorrect:** Have you received an *invite* to Sofia's party?

IRREGARDLESS: This incorrect form of *regardless* is often misused by speakers and writers because of its similarity to words such as *irresponsible, irrational,* and *irregular.* It is not acceptable.

> **Incorrect:** Larry seemed determined to go *irregardless* of my objections.

IRRITATE, AGGRAVATE, ANNOY: See *aggravate, annoy, irritate.*

IT'S: *It's* is the contracted form of *it is;* do not use *it's* as the possessive form of *it,* which is *its* without the apostrophe.

> **Incorrect:** The dog spat out *it's* chew toy at my feet.
> **Correct:** The dog spat out *its* chew toy at my feet.

JIBE, JIVE, GIBE: See *gibe, jibe, jive.*

JUDGEMENT, JUDGMENT: *Judgment* is the more frequent spelling; the other spelling, *judgement* (chiefly British and Canadian), is sometimes considered an error.

JUST: Do not use *just* to mean "completely, simply, quite." *Just* means "fair, even-handed, impartial, honest" or "only, precisely" and "barely."

> **Correct:** These potato chips have *just* enough salt.
> **Correct:** That meteorite *just* missed Jowana.
> **Incorrect:** Antonia looked *just* lovely in her gown.
> **Correct:** That painting is *simply* beautiful.

KIND, SORT: These two words are singular forms and require singular demonstrative modifiers. *Kinds* and *sorts* are plural and require plural demonstrative modifiers.

> **Correct:** That *kind* of couch would be perfect in my living room.
> **Incorrect:** Not many people like those *sort* of programs.

KIND OF, SORT OF: Do not use these two expressions as adverbs to mean "somewhat, rather, after a fashion."

>**Incorrect:** The new senator was *kind of* naive about politics.
>**Incorrect:** After the game, I was *sort of* tired.

KIND OF A, SORT OF A: Omit the *a*. Usually, the article is placed *before* the first noun, not after the preposition.

>**Incorrect:** Do you enjoy this *kind of a* performance?

LADY, GENTLEMAN: See *gentleman, lady*.

LAST, LATEST: *Last* is final; *latest,* most recent.

>**Correct:** Barbara's *latest* novel has become a bestseller.

LATER, LATTER: *Later* is the comparative of *late* and means "more late"; alternatively, *later* means "at a time in the future." *Latter* refers to the second of two. If more than two are named, use *last* or *last-mentioned* instead of *latter*.

>**Correct:** I will mow the lawn *later* this afternoon.
>**Correct:** Of the two options you presented, I prefer the *latter*.

LATEST, LAST: See *last, latest*.

LATTER, LATER: See *later, latter*.

LAY, LIE: To *lay* means "to put" or "to place." To *lie* means "to rest" or "to recline." For more information, refer to the section titled "Troublesome Verbs" in Chapter 3, "Verbs."

>**Correct:** Just *lie* there a moment until your head clears.
>**Correct:** I *laid* the book on the shelf.

LEAD, LED: *Lead* (verb) is the present-tense form; *led* is the past-tense and past-participle forms.

>**Correct:** The sergeant stepped forward to *lead* his men.
>**Incorrect:** Ricky *lead* the race until the final lap, when he was overtaken by Jimmy.

LEARN, TEACH: *Learn* means "to acquire knowledge"; *teach* means "to impart knowledge."

>**Correct:** I will *learn* from you if you will *teach* me.

LEAVE, LET, PERMIT, ALLOW: See *allow, leave, let, permit.*

LED, LEAD: See *lead, led.*

LEND, LOAN: *Lend* is a verb meaning "to make a loan." *Loan* is a noun meaning "the result of lending."

> **Correct:** In order to pay for college, Joseph obtained a *loan.*
> **Correct:** Can anyone here *lend* me a dollar until tomorrow?

LESS, FEWER: See *fewer, less.*

LET, PERMIT, ALLOW, LEAVE: See *allow, leave, let, permit.*

LIABLE, LIKELY, APT: See *apt, liable, likely.*

LIE, LAY: See *lay, lie.*

LIKE, AS, AS IF: See *as, as if, like.*

LIKE, LOVE: *Like* refers to taste or preference; *love* expresses affection.

> **Correct:** I *like* swimming in a heated pool.

LIKE, SUCH AS: Do not use *like* to mean *such as.*

> **Incorrect:** I enjoy eating Indian dishes, *like* chicken curry.
> **Correct:** It's wise to wear a helmet when engaging in certain activities, *such as* riding a motorcycle.

LIKELY, APT, LIABLE: See *apt, liable, likely.*

LITERALLY, FIGURATIVELY: See *figuratively, literally.*

LOAN, LEND: See *lend, loan.*

LOCATE: Do not use this verb to mean *settle. Locate* means "to discover, to find"; *settle* means "to put into place or to establish in a permanent location."

> **Incorrect:** Our former neighbors decided to *locate* in Seattle.
> **Correct:** They *located* a fertile valley and *settled* there permanently.
> **Correct:** Instead of continuing to follow the wagon train west, the Smith family *settled* in Kansas in 1842.

The definitions of these words tend to overlap with respect to location or establishing a location.

LOOSE, LOSE: *Lose* means "to cease having." *Loose* as a verb means "to set free"; as an adjective, it means "free, not fastened."

Correct: *Loose* the moorings so that we may set sail.
Correct: Is that button *loose?*
Correct: Try not to *lose* the money your father gave you.

LOSE OUT: The *out* is superfluous.

Incorrect: I was afraid that he would *lose out* in the race.

LOTS, LOTS OF, A WHOLE LOT, A LOT: See *a lot, a whole lot, lots, lots of.*

LOTS OF, A WHOLE LOT, A LOT, LOTS: See *a lot, a whole lot, lots, lots of.*

LOVE, LIKE: See *like, love.*

LUXURIANT, LUXURIOUS: *Luxuriant* means "profuse in growth"; *luxurious* pertains to luxury.

Correct: My neighbors' lawn is certainly *luxuriant.*
Correct: Riding in a limousine is a *luxurious* way to travel!

MAINTAIN, ASSERT: See *assert, maintain.*

MAJORITY, PLURALITY: *Majority* is more than half the total; *plurality* is the greatest of three or more numbers but less than half.

Correct: As a customer-support representative, Stacy spends the *majority* of her time at work on the phone.
Correct: Thirty votes were cast: Bill had 14; Carla had 9; Sam had 7. Bill had a *plurality* of the votes.

MATH: Avoid this shortening of *mathematics* in formal writing.

Incorrect: *Math* used to be my favorite subject, but now I prefer social studies.

MAY, CAN: See *can, may.*

MAY, MIGHT: The past tense form of *may* is *might.* That is, *may* expresses present or future intentions or possibility; *might* expresses past situations.

Correct: I *may* go to the game; I'm not certain.
Correct: I *might* have done it; I don't remember clearly.

Might is used in other special situations. For instance, *might* is used to state hypothetical situations.

Correct: If the moon were brighter, we *might* be able to go outside without our flashlights.

Might is also used to express weaker possibility or probability than *may*.

> **Correct:** Sandy *may* become a doctor someday.
>   (A reasonable possibility exists.)
> **Correct:** Of course I can run a four-minute mile. I *might* even be able to do it in high heels.
>   (The possibility is weak or nonexistent.)

MAY BE, MAYBE: Do not confuse the verb form *may be* with the adverb *maybe*, which means "perhaps."

> **Correct:** I think we *may be* going the wrong way.
> **Correct:** *Maybe* we should turn around.

MAY OF: Avoid this corruption of *may have*.

> **Incorrect:** Cynthia *may of* telephoned, but I'm not certain.

MAYBE, MAY BE: See *may be, maybe*.

MEDIA, PHENOMENA, STRATA, DATA: See *data, media, phenomena, strata*.

MESSRS.: The plural of *Mr., Messrs.* should never be used without a name or names following it.

MIGHT, MAY: See *may, might*.

MIGHT COULD: This is a corruption of *may be able to*.

> **Incorrect:** We *might could* finish the project before Saturday.

MIGHT OF: Avoid this corruption of *might have*.

> **Incorrect:** We *might of* made it home in time had Xander not stopped to chat with Zach.

MIGHTY: *Mighty* means "strong"; do not use it to mean "very."

> **Incorrect:** There are times when I become *mighty* discouraged.

MORAL, MORALE: Distinguish the adjective *moral* from the noun *morale*.

> **Correct:** The *moral* standards of the community are beyond reproach.
> **Correct:** The team's *morale* was really high after the win.

MOST, ALMOST: See *almost, most*.

MOSTLY: *Mostly* means "almost entirely." Avoid using *mostly* to mean "in the greatest degree."

> **Correct:** The students were *mostly* freshmen.
> **Incorrect:** The people *mostly* affected by the new regulations are hunters.

MS.: This is an accepted title for a woman whose marital status is unknown or irrelevant to the situation.

MUCHLY: This is an unacceptable form of *much*.

> **Incorrect:** Mother was *muchly* disturbed when Betsy broke curfew.

MUST OF: Avoid this corruption of *must have*.

MUTE, STUPID, DUMB: See *dumb, mute, stupid*.

MUTUAL, COMMON: See *common, mutual*.

MYSELF, YOURSELF, HIMSELF: See *himself, myself, yourself*.

NEARLY, PRACTICALLY: *Practically* means "virtually" or "for all intents and purposes"; *nearly* means "almost" or "closely, as in space or time."

> **Correct:** Andy and Tonya have been together for so long, they're *practically* married.
> **Correct:** Pat *nearly* fell after tripping over the vine.

NECESSITY: Use *of* with this word, not *to*.

> **Correct:** One *necessity of* teachers is classrooms with ample lighting.

NEEDS, WANTS: *Wants* are things that one desires; *needs* are things required to continue as planned or hoped.

> **Correct:** His *wants* are few: a new fishing pole and some lures.
> **Correct:** Having been rescued, the survivor's primary *needs* involve food and rest.

NEITHER, EITHER: See *either, neither*.

NO ACCOUNT, NO GOOD: Avoid these two expressions to mean "worthless" or "of no value."

> **Incorrect:** His check again proved to be *no good*.

NO PLACE: Avoid this corruption of *nowhere*.

> **Incorrect:** There's *no place* like home.

NOT HARDLY: This is a double negative. Omit *not*. See *hardly, scarcely*.

> **Incorrect:** Tracey *didn't hardly* know her ABCs!

NOTORIOUS, FAMOUS, INFAMOUS: See *famous, infamous, notorious*.

NOVICE, AMATEUR: See *amateur, novice*.

NOWHERE NEAR: Avoid this expression to mean "not nearly."

> **Incorrect:** Your essay is *nowhere near as* good as it should be.
> **Correct:** The manuscript in its present form is *not nearly* acceptable.

NUMBER, AMOUNT: See *amount, number*.

O, OH: Both are interjections. *O* is used in a very formal direct address, is always capitalized, and is never followed by a mark of punctuation. *Oh* expresses a wish, grief, pain, or surprise and is always followed by a comma or an exclamation mark. See the section titled "Interjections" in Chapter 5, "Function Words."

> **Correct:** The *Star-Spangled Banner* starts with this line: "*O* say can you see by the dawn's early light."
> **Correct:** *Oh*, how I wish I were taller!

OBSERVANCE, OBSERVATION: *Observance* is the act of recognizing a holiday or honoring a special event. *Observation* refers to watching something or keeping a person or group under scrutiny.

> **Correct:** The banks will be closed in *observance* of the legal holiday.
> **Correct:** The ailing puppy was kept under *observation* by the veterinarian.

OF: See *could of, had of, ought to of*. *Of* is never a substitute for *have*.

> **Incorrect:** You should *of* told him what you thought.

OFF OF: The *of* is unnecessary.

> **Incorrect:** The paper has blown *off of* my desk.

OH, O: See *O, oh*.

OK, O.K., OKAY: Avoid these expressions in formal contexts.

ONE ANOTHER, EACH OTHER: See *each other, one another*.

ONLY: Be certain that *only* is used only in conjunction with the word it is meant to modify.

Correct: *Only* he wanted to eat the fish.
 (He was the only one who wanted to eat the fish.)
Correct: He wanted *only* to eat the fish.
 (The only activity he wanted to perform with the fish was eating it. He did not, for example, wish to release it into the water.)
Correct: He wanted to eat *only* the fish.
 (He didn't wish to eat anything but the fish.)

OR: Do not use *or* with *neither.*

 Incorrect: *Neither* Don *or* Drew wrote to me after they moved.
 Correct: *Neither* Don *nor* Drew wrote to me after they moved.

OTHER, OTHERWISE: Use *other* as an adjective and *otherwise* as an adverb.

 Correct: The carpenter did some *other* work for my neighbors.
 Correct: You are an excellent writer; don't let anyone say *otherwise!*

OTHER TIMES: Use *at other times.*

 Incorrect: Sometimes I like being with people; *other times* I prefer to be alone.

OTHERWISE, OTHER: See *other, otherwise.*

OUGHT TO OF: Avoid this corruption of *ought to have.*

 Incorrect: You *ought to of* told me that Carrie's mother was sick!

OUT LOUD: Avoid this expression; use *aloud.*

 Incorrect: It's fine to think that; to say it *out loud* is another thing entirely.
 Correct: Would you please read *aloud?*

OUTSIDE OF, INSIDE OF: See *inside of, outside of.*

OVER WITH: The *with* is superfluous.

 Incorrect: We were really pleased when the storm was finally *over with.*

OWN UP: Do not use this expression to mean "admit, confess."

 Incorrect: Fortunately, the suspect *owned up* to the robbery, thereby putting an end to the investigation.

P.M., A.M.: See *A.M., P.M.*

PARDON, EXCUSE: See *excuse, pardon.*

PARTY, PERSON, INDIVIDUAL: See *individual, party, person.*

PASSED, PAST: *Passed* means "exceeded, gained the lead" or "caused someone to receive something." *Past* means "(in) a bygone time."

> **Correct:** As they neared the finish line, Miranda *passed* Eleanor to claim the lead.
> **Correct:** The gambler *passed* his partner an ace under the table.
> **Correct:** Automobiles were much easier to work on in the *past.*

PEDAL, PEDDLE, PETAL: *Pedal* is either a verb meaning "to push with one's foot" or a noun meaning "that which is pushed with the foot." *Peddle* means "to sell or distribute something." *Petal* is a leaflet of a flower blossom.

> **Correct:** We must *pedal* faster if we wish to be home by noon.
> **Correct:** He attempted to *peddle* his ideas to a disbelieving audience.

Correct: Sprinkling rose *petals* as she walked, the flower girl preceded the bride down the aisle.

PERCENT: Use this expression only *after* a number. Do not use *percent* to mean *percentage.* Do not use *per cent.*

> **Incorrect:** A large *percent* of the students were unable to hear the speaker.

PERMIT, ALLOW, LEAVE, LET: See *allow, leave, let, permit.*

PERSON, PARTY, INDIVIDUAL: See *individual, party, person.*

PERSONAL, PERSONNEL: *Personal* means "belonging to someone," "private," or "confidential." *Personnel* refers to people associated with an organization such as a business.

> **Correct:** Fred's *personal* plane was waiting to take us to Washington.
> **Correct:** The *personnel* of the First Armored Division were ready for the inspection.

PETAL, PEDAL, PEDDLE: See *pedal, peddle, petal.*

PHASE: See *faze, phase.*

PHENOMENA, STRATA, DATA, MEDIA: See *data, media, phenomena, strata.*

PHONE: Avoid this shortening of *telephone* in formal contexts.

> **Incorrect:** No one is to use the *phone* without permission.

PHOTO: Avoid this shortening of *photograph* in formal contexts.

> **Incorrect:** This *photo* serves as evidence against the defendant.

PIECE: Do not use *piece* to mean "distance, short distance."

> **Incorrect:** Several of us walked down the road a *piece*.

PLAN ON: Use *plan to*.

> **Incorrect:** Don't *plan on* eating until after we return.
> **Correct:** Our group *plans to* be in Paris next summer.

PLENTY: Do not use *plenty* as an adverb to mean "quite" or as an adjective before a noun.

> **Incorrect:** That driver was *plenty* clever to find a good route.
> **Incorrect:** There are *plenty* apples for all of you.

PLURALITY, MAJORITY: See *majority, plurality*.

POSTED: Do not use *posted* to mean "informed."

> **Incorrect:** I'll keep you *posted* on the situation.

PRACTICABLE, PRACTICAL: *Practical* means "useful, not theoretical." *Practicable* means "capable of being put into practice."

> **Correct:** A screwdriver is a very *practical* tool to own.
> **Correct:** John submitted a *practicable* plan to his supervisor.

PRACTICALLY, NEARLY: See *nearly, practically*.

PRECEDE, PROCEED: *Precede* means "before"; *proceed* means "continue."

> **Correct:** Shall we *proceed* with the investigation?
> **Correct:** Stephanie *preceded* Susannah in line.

PRETTY: Avoid this word as an intensifier. Use *very, somewhat, greatly, rather*.

> **Incorrect:** Greg is *pretty* good at math, but Sean is even better.

PRINCIPAL, PRINCIPLE: *Principal* means "first, leader, chief"; *principle* means "a general truth, a basic law, moral standard."

> **Correct:** The *principal* disagreement involved salary.
> **Correct:** Some *principles* of physics can be difficult to grasp.

PROCEED, PRECEDE: See *precede, proceed*.

PRODUCE, PRODUCTS: *Produce* means "raw material, agricultural products"; *products* means "manufactured items."

Correct: Because of the flood, the farmer could not get his *produce* to market.
Correct: What *products* do you use to care for your lawn?

PROMINENT, EMINENT, IMMINENT: See *eminent, imminent, prominent*.

PROPOSITION: Do not use this word in the sense of "*proposal, scheme, project,* or *undertaking*." A *proposition* is a statement of truth.

Incorrect: All of us listened attentively to the unusual *proposition* contained in the motion.

PROVIDING: Do not use this word in the sense of *if;* use *provided*.

Incorrect: We should like to hear more of this plan, *providing* you are not too tired to discuss it with us.

PUT IN: Do not use this expression to mean *spent, occupied, applied*.

Incorrect: I *put in* for promotion yesterday.
Incorrect: I *put in* six hours at work this morning.

QUITE: *Quite* means "entirely" or "all the way" and must not be used in the sense of *rather, somewhat, considerably,* or any other word of degree.

Correct: You are *quite* correct in your analysis of the facts.
(*Quite* correct means "entirely correct," not "almost correct.")

Further, *quite* should not be followed by a noun.

Incorrect: He caught *quite* a few fish before breakfast.
Incorrect: We carried *quite* a load of wood to the kitchen door.

QUOTATION, QUOTE: *Quote* is a verb. Do not misuse it as the noun *quotation*.

Incorrect: That statement is a *quote* from your last speech, Senator.

RAISE, RISE: *Raise* means "to lift something or force something upward"; *rise* means "to go higher, to gain elevation." See the section titled "Troublesome Verbs" in Chapter 3 for more information.

Correct: *Raise* your hand if you know the answer.
Correct: When Ellen received straight A's, she saw her grade point average *rise*.

RARELY EVER, SELDOM EVER, SELDOM OR EVER: Do not use any of these expressions for *seldom if ever, rarely if ever,* or *hardly ever*. In the cases of *seldom ever* and *rarely ever,* simply omit *ever* or change *seldom* and *rarely* to *hardly*.

Correct: The stars *seldom* appear as bright as they do tonight.

REAL: Do not use *real* to mean "very" or as a substitute for *really* or *very*. *Real* means "genuine" or "authentic."

> **Incorrect:** I am *real* sorry for your loss.
> **Correct:** We all suffered a *real* setback in our plans.

REASON IS BECAUSE: Use *reason is that*. See *because*.

> **Incorrect:** His *reason* for being late *was because* he could not find his hat.
> **Correct:** Kristin's *reason* for leaving early *was that* she felt ill.

REASON WHY: The *why* is redundant. See *reason is because*.

REBUT, REFUTE: Do not use these terms interchangeably. To *refute* is to prove something wrong; to *rebut* is to put forth an argument or evidence in an attempt to prove that something is wrong.

> **Correct:** Kate's attorney *rebutted* Nicole's claim by producing signed affidavits stating the contrary.
> **Correct:** During the course of her rebuttal, Jenny *refuted* Kathy's statements.

REFER, ALLUDE: See *allude, refer*.

REFER BACK: The *back* is superfluous. If more than one reference is made to an item, use *refer again*.

> **Incorrect:** *Refer back* to page 14 for an explanation of the answer.

REFUTE, REBUT: See *rebut, refute*.

REPUTATION, CHARACTER: See *character, reputation*.

RESPECTABLY, RESPECTIVELY: *Respectively* means "in a certain order"; *respectably* means "deserving of respect."

> **Correct:** Alyson and Heather were elected president and vice president, *respectively*.
> **Correct:** Although Stanton did not win the race, he certainly performed *respectably*.

REST, BALANCE: See *balance, rest*.

REVEREND, HONORABLE: See *honorable, reverend*.

RIGHT: Do not use *right* to mean "very" or "extremely."

> **Incorrect:** He was a *right* jolly soul.

RIGHT ALONG: Do not use this expression to mean "continuously."

> **Incorrect:** It rained *right along* for the entire evening.

RIGHT AWAY: Do not use this expression to mean "immediately" except for informal writing.

>**Incorrect:** I'll bring you your supper *right away*.

RISE, RAISE: See *raise, rise.*

SAID: Use *said* as an adjective meaning "before-mentioned" only in legal documents.

>**Correct:** Evidence shows that the *said* meeting did not take place.

SALARY, WAGES: *Salary* is a fixed amount of pay as remuneration for administrative, supervisory, or professional effort; *wages* refers to pay—usually at an hourly rate—for labor or physical effort.

>**Correct:** Although the cost of living has risen, my annual *salary* has not kept pace.
>**Correct:** This week's *wages* were more than last week's because I worked several hours of overtime.

SAME, SUCH: Use these two words as substitutes for *it, this,* or *that* only in legal documents.

SAYS: This is a corruption of *said* when reporting past conversations.

>**Incorrect:** Then I *says* to him, "Goodbye forever!"
>**Correct:** Sal sometimes *says* the strangest things.

SCARCELY, HARDLY: See *hardly, scarcely.*

SELDOM EVER, SELDOM OR EVER, RARELY EVER: See *rarely ever, seldom ever, seldom or ever.*

SET, SIT: To *set* means "to put" or "to place." To *sit* means "to rest." See the section titled "Troublesome Verbs" in Chapter 3 for more information.

>**Correct:** She often *sits* by the window to read.
>**Correct:** I *set* the dog's water bowl on the floor.

SEWAGE, SEWERAGE: *Sewage* is waste material; *sewerage* is the system of pipes or channels for drainage.

>**Correct:** The city has proposed a bond issue to extend *sewerage* to the outlying residential areas.

SEX, GENDER: See *gender, sex.*

SHALL, WILL: *Shall* is used with the first-person pronoun; *will* is used with second- and third-person pronouns. For more information about the use of these verbs, refer to Chapter 3.

> **Correct:** I *shall* sing to you.
> **Correct:** You *will* be the first speaker tomorrow evening.

SHOULD OF: Avoid this corruption of *should have*.

> **Incorrect:** I knew we *should of* brought an umbrella; I'm getting rained on!

SHOW UP: Do not use this expression to mean "expose" or "arrive."

> **Incorrect:** At what time did he *show up?*
> **Incorrect:** I intend to *show up* Danica at the race track today.

SICK, ILL: See *ill, sick.*

SIT, SET: See *set, sit.*

SINCE, BECAUSE: See *because, since.*

SITE, CITE: See *cite, site.*

SIZE: Do not use *size* to mean "sized."

> **Correct:** What *sized* hat does your uncle wear?
> **Incorrect:** What *size* home do you want to buy?

SIZE UP: Do not use this expression to mean "estimate, judge, evaluate."

> **Incorrect:** After some serious observation, the officer *sized up* the situation.

SO . . . AS. . . , AS . . . AS. . . : See *as . . . as. . . , so . . . as. . . .*

SOME: Do not use *some* as an adjective to intensify (for instance, in place of *rather* or *somewhat*). Use *some* only to indicate amount or quantity.

> **Incorrect:** That is *some* car!

SORT, KIND: See *kind, sort.*

SORT OF, KIND OF: See *kind of, sort of.*

SORT OF A, KIND OF A: See *kind of a, sort of a.*

STANCH, STAUNCH: The verb *stanch* means "to stop the flow of"; the adjective *staunch* means "firm and steadfast." Although *staunch* can be substituted for *stanch*, *stanch* cannot be substituted for *staunch*.

Correct: Using a tourniquet on the victim's arm, the EMT was able to *stanch* the flow of blood.
Correct: The university's president is a *staunch* defender of students' rights.
Incorrect: Christine is a *stanch* supporter of the mayor.

STANZA, VERSE: *A stanza* is a group of lines; a *verse* is one line.

Correct: The second *stanza* contains six *verses*.

STARTLE, FRIGHTEN: See *frighten, startle*.

STATIONARY, STATIONERY: *Stationary* means "fixed, unmoving, unmovable"; *stationery* is paper made especially for correspondence.

Correct: Dorinda wrote me a letter on the most elegant *stationery*.
Correct: The guards at Buckingham Palace stand *stationary* for hours at a time.

STATUE, STATURE, STATUTE: *A statue* is a figure, a graven image; *stature* is height or image; a *statute* is a written law.

Correct: Our legislature placed this *statute* on the books two years ago.
Correct: Julia's *stature* makes her an ideal candidate for the volleyball team.
Correct: The *statue*, called Winged Victory, is among the most visited of the treasures of the Louvre.

STAUNCH, STANCH: See *stanch, staunch*.

STIMULANT, STIMULUS: *Stimulant* is that which increases physical or vital energy; *stimulus* is that which increases emotional or mental energy.

Correct: The doctor gave the patient a prescription for a *stimulant*.
Correct: Your remarks served as a *stimulus* for our new thinking on this matter.

STRANGE, FUNNY: See *funny, strange*.

STRATA, DATA, MEDIA, PHENOMENA: See *data, media, phenomena, strata*.

STUPID, DUMB, MUTE: See *dumb, mute, stupid*.

SUCH: *Such* is followed by *as* to introduce a relative clause and by *that* to introduce a clause indicating a result. Do not use *such* to mean "very." Refer to the section titled "Clauses" in Chapter 9, "Sentence Parts," for more information about clauses.

Incorrect: This is *such* a pleasant evening.
Correct: The movie was *such that* I had to walk out halfway through.

SUCH, SAME: See *same, such.*

SUCH AS, LIKE: See *like, such as.*

SUIT, SUITE: In its common usage, *suit* refers to items of apparel that serve as a unit and are meant to be worn together. *Suite* means "related things that are intended to be used as a single set" or "connecting rooms."

> **Correct:** My sister bought a new *suit* to wear to her friend's wedding.
> **Correct:** The conference was held in a *suite* of rooms at the new convention center.

SUPERIOR: This word should not be followed by *than;* use *to.*

> **Incorrect:** Does this material seem *superior than* the one we saw earlier?

SURE: Do not use *sure* as an adverb. Use *surely* or *certainly.*

> **Incorrect:** I *sure* hope we don't get any more rain tonight.
> **Correct:** *Surely* this is the last snow of the season!

SURE AND, TRY AND: Use *try to, sure to.*

> **Incorrect:** Be *sure and* write to us while you are away.

SUSPECT, EXPECT: See *expect, suspect.*

TAKE, BRING: See *bring, take.*

TAKE AND: This combination is often superfluous and can be omitted in most sentences.

> **Incorrect:** Take the ball and hit it with your racket.
> **Correct:** Hit the ball with your racket.

TAKE SICK: Do not use this expression for *become ill.* See *ill, sick.*

> **Incorrect:** The mare *took sick* on Tuesday, but she seems better now.

TAKE STOCK IN, BANK ON: See *bank on, take stock in.*

TEACH, LEARN: See *learn, teach.*

TEND TO: The *to* is superfluous.

> **Incorrect:** Noreen went outside to *tend to* the garden.

TENDERHOOKS: This is a corruption of the term *tenterhooks,* meaning "in a state of tension."

THAN, THEN: *Than* is a conjunction used in comparisons; *then* is an adverb used to refer to a period or moment of time.

> **Correct:** Bill was able to catch fish much more quickly *than* I was.
> **Correct:** We all watched the sunset; *then* it was time to go home.
> **Correct:** First we had rain, *then* we had snow; overall, though, we had more of the former *than* the latter.

THAT: Do not use *that* as an adverb.

> **Incorrect:** I know I didn't do *that* badly on the test.

THAT, WHICH: Although many people use *that* and *which* interchangeably, they should not be so used. *That* should be used only to introduce a restrictive clause; *which* should be used only to introduce a nonrestrictive clause: For more information about the correct use of *that* and *which*, refer to Chapter 9.

> **Correct:** The skirt *that* I wore to work was torn.
> (This sentence implies that there is more than one skirt; the speaker is referring specifically to the one she wore. This is a restrictive clause.)
> **Correct:** The skirt, *which* I wore to work, was torn.
> (In this sentence, the clause *which I wore to work* simply provides more information about the skirt in question; if the clause were removed, the sentence's essential meaning would still be conveyed. This is a nonrestrictive clause.)

THAT, WHO: Use *who* instead of *that* to refer to persons.

> **Incorrect:** I caught the boy *that* broke the window.
> **Correct:** The man *who* repaired our car is a good mechanic.

THAT THERE, THEM THERE, THESE HERE, THIS HERE: These are all corrupt forms of *this, that, these, those*.

> **Incorrect:** *That there* raccoon ate my garbage!

THEM: Do not use *them* as an adjective. Use *these* or *those*.

> **Incorrect:** How do you like *them* apples?

THEM THERE, THESE HERE, THIS HERE, THAT THERE: See *that there, them there, these here, this here*.

THEN, THAN: See *than, then*.

THESE HERE, THIS HERE, THAT THERE, THEM THERE: See *that there, them there, these here, this here*.

THESE KIND, THESE SORT: See *kind, sort*.

THIS HERE, THAT THERE, THEM THERE, THESE HERE: See *that there, them there, these here, this here*.

THOUGH, ALTHOUGH: See *although, though*.

THUSLY: Use *thus*, except in pointing out method or direction (adverbial function).

> **Correct:** According to the excavations, the ancient river flowed *thusly*.
> **Correct:** Nancy was clearly the strongest applicant, *thus* she got the job.

TOWARD, TOWARDS: Avoid *towards*.

> **Correct:** Although Stephen used to be a staunch conservative, he has since moved *toward* the left on some issues.

TRY AND, SURE AND: See *sure and, try and*.

UN-, IN-: See *in-, un-*.

UNINTERESTED, DISINTERESTED: See *disinterested, uninterested*.

UNIQUE: This word means "one of a kind" and does not admit of comparison.

> **Incorrect:** His rock collection is the most *unique* on campus.

UNITED STATES: When *United States* is used as a noun, it is always preceded by *the*.

> **Correct:** The results of this election will determine who is the next president of *the United States*.

VERSE, STANZA: See *stanza, verse*.

VOCATION, AVOCATION: See *avocation, vocation*.

WAGES, SALARY: See *salary, wages*.

WAIT ON: Do not use this expression in place of *wait for*. *Wait on* means "to serve," as in a restaurant.

> **Correct:** When John took me to dinner, his friend Tim, a server at the restaurant, *waited on* us.
> **Correct:** We will *wait for* you until dark.

WANT: *Want* should not be followed by a *that* clause.

> **Incorrect:** Robert *wanted that* no one would interrupt him this morning.

WANTS, NEEDS: See *needs, wants*.

WANT IN, WANT OUT, WANT UP, WANT DOWN, WANT OFF, WANT THROUGH: These expressions are corruptions of *wish to come in* and the like.

> **Incorrect:** I *want off* this roller coaster—it's making me sick!

WAYS: Do not use *ways* to mean "distance."

> **Incorrect:** Walk *a ways* with me and tell me about your day.

WELL, GOOD: See *good, well*.

WHERE: Do not use *where* for *that* to introduce a noun clause.

> **Incorrect:** I read *where* the election will be postponed.

WHERE AT: The *at* is redundant and must be omitted.

> **Incorrect:** We think we know *where* the hidden treasure is *at*.

WHERE TO: The *to* is redundant.

> **Incorrect:** *Where* do you want me to drive you *to?*

WHETHER, IF: See *if, whether*.

WHICH, THAT: See *that, which*.

WHILE: Avoid using *while* as a substitute for *and* or *but* as a coordinating conjunction. *While* refers to time.

> **Incorrect:** Felix enjoys opera, *while* I enjoy blues.
> **Correct:** Griffin enjoys country music, *but* I prefer pop.

WHO, THAT: See *that, who*.

WILL, SHALL: See *shall, will*.

WIN OUT: The *out* is redundant.

> **Incorrect:** Let's hope that our team *wins out* in the end.

WORSE: Do not use *worse* to mean *more*.

> **Incorrect:** The children wanted ice cream *worse* than they wanted broccoli.

WORSE, WORST: *Worse* is used to describe the less appealing of two options; *worst* describes the least appealing option among three or more.

> **Incorrect:** I'm having the *worse* day of my life.
> **Incorrect:** Of the twins, Carly is by far the *worst*.

WORST WAY: Do not use this expression to mean *very much*.

> **Incorrect:** I want some pizza in the *worst way*.
> **Correct:** He very much *wanted* to go to Hawaii.

WOULD HAVE: Do not use *would have* to mean *had*.

> **Incorrect:** If he *would have* asked me, I would have helped him move.
> **Correct:** *Had we* purchased stock then, we'd be rich by now.
> **Correct:** I *would have* done that had I been asked.

WOULD OF: This is a corrupt form of *would have*.

> **Incorrect:** I *would of* rather gone to a movie than to a ball game.

WOULD RATHER, HAD BETTER, HAD RATHER: See *had better, had rather, would rather*.

YOU ALL: Use this expression only in a plural sense for emphasis.

> **Correct:** I don't love just some of you; I love *you all!*

YOU WAS: This is corrupt form of *you were*.

> **Incorrect:** I told Kevin *you was* on your way home.

YOURSELF, HIMSELF, MYSELF: See *himself, myself, yourself*.

Glossary

A

absolute adjective   An adjective that expresses within itself the highest degree of comparison, an absolute quantity, and thus will not submit to further comparison. Examples of such words are *unique, perfect, round, square, honest, vertical, horizontal, perpendicular, exact, endless, frozen, dead, full, empty,* and *straight*.

abstract noun   A noun that names a quality, an attribute, an idea, or anything not having physical properties. Such words as *goodness, love, truth,* and *mercy* are included in this category. Many abstract nouns employ the suffixes *ness* (*goodness*), *ty* (*loyalty*), and *th* (*truth*) to name ideas and intangible qualities.

active voice   A verb voice in which the subject of the verb is the actor, or the doer of the action.

acute accent   An accent (´) placed over a vowel to indicate length or high pitch, or to indicate primary stress of a syllable.

adjectival complement   A complement that restricts or completes the meaning of an adjective in a sentence.

adjective   A word that describes or limits a noun or pronoun. An adjective identifies by placing restrictions on any noun with which it is associated. For example, the adjective *small* in the phrase "the small boy" not only describes the boy but also limits the focus to a certain boy, not just any boy—specifically, to the *small boy*.

adjective clause   A clause that, like a single-word adjective, modifies a noun or pronoun. It is introduced by a relative pronoun (*who, whose, whom, which,* or *that*) or by a subordinate conjunction (*where, when,* or *why*).

adjunct   A form of adverbial that is integrated to some degree in the sentence or clause structure and typically informs as to space, time, process, or focus (*in my neighborhood, next week, easily, primarily*).

adverb   A word that modifies a verb, an adjective, or another adverb. In certain constructions, an adverb may also modify a preposition, conjunction, verbal, noun, or pronoun. As a general rule, adverbs tell how, when, where, why, under what conditions, and to what extent.

adverb clause   A clause that, like a single-word adverb, modifies a verb (including the verb form in a verbal—that is, a gerund, an infinitive, or a participle), an adjective, or an adverb. Adverb clauses are introduced by subordinating conjunctions such as *even if, as though, when, although, because, as long as, as, until, before, than, wherever, while, whenever, though, after, whether, since, whereas, so that, provided that, where, as if, in order that,* and *as soon as.*

adverbial   An optional element in sentence or clause structure. Adverbials come in three main forms: adjuncts, conjuncts, and disjuncts.

adverbial complement   A complement that functions as an adverb and is necessary to complete the meaning of the sentence that contains it. Adverbial complements are similar to subject complements but usually convey the meaning of location, direction, progression, duration, condition, circumstance, or purpose.

adverbial conjunction   An adverb that serves to connect independent clauses: *however, nevertheless, moreover, then, therefore, thus,* and *consequently.*

antecedent   The expression to which another expression refers. For example, in the sentence "The person who gave you that book is my sister," *person* is the antecedent of *who gave you that book.*

apostrophe   A punctuation mark (') used to form possessives and various other semantic relationships, such as characterization, origin, measure, and so forth. In addition, apostrophes are used in contractions, as well as to indicate missing letters.

appositive   A word, phrase, or clause usually located after a nominal (a noun, noun phrase, or noun substitute) to identify, explain, or describe the nominal. Although adjectives may be used in apposition, appositives are usually nouns and pronouns. For example, in the sentence "Pirmin Zurbriggen, the greatest ski-racer of his generation, retired some time ago," the appositive is *the greatest ski-racer of his generation.*

appositive adjective   An adjective (or set of adjectives) that follows the words it modifies. These adjectives are usually used in pairs and employ the conjunction *and* or *but* between them.

article   A member of a small group of words (*a, an, the*) used with nouns to limit or define the noun.

aspect   The way the time of a situation is regarded. Aspects are expressed by a combination of an auxiliary and a main verb.

attributive adjective   An adjective found immediately before the word(s) it modifies.

auxiliary   One of a small set of verbs that combine with a main verb to express various shades of meaning, usually of time or voice. The three primary auxiliaries are *be, have,* and *do.*

B

brackets   Punctuation marks ([ ]) used to enclose explanations within parentheses or in quoted material when the explanation is not part of the quotation and to rectify a mistake such as may appear in a book or another manuscript.

C

case   The form of a pronoun. The case of some pronouns, chiefly personal pronouns, changes depending on their placement in a sentence. Pronouns being used as a subject of a sentence or clause are said to be in the *nominative case;* pronouns being used as an object are in the *objective case;* and pronouns being used to show ownership or similar relationships are in the *possessive case.*

cedilla   A diacritical mark (ç), which is placed under a letter to indicate an alteration or modification of the letter's usual phonetic value.

circumflex   A diacritical mark (ˆ) originally used in Greek over long vowels to indicate a rising-falling tone; used in other languages to mark length, contraction, or a particular vowel quality.

clause   A sentence or sentence-like construction within another sentence.

cliché   A word or phrase that is overused or has grown trite.

collective noun   A singular noun that refers to more than one thing as members of a single unit. Some examples are *herd* (the single unit *herd* is made up of the individual members—cows, for example), *flock, jury, bunch, throng, committee, company, class, team, tribe, school* (of fish), *army, platoon, family,* and *Congress.*

colon   A punctuation mark (:) used after the salutation of a business letter; before a list of any kind that is introduced formally by such words as *the following* or *as follows,* by a number, or by any other "pointing out" expression; before a long and formal statement; between main clauses when the second clause explains or restates the first; and between numbers expressing the time by the clock, between the volume and page number of a magazine, between chapter and verse of a Bible passage, and between the title and subtitle of a book when the subtitle explains the title.

comma   A punctuation mark (,) used to separate words, phrases, and clauses written in a series.

common noun   A noun that is the name of a thing in general. Common nouns are divided into two groups: count nouns and mass nouns. See also *count noun, mass noun.*

comparative clause   A clause containing a comparison.

complement   A noun, an adjective, a pronoun, or a phrase added to a verb to complete the predicate of a sentence. The complement provides information about a clause's subject or object.

complex sentence   A sentence that contains one main clause; embedded in that main clause are one or more subordinate clauses.

compound sentence   A sentence that contains multiple main clauses, which are often linked by a coordinating conjunction (*but, and,* and so on). Alternatively, a semicolon may be used to unite the two clauses. Clauses may also be linked with a conjunct, such as *however, therefore,* and the like.

concrete noun   A noun that names a thing that has physical properties—that is, a thing that is a tangible item. Some examples of concrete nouns are *wood, rain, smoke, Mr. Peterson, ghost, car, moon, wind, pencil, Jennifer, sunshine, story, lie,* and *Saturday.*

conjunct   An adverbial that indicates logical relationships between sentences or clauses. Conjuncts are mainly adverbs or prepositional phrases (*therefore, however, nonetheless, on the other hand,* and so on).

conjunctive adverb   An adverb used to connect subordinate clauses to the remainder of the sentence. The most widely used conjunctive adverbs are *where, when, whenever, while, as, why, before, after, until,* and *since.*

conjunction   A connective word that joins single words, phrases, or clauses to the rest of the sentence.

coordinate clause   A clause connected to one or more other clauses of equal status. Such clauses are joined through the use of coordinating conjunctions such as *for, and, nor, but, or,* and *yet.*

coordinating conjunction   A word that connects elements of equal rank in the sentence. The sentence elements may be single words, phrases, or clauses.

copular prepositional verb   A prepositional verb (combination of verb plus preposition) that is complemented by a subject complement. Examples include *sound like, turn into,* and *serve as.*

copular verb   See *copulative verb.*

copulative verb   Also called a *copular verb,* a verb that usually patterns with a modifier or noun (or noun substitute) that is necessary to complete the meaning of the sentence. The most common copulative verb is *be;* others include *become, feel, get,* and *seem.*

correlative conjunction   A conjunction that functions normally, except that it patterns in a pair. The correlative conjunctions are *either . . . or, neither . . . nor, whether . . . or, both . . . and,* and *not only . . . but also.*

count noun   A noun that identifies individual items, either singly or as members of groups.

D

declarative sentence   A sentence whose primary role is to make a statement.

definite article A word (*the*) denoting a definite noun phrase, as in *the woman*. In this case, the speaker or writer refers to a specific woman (*the woman*), not just any woman (*a woman*).

demonstrative A word whose role is to locate a referent in relation to a speaker, an addressee, or some other person. Examples of demonstratives are *this* and *that*.

demonstrative pronoun A pronoun that serves to point out particular persons, places, or things, even though they may not be named directly.

dependent clause A clause that cannot stand alone. Also called a *subordinate clause*.

determiner A word that introduces and limits a noun phrase. Determiners specify number and quantity (*all, both, two, many, several*) or convey the denotation of a noun phrase (*a/an, the, my, this*).

diacritical mark An accent, diacritical, or special alphabetic character for a native word. The diacritical marks most commonly used in European and Asian languages written in the Latin alphabet are the acute accent (´), the grave accent (`), the dieresis (¨), the umlaut (¨), the circumflex (ˆ), the tilde (˜), and the cedilla (ç).

dieresis A diacritical mark (¨) placed over a vowel to indicate that it is pronounced in a separate syllable. See also *umlaut*.

direct object A major sentence element contained in many predicates. Direct objects occur in sentences that have transitive verbs. To identify direct objects, one may ask a "what" question or a "who" question in conjunction with the verb. For example, examine the sentence "Joseph found a silver coin in the street." Then, ask the "what" question: What did Joseph find? He found a silver coin. *Silver coin*, then, is the direct object.

disjunct An adverbial that evaluates or comments on the act or truth of speaking or writing. Style disjuncts—which may be adverbs, prepositional phrases, finite clauses, and non-finite clauses—comment on the act of speaking or writing (*truthfully, in short, frankly speaking, since you mentioned it*). Content disjuncts, on the other hand, evaluate or comment on the truth value of what is said (*probably, unfortunately*).

E

ellipsis A punctuation mark (. . . or . . . .) used to indicate an omission from a quotation.

em dash A punctuation mark (—) used to indicate an important break in thought or in sentence structure; to set off an appositive that is a series; to mean *namely, in other words, that is,* and similar expressions that precede explanations; to indicate speech that is broken or faltering; and after an incomplete sentence (in which case the em dash should be used without a period).

en dash   A punctuation mark (–) used to connect continuing (that is, inclusive) numbers, as in dates, time, or reference numbers; to indicate a single period or season spanning parts of two successive calendar years; and in place of a hyphen in cases of compound adjectives when one element of the adjective is an open compound or when multiple elements are hyphenated compounds.

exclamation point   A punctuation mark (!) used after a strong interjection or after phrases or sentences that show strong emotions.

exclamatory sentence   A sentence that conveys a strong emotion. These types of sentences, which often contain no verb, sometimes consist of the word *what* or *how* followed by a noun phrase.

F

first person   A manner of speaking or writing that refers to the speaker or writer through the use of certain linguistic sets, such as pronouns and verb forms. For example, the sentence "I ate fish for dinner" is in the first person, as indicated by the use of the pronoun *I*.

function word   A word that has a grammatical (syntactic) role in a sentence or clause as opposed to a lexical (semantic) meaning. Also called *structure words*, function words include determiners, prepositions, conjunctions, interjections, and auxiliary verbs.

G

gerund   A word that ends in *ing* that shares characteristics of nouns and verbs. For example, in the sentence "Sculpting hedges is Robyn's favorite activity," the gerund *sculpting* requires a direct object (*hedges*) in the same way many verbs require direct objects. At the same time, the phrase *sculpting hedges* acts as the subject of the sentence, much as nouns do.

gerund phrase   A phrase recognized by two means, one of description and one of function. First, the gerund phrase is recognized by its characteristic verb form with an *ing* ending, although this is not always a surefire means of spotting a gerund. In addition to the *ing* ending, the gerund phrase functions in a sentence in a manner similar to that of a noun. Of course, because this discussion concerns phrases, other words besides gerunds must be included with the gerund to form the phrase.

grave accent   A diacritical mark (`) placed over a vowel to indicate length or low pitch, or to indicate secondary stress of a syllable.

guide word   A key word that controls a preposition.

H

hedge word   A word used to help a speaker or writer avoid making an absolute statement, such as *alleged* in "The alleged burglary occurred last night." In general, these should be avoided.

hyphen   A punctuation mark (-) used between words that act as a single adjective modifier (including coined ones) preceding the word being modified; in two-word fractions when the fraction is a single adjective that modifies directly; in numbers from *twenty-one* through *ninety-nine*; after a prefix that has been attached to a proper noun; after *self* and *all* when these words are prefixed to nouns; in compound titles containing *vice, ex,* and *elect;* in words when there may be doubt as to meaning; when the joining of a prefix with the root causes an awkward combination of letters; and to show the omission of a connecting word. In addition, a hyphen should be used to divide a word at the end of a line.

I

idiom   An expression that is peculiar to itself grammatically or that has a meaning that cannot be derived from the conjoined meaning of its elements.

imperative mood   A mood used to state a request, command, or suggestion.

imperative sentence   A sentence that gives an order or issues a command.

indefinite article   A word (*a, an*) that denotes an indefinite noun phrase, as in *a woman*. In this case, the speaker or writer is not discussing a particular woman.

indefinite pronoun   A word that is substituted for a noun without referring to a definite person, place, or thing.

indefinite relative pronoun   A pronoun that introduces a noun clause. The indefinite relative pronouns are *who, whom, what, whoever, whomever, whatever,* and *whichever*.

independent clause   A clause that, although it lacks the capitalization and punctuation of a sentence, could stand alone, grammatically speaking.

indicative mood   A mood used to state a fact or to ask a question. The indicative mood is the form common to most sentences, whether declarative or interrogative.

indirect object   A part of the predicate that occurs in a sentence containing a direct object and identifies the person/thing to whom or for whom something is done or given or of whom a question is asked. Indirect objects are usually nouns or pronouns. For example, in the sentence "I told Maria the truth," *Maria* is the indirect object.

infinitive The word *to* followed by the root form of a verb, such as *run, jump, play, work, buy, see,* and so on. Infinitives, then, look like this: *to run, to jump, to play, to work, to buy, to see.*

infinitive phrase A phrase that contains an infinitive and words that pattern with it—modifiers, objects, and subjects. An infinitive may have an object—in this case called an *object of the infinitive* rather than a *direct object.*

inflection An affix that expresses a grammatical relationship, such as the plural *s* in *candidates* and the *ed* ending in *wanted.* In English, inflections are always suffixes.

intensifier An adverb that adds emphasis to or amplifies an adjective. The word *intensifier* is also used to describe an adjective that creates an emphasizing or amplifying effect.

intensive pronoun A pronoun that is similar to the reflexive pronoun except in its function within a sentence. An intensive pronoun usually appears immediately following a noun or pronoun and lends emphasis to the noun or pronoun that it follows.

interjection A word or phrase "injected" into a sentence to express strong feeling or sudden emotion.

internal punctuation Punctuation that separates, divides, and points out elements within an expression, thereby developing clarity and specific identity.

interrogative adverb An adverb used in asking a question, as in *"Where* have you been?" *"When* were you in Texas?" and *"Why* did you burn that picture?"

interrogative pronoun A pronoun used when asking a question. The interrogative pronouns are *who, whom, whose, which,* and *what.*

interrogative sentence A sentence that asks a question.

intransitive verb A verb that shows action of some sort but does not require a direct object. Examples include *swim, run, walk, talk,* and so on.

italics A style of font used for names of books, magazines, newspapers, long plays, long poems (book length), motion pictures, musical productions, works of art, ships, aircraft, and trains. Italics should also be used for words, letters, figures, and symbols referred to by name; for foreign words and phrases; and to lend emphasis.

L

linking verb A verb that requires a subject complement to complete the meaning of a sentence. Linking verbs are also copulative verbs. Any verb that can be substituted in the place of the word *looked* is probably a linking verb. Some common linking verbs include *appear, become, grow, remain, seem, get, look, sound, smell, feel, taste,* and *continue.*

M

mass noun   A noun that identifies undifferentiated mass—that is, things not usually considered countable by individual items. Sometimes called *non-count noun*.

misplaced modifier   A modifier located in a place other than near the word it modifies, therefore seeming to modify a word other than that it is intended to modify.

N

nominal relative clause   A clause used as a noun substitute. The relative pronouns *who, whoever, whom, whomever, that, which, whichever, what,* and *whatever* may introduce nominal relative clauses.

nominative case   See *case*.

non-count noun   See *mass noun*.

nonfinite verb   See *verbal*.

nonrestrictive clause   A clause that may be omitted from a sentence without a loss of the basic meaning of the sentence. These types of clauses, which are also called *nonessential clauses,* should be set off by commas.

noun   A word that names a person, place, or thing.

noun clause   A clause that functions in a sentence just as a noun functions. A noun clause is usually introduced by one of the following words: *that, who, what, where, when, why, how, which,* or *whether*.

noun phrase   A phrase (which may consist of only a single noun) that can be used in a sentence just as a noun is used: as the subject, direct object, indirect object, subject complement, object complement, object of a preposition, object of an infinitive, subject of an infinitive, and so on.

O

object complement   A word or phrase that describes or "completes" the direct object, usually by adding a noun or an adjective immediately after the direct object.

objective case   See *case*.

P

parentheses   Punctuation marks [( )] used to enclose parenthetical material that is only remotely connected with the content; to enclose references, directions, and incidental explanatory matter; to enclose figures repeated to ensure accuracy; and to enclose figures or letters used to mark divisions or enumerations that run into the text. In addition, you can use a question mark within parentheses after a word or a statement of which the accuracy is questionable.

participial phrase   A phrase that contains a participle. Such phrases can follow noun phrases; can function like subordinate clauses to indicate time, result, reason, and so on; or can follow an object and a verb of the senses. Participial phrases are generally used as adjectives.

participial preposition   A preposition that takes the *ing* form of certain verbs, such as *assuming, barring, beginning, considering, following, including, involving, regarding,* and a few others.

participle   A nonfinite form of a verb—that is, a verb that does not indicate tense. A participle combines characteristics of a verb with those of an adjective. Except for irregular verbs, the present participle of any verb ends in *ing;* the past participle of a regular verb is identified with the past tense, ending in *ed.* Participles are used to introduce participial phrases.

parts of speech   Word classes—that is, the different types of words contained in a language. In English, the parts of speech are nouns, pronouns, adjectives, verbs, adverbs, interjections, and function words (prepositions, conjunctions, and the like).

passive voice   A verb voice in which the actor–action–patient elements pattern in a reverse order from active voice. In such sentences, the actor remains passive and often patterns as the object of a preposition at the end of the sentence. The element that is the direct object in a sentence in the active voice becomes the subject of the sentence in the passive voice.

past participle   See *participle*.

period   A punctuation mark (.) used after a declarative sentence; after an imperative sentence that is a polite request; after an indirect question; after a polite request that is put in the form of a question; after each initial in a proper name and after most abbreviations; as a decimal point; and after each numeral or letter division in an outline except those enclosed in parentheses.

personal pronoun   A pronoun used when a writer or speaker wishes to employ a substitute for a word that refers to a person, either himself or someone else (or, in the case of *it,* a thing).

phrasal preposition   A unit of two or more words serving as a single preposition. Often a phrasal preposition is itself a prepositional phrase.

phrase   A group of words not containing a subject and predicate that, together, function as a part of speech (noun, verb, adjective, adverb, preposition, and so on). The various types of phrases include noun phrases, prepositional phrases, and verbals.

plural   More than one (as opposed to singular).

possessive case   See *case*.

postponed preposition   A preposition that patterns after its object.

predicate   The part of the sentence that makes an assertion or a denial about the subject of that sentence; that is, it represents what is said about the sentence's subject. For example, in the sentence "Cammy gave up skiing to become a champion snowboarder," *Cammy* is the subject, and *gave up skiing to become a champion snowboarder* is the predicate.

predicate adjective   An adjective that occurs after a linking verb or after a form of the verb *to be* and that modifies the subject of that verb. As the name implies, these adjectives occur in the predicate of a sentence or clause, but they must modify the subject of the sentence or clause to be considered predicate adjectives.

prefix   An affix attached to the beginning of a word, root, or phrase.

preposition   A word or, in some instances, a short word group that functions as a connector between sentence elements. The element that it connects and patterns with is usually a noun and is identified as the *object of the preposition*.

prepositional phrase   The combination of a preposition and the object of that preposition, and all words that pattern with it.

present participle   See *participle*.

pronoun   A word that can be substituted for a noun, two or more other pronouns, or a noun phrase without changing the meaning of the sentence or the basic construction pattern of the sentence.

proper adjective   An adjective derived from a proper noun or a proper noun used as an adjective. These adjectives are generally written with capital letters.

proper noun   A noun that names specific things that are identified with an individual name.

Q

quantifier   A word that indicates a relative or indefinite quantity. Examples include *all, many, several,* and *few*. These are distinguished from numerals, which provide an absolute indication of quantity (for example, "*nine* ladies dancing").

question mark   A punctuation mark (?) used after a direct question; after each incomplete question in a series; and in parentheses to indicate historical doubt or uncertainty.

quotation mark   A punctuation mark (" " or ' ') used for quotations that employ the exact words from some source (either spoken or written).

R

reflexive pronoun   A pronoun that reflects a person or thing already identified. Reflexive pronouns are used when the subject of a sentence performs an action on itself or refers to itself in some other way.

relative pronoun   A pronoun that connects adjective or noun clauses to other elements of the sentence. That is, a relative pronoun substitutes for the noun being modified by an adjective clause and relates that clause to the noun.

restrictive clause   An adjective clause that is necessary in order to restrict the meaning of the sentence; in other words, restrictive clauses indicate the essential meaning of the sentence. Adjective clauses beginning with *that* are always restrictive clauses.

S

second person   A manner of speaking or writing that refers to the addressee through the use of the pronoun *you*. For example, the sentence "You ate fish for dinner" is in the second person.

semicolon   A punctuation mark (;) used between main clauses that are not joined by *and, or, for, nor, but, so,* or *yet;* between main clauses that are joined by *and, or, for, but, nor, so,* and *yet* if there is a comma within any one of the main clauses; between the items in a series if any one of the items contains commas; and before such explanatory words and phrases as *namely, for example, in fact,* and *that is.*

sentence modifier   An adverbial that relates to the entire sentence as opposed to relating to any separate element within the sentence. Sentence modifiers are usually set off by commas.

simple adverb   A one-word adverb that modifies the word or phrase appearing next to it.

simple preposition   A preposition made up of either a simple or compound word: *up, down, in, into, from, to, with, inside, around, before, upon, along, without,* and so on.

simple sentence   A sentence that consists of one main clause with no coordinate or subordinate clause.

singular   One, as opposed to two or more (plural).

squinting modifier   Similar to a misplaced modifier, a modifier that is placed in a sentence in such a manner that it could modify either of two nouns in the sentence.

structure word   See *function word.*

subject   A sentence element that represents a person or thing of which something is said, usually the noun, pronoun, or noun phrase in a sentence or clause that comes before the verb or, in the case of interrogative sentences, after the verb. For example, in the sentence "Alexia began taking ballet lessons at the age of five," *Alexia* is the subject of the sentence; it is being said of her that she *began taking ballet lessons at the age of five.*

subject complement   The complement of a copulative verb such as *be* or *seem*. The subject complement may be an adjective phrase, an adverb phrase, or a prepositional phrase, as well as a noun phrase or a nominal clause.

subjunctive mood   A mood used to express a condition contrary to fact, a wish, a supposition, a prayer, or a doubt, as well as in *that* clauses. The subjunctive mood is most commonly employed, however, in contrary-to-fact statements, as in "If I were rich, I'd quit my job."

subordinate clause   See *dependent clause.*

subordinating conjunction   A conjunction that connects two clauses of unequal rank. Subordinating conjunctions begin dependent clauses (usually adverb clauses) and show the relationship of those dependent clauses to the independent clauses of which they are a part. Some subordinating conjunctions include *if, because, after, since, when, while, until, unless, although, for* (meaning *because*), *wherever, than,* and *as.* The relative pronouns *who, whom, whose, which, what,* and *that* also function as subordinating conjunctions.

suffix   An affix attached to the end of a word, root, or phrase.

T

tense   Refers to the time of a situation. Tenses are indicated by the form of the verb.

terminal punctuation   Punctuation that brings something, such as a sentence or an abbreviation, to an end.

third person   A manner of speaking or writing that refers to neither the speaker/ writer nor the addressee. For example, the sentence "He walked to the corner store" is in the third person, as indicated by the use of the pronoun *he.*

tightening   In writing, the act of eliminating unnecessary words in prose.

tilde   A diacritical mark (˜) placed over the letter *n* to denote the sound *ny* or over vowels to indicate nasality.

transitional device   In writing, a device that helps ease prose from one point to the next.

transitional expression   The main type of transitional device. There are several types of transitional expressions: contrast and qualification, continuity, cause and effect, exemplification, and summation.

transitive verb   A verb that patterns with a direct object—that is, it expresses an action that directly affects a grammatical unit (usually a noun or pronoun) elsewhere in a clause or sentence. Stated another way, a transitive verb shows an action that is "passed on" to the direct object.

U

umlaut   A diacritical mark (¨) placed over a vowel to indicate a more central or front articulation.

V

VAC   See verb-adverbial composite.

verb   A word that expresses an act, an occurrence, or a state of being.

verb-adverbial composite (VAC)   A word used as a preposition or as a single-word adverb linked to a verb.

verbal   A type of phrase that incorporates a verb form into its basic construction. Verbals, which include infinitives, gerunds, and participles, are employed as grammatical units within sentences, usually as nouns or modifiers. They are often classified as non-finite verbs because they are not inflected (do not change form) to indicate person, number, or tense.

W

word class   See *parts of speech*.

INDEX